Our Forests
Our Future

Report of the World Commission on Forests and Sustainable Development

Emil Salim and Ola Ullsten
Co-Chairmen

Cambridge
University Press

PUBLISHED BY THE PRESS SYNDICATE OF THE UNIVERSITY OF CAMBRIDGE
The Pitt Building, Trumpington Street, Cambridge, United Kingdom

CAMBRIDGE UNIVERSITY PRESS
The Edinburgh Building, Cambridge CB2 2RU, UK
http://www.cup.cam.ac.uk
40 West 20th Street, New York, NY 10011-4211, USA http://www.cup.org
10 Stamford Road, Oakleigh, Melbourne 3166, Australia

First published 1999

Printed in the United Kingdom

Typeface Times 10 auto System QuarkXPress® [WCFSD]

A catalogue record for this book is available from the British Library

ISBN 0 521 66021 1 hardback
ISBN 0 521 66956 1 paperback

ESTS

TURE

...that if action
...maintaining a
...ation of plants
...many parts of
...ss.

...pend on forests for their livelihood, the World Commission on Forests and Sustainable Development (WCFSD) concludes: 'We must urgently choose a path that respects the ecological values of forests while recognising their role in social and economic development.'

Key recommendations in the report include:

- the global nature of the forest crisis requires decisive international leadership and action;
- governments must ensure that the public interest prevails over private interests;
- prices and policies that truly reflect all benefits provided by forests are needed to change wasteful production and consumption patterns;
- protection of the remaining primary forests requires that future demand for wood products must be met through plantation and secondary forests;
- community involvement in decision-making is essential for sustainable management of forests.

Our Forests... Our Future is a compelling and well-documented appeal from a group of respected individuals with backgrounds in politics, policy, science and forestry from 24 different countries in both the North and the South. Due to its independence and broad international representation, the Commission has been able to address the most significant global forest issues from a fresh and unique perspective.

Contents

List of Figures

List of Tables

List of Boxes

Foreword

Since the answers to fundamental and serious concerns are not at hand, there is no alternative but to keep on trying to find them.
(WCED – The Brundtland Commission, 1987)

A dozen years ago the Brundtland Commission, later supported by the UNCED process, set a new paradigm for the world: Sustainable Development. It is a term that implies two concepts: the concept of needs and the concept of limits. The needs of present and future generations must be met with the full support of human ingenuity but within the limits of a stable biosphere. For the forests this requires that if we want to benefit from the material goods and services of the forests, it has to be done in a way that does not jeopardize their ecological functions. Both forests and development have to be sustained.

That is not what we are doing today. True, steps in the right direction are being taken both by governments and by the private sector. Still the general trend is that the delicate ecological balance that forests and other natural resources maintain is constantly being upset. We are drawing on the world's natural capital far more rapidly than it is regenerating. Rather than living on the 'interest' of the 'natural capital', we are borrowing from poorer communities and from future generations.

In this report the World Commission on Forests and Sustainable Development proposes a plan for how the world's forests can be used without being abused and outlines what it takes in terms of policies and institutions for such a plan to be implemented.

The Commission appeciated that the complex intertwining of the earth's ecology, the world's economy, and the well-being of its people is tied up with considerations about power and poverty and equity. Consequently the Commission sought out the opinions of those whose lives are directly connected with forests. It did this through five public hearings held in Asia, Africa, the Commonwealth of Independent States and Europe, Latin America and the Caribbean, and North America.

We met with forest-dwelling and other local communities in developing countries who are directly dependent on forests for their economic, social, cultural and spiritual well-being. We listened to farmers from countries in the North and South who rely on forests and trees for agricultural productivity and sustenance. We heard executives and their employees from forest industries in different parts of the world who supply wood products to society. We took careful note of what scientists, economists, foresters, government officials, and other specialists involved in national and international forest policy had to say. We listened to and read written submissions from individuals and community-based organisations and met with national and international NGOs.

Contributions from these groups, all of which have their stake in the future of the world's forests, form the basis of the Commission's conclusion and recommendations. Most of these submissions support the Commission's conclusion that we are faced with a forest crisis, and one with many dimensions. These range from highly visible expression of barren, degraded land in many developing countries to the less visible loss of biodiversity, forest decline, and negative impacts on global ecological cycles such as climate change.

In whichever form the crisis appears it needs our urgent attention. We have a choice to make. Can we afford to continue on a path of unsustainable development, depleting our natural capital, or are we willing to risk a change in direction towards sustainable development that may involve some short-term political risks? Often, new directions may involve policies that do not maximise immediate economic returns, but focus instead on maximising long-term human and ecological well-being.

The report suggests that at this juncture a change in direction is still economically and politically possible. The costs may be too much if we further delay action to change direction. To facilitate this change, the Commission advocates radical reform of policies, calls for a new political agenda, greater civil society involvement, and more science in policy.

We have to slow deforestation, support sustainable forest management, preserve the remaining primary forests, and support policies that increase forest cover.

We have to correct the prices on wood products so as to reflect the real costs of extracting timber and fibre from the world's forests. We have to develop financial methods of capturing the value of the services that forests provide.

We have to introduce institutional reforms that enable active involvement of people at local and national levels in decision-making processes concerning the use and management of forests.

We have to make international trade and development cooperation policies to support national efforts in developing countries to use forests for alleviating poverty.

We have to build active partnerships between the private and the public sector that would promote sustainable forest management policies.

These are all challenges that require astute and far-sighted political leadership. It involves politically sensitive issues like the right to use and own forest land, implementing policies to reflect the rights of indigenous people, transparency in the process of selling timber concessions, the removal of perverse subsidies, stumpage fees that reflect true costs, trade policies based on equity and fairness, fighting corruption, and shifting the balance of power over an important natural resource to people who depend on them.

The whole forest issue is about people, sometimes illustrated in a direct and brutal way. When some 10,000 people drowned in mud and water in Central America in November 1998 the blame was on Hurricane 'Mitch', the worse of its kind in a long time. This was only half of the truth about that tragic event. The other half is about land mismanagement in the region. Big cash crop farms, often multinational, have gradually taken over the fertile plains and driven poor families to cultivate and collect firewood from marginal land and forested mountain hillsides. As expected, these lands have become eroded, causing unprotected soil to wash away by forceful rains, forming mudslides which killed everything in their path.

Similar examples can be taken from many parts of the world. Environmental degradation is self-inflicted by humans and is in the main a political issue; deforestation is no exception. We know why forests in the millions of hectares every year are being destroyed. We know a lot about the means needed for arresting this trend. The world possesses more financial resources and more sophisticated technology, including means of communication, than ever before. The awareness among the public is growing. What we are waiting for are politicians and civil society leaders who dare to challenge the variety of vested private interests that stand in the way of applying new policies.

We want so much from our forests. Everything from timber and fibre to scenery and tranquillity. From jobs and profits to an undisturbed habitat for wildlife and flora. We want forests to leave room for roads and cities and fields for growing crops and grazing cattle, and yet we want the forest area to grow in size to become more effective as a carbon sink. Different stakeholders can be linked to one or more of these interests. Many of us have a stake in one or all of the benefits that forests have to offer.

Identifying the multiple interests is necessary for the political process and the Commission has done that through its public hearings. But, simply framing policies based on compromises between stakeholders is not easy, nor is it that meaningful. Government policies have to reach beyond the private interests of individuals and groups and try to make an enlightened interpretation of what is in the public interest. Each group interest cannot be accorded the same legitimacy. The ecological and social functions of forests will have to be prioritized. This report clearly shows that we need all the services forests provide, be they be economic, social or ecological.

We did not think it would be possible to issue a set of universal prescriptions valid for all sorts of forests in all parts of the world, and in countries with widely varying political traditions and systems. A recommendation that may be useful for industrial forest management in areas with low population densities as in Canada and the Scandinavian countries may not apply to the rainforests of the Amazon and Southeast Asia. Similarly, the reverse holds true.

By going beyond traditional forestry with its focus on wood production, to the multiple role of forests in providing local and global ecological, social and economic benefits, we feel it is easy to justify the holistic solutions to the forest crisis that we have recommended in this report. In doing so, we have emphasised the concept that the world's forests are held in trust by different countries, all with responsibilities for their health and survival.

We hope that our report will give impetus, encouragement and support to others who are unified in similar deep concerns about the current state of the world's forests, and in the search for ways of sustaining both forests and development.

Ola Ullsten
Co-Chairman

Emil Salim
Co-Chairman

The World Commission on Forests and Sustainable Development

Immediately after the Earth Summit in 1992, Ola Ullsten, former Prime Minister of Sweden, and Emil Salim, former Minister of Population and Environment of Indonesia, convened a series of meetings of world forest leaders to seek a way forward from the deeply divided positions on forests between North and South.

Following calls for action from many concerned groups around the world, they responded in 1994 to a proposal by the InterAction Council of Former Heads of State and Government, at that time headed by former Chancellor Helmut Schmidt of Germany, to establish an independent World Commission on Forests and Sustainable Development.

The mandate that the Commission was given by the InterAction Council was to:

- Increase awareness of the dual function of world forests in preserving the natural environment and contributing to economic development;
- Broaden the consensus on the data, science, and policy aspects of forest conservation and management;
- Build confidence between North and South on forest matters with emphasis on international cooperation.

Twenty-three other persons were invited to join the Commission as members. Together they brought a wide variety of backgrounds and perspectives to bear on the work. All of them served in their individual capacity, and the Commission functioned as an independent body.

With the assistance of the Woods Hole Research Centre in Massachusetts, USA, the Commission's secretariat was recruited and established in Geneva, with forestry expert John Spears as Secretary-General. The Commission records its deep appreciation for the invaluable services and dedicated support of the members of its Secretariat.

The Commission began its work in June 1995. From the outset, it decided to seek a citizens' perspective on the issues, especially among those whose lives are most directly affected by forests and trees. Between March 1996 and September 1997, five Public Hearings were held. In addition to submissions from several thousand members of the public, the Commission had the benefit of technical papers it commissioned and opinion it invited from numerous specialists. The Commission records its deep appreciation for all of these inputs, which have been invaluable in enabling it to consider the many and complex factors involved in considering the challenge of sustaining forests and development.

The process in which the Commission engaged and the preparation of this Report would not have been possible without the faith which so many governments and agencies placed in the Commission and in its approach, and the financial support which they made available. The Commission records its deep appreciation to all of them. These technical and financial sources of support are listed in the Acknowledgements and Annex 4.

During the final stages of its work and while awaiting the preparation and publication of its Report, the Commission liaised with several organisations about its conclusions and proposals, several of which are already being actively pursued by partner organisations. With the facilitation of the International Institute for Sustainable Development, this process will continue until the end of 1999 as a means of supporting those follow-up activities already in process and helping to put other proposals into motion. This immediate follow-up effort will be under the direction of Ola Ullsten and Emil Salim on behalf of the rest of the Commission. Individual Commissioners are also actively continuing this work in their own countries and communities.

Co-chairmen:

Emil Salim, *Indonesia*
Professor, Former Minister of State for Population and Environment

Ola Ullsten, *Sweden*
Former Prime Minister of Sweden

Members:

Emeka Anyaoku, *Nigeria*
Commonwealth Secretary-General, Former Foreign Minister of Nigeria

Charles Caccia, *Canada*
Member of Parliament, Chairman of Parliamentary Committee on Environment and Sustainable Development, Former Minister of Environment

Kamla Chowdhry, *India*
Chair, Society for Promotion of Wastelands Development,
Former Chairperson, National Wastelands Development Board

Angela Cropper, ***Trinidad and Tobago***
Former Executive Secretary, United Nations Convention on Biological Diversity

Christine Debrah, ***Ghana***
Former Executive Director, Environmental Protection Council

B.C.Y. Freezailah, ***Malaysia***
Executive Director, International Tropical Timber Organization (ITTO)

José Goldemberg, ***Brazil***
Professor, Former Minister of Education, Environment, Health, Science and Technology

Wakako Hironaka, ***Japan***
Member, House of Councillors, Former Minister of Environment

Yolanda Kakabadse, ***Ecuador***
Executive President, Fundacion Futuro Latino Americano, President, IUCN

Speciosa Wandira Kazibwe, ***Uganda***
Vice President and Minister of Agriculture, Animal Husbandry and Fisheries

LI Lukang, ***China***
Chief Adviser for International Cooperation, Ministry of Forestry

Hemmo Muntingh, ***The Netherlands***
Founder of Global Legislators Organisation for a Balanced Environment (GLOBE)

David Pearce, ***UK***
Associate Director, Centre for Social and Economic Research on the Global Environment

Manuel Rodriguez, ***Colombia***
Director, Andean Center for Sustainable Development, Foundation for Higher Education, Former Minister of Environment

Kazimierz Rykowski, ***Poland***
Professor of Forestry and Forest Protection, Deputy Director of The Forest Research Institute, Former Chairman of FAO Forestry Commission

Jorge Miles da Silva (Terena), ***Brazil***
Member, Latin American and Caribbean Commission on Development and Environment, Former Regional Director for Indigenous Affairs, IFAD

José Sarukhán Kermez, ***Mexico***
National Coordinator, Mexican National Commission on Biodiversity (CONABIO), Former Rector, National University of Mexico

M.S. Swaminathan, ***India***
Director, Centre for Research on Sustainable Agricultural and Rural Development, Former President, IUCN, Former Director General, International Rice Research Institute

Margaret Taylor, ***Papua New Guinea***
Former Ambassador of PNG to the USA

Mostafa Terrab, ***Morocco***
Executive Secretary of the Middle East/North Africa Economic Summit

Klaus Topfer, ***Germany***
Former Federal Minister for Building Construction and Urbanism, Former Chairman of the UN/CSD

Nikolay N. Vorontsov, ***Russia***
Vice President, Russian Academy of Natural Sciences, Former Minister of Environment

George M. Woodwell, ***USA***
Director, The Woods Hole Research Center

Jong-Tack Yoo, ***Republic of Korea***
President, Taegu Kyungbuk Development Institute and Visiting Professor Yeung-Nam University, Former ViceMinister, Ministry of Agriculture and Forestry

Chair, Scientific Committee:
George M. Woodwell

Chair, Editorial Committee:
Angela Cropper

Secretary-General:
John Spears

World Commission on Forests and Sustainable Development
c/o International Institute for Sustainable Development
161 Portage Avenue East, 6th Floor
Winnipeg, Manitoba R3B 0Y4, Canada
Tel: 1 204 958 7700; Fax: 1 204 958 7710
Website: http://iisd/ca/wcfsd

Acknowledgements

The Commission has received advice and support from a large group of people. Many have made oral or written submissions during the Commission's public hearings, others have functioned as resource persons during certain phases of the Commission's work or through its duration. We are grateful to them all. We have also highly appreciated the assistance in many forms that has been rendered to the Commission by many governmental, non-governmental and private institutions. Throughout its work the Commission has been supported by a small staff, an active group of resource persons and by local organisers of the Commission's public hearings. Their dedication and tireless efforts are especially appreciated.

The Commission commends the role of The Woods Hole Research Center (WHRC), which first launched the idea of an independent commission on forests, and which continued as an unwavering partner in bringing the idea to fruition and in completion of this report. The Commission is equally grateful to the InterAction Council (of former Heads of State and Government) for having 'godfathered' the Commission.

Without the financial support from Governments, Business Associations, Private Foundations and International and Regional Organisations it would not have been possible to pursue an ambitious work programme which included five regional public hearings. Early and very generous contributions enabled the Commission to commence its work and to obtain other financial support from many other equally generous sources. The facilitation of WHRC, UNDP and IISD has been invaluable in this process. The Commission is grateful to all these contributors.

The Commission attempts to recognise all these individuals and institutions in Annex 4. However, given the open, participatory and diffuse nature of the Commission's process, it is possible that some sources may not have been specified – we regret those instances.

The Commission conveys its appreciation to all who supported its efforts, and for their belief in the usefulness of an independent non-governmental process to examine the issues of forests and sustainable development.

Acronymns

ACS	Association of Caribbean States
APEC	Asia-Pacific Economic Cooperation
ASEAN	Association of Southeast Asian Nations
CARICOM	Caribbean Community
CBD	Convention on Biological Diversity
CIDA	Canadian International Development Agency
CIFOR	Center for International Forestry Research
CITES	Convention on the International Trade in Endangered Species of Wild Fauna and Flora
COAMA	Coalicion Orinoquia Amazonia
EC	European Community
EEPSEA	Economy and Environment Program for Southeast Asia
EU	European Union
FAO	Food and Agriculture Organization of the United Nations
FCI	Forest Capital Index
FSC	Forest Stewardship Council
G-8	Group of Seven plus Russia
GDP	Gross Domestic Product
GEF	Global Environment Facility
GFIS	Global Forest Information Service
GIS	Geographic Information Systems
GLOBE	Global Legislators Organization for a Balanced Environment
ICARDA	International Center for Agricultural Research in Dry Areas
ICRAF	International Centre for Research in Agroforestry
IDRC	International Development Research Centre
IFF	Intergovernmental Forum on Forests
IFPRI	International Food Policy Research Institute
IIED	International Institute for Environment and Development
IISD	International Institute for Sustainable Development
IMF	International Monetary Fund
IPF	Intergovernmental Panel on Forests
ISO	International Organization for Standardization
ITTO	International Tropical Timber Organization
IUCN	The World Conservation Union
JFM	Joint Forest Management
MAI	Multilateral Agreement on Investment
NAFTA	North American Free Trade Agreement
NGO	Non-Governmental Organisation
ODA	Overseas Development Agency
OECD	Organisation for Economic Co-operation and Development
SAARC	South Asian Association for Regional Cooperation
SADCC	Southern African Development Coordination Conference
SAREC	Swedish Agency for Research Co-operation with Developing Countries
SIDA	Swedish International Development Agency
SPREP	South Pacific Regional Environment Programme
UN/ECE	United Nations Economic Commission for Europe
UNCED	United Nations Conference on Environment and Development
UNDP	United Nations Development Programme
UNEP	United Nations Environment Programme

UNFCCC	United Nations Framework Convention on Climate Change
US AID	United States Agency for International Development
WCED	World Commission on Environment and Development (or Brundtland Commission)
WCFSD	World Commission on Forests and Sustainable Development
WCMC	World Conservation and Monitoring Centre
WCS	World Conservation Strategy
WRI	World Resources Institute
WTO	World Trade Organization
WWF	World Wildlife Fund for Nature

Quotations and edited statements of submissions made to the Commission at its public hearings or through private communication appear throughout this report. These reflect opinions presented to the Commission, and do not necessarily reflect the views of the Commission.

1

FORESTS IN CRISIS

The evolution of the human economy has passed from an era in which manmade capital represented the limiting factor in economic development (an 'empty' world) to an era in which increasingly scarce natural capital has taken its place (a 'full' world)... In this new full-world era investment must shift from manmade capital accumulation toward natural capital preservation and restoration.
(Daly, 1993)

1.1 The nature of the crisis

management of forests needs to be imbued with a public purpose

The rich green mantle of forests that once covered nearly half of the earth's land surface is being replaced by a chequered landscape of cities, highways, agricultural fields, pastures, degraded woodlands, forest plantations and land degraded by salinisation and erosion. Much of the forest that remains is being progressively impoverished, and all is threatened. It is not just the fact of this decline in forest cover and quality that constitutes the crisis: it is the global loss of forest functions in maintaining a habitable earth.

The crisis arises because of the importance of forests for environment, for economy, and for society; because of rapidly expanding human demands on forests; because today's economic and political systems permit patterns of use and management that lead to erosion of the forest capital; because of the complacency of those with political power and authority, many of whom ignore or overlook the importance of forests to human and planetary security.

Forested lands have always been used, and will continue to be used, to meet human needs for food, fibre, fuel, shelter and other amenities. The challenge addressed by this report is that the area of forest cover and the internal integrity of forest ecosystems are being lost as the result of excessive human demands and short-sighted use of the landscape.

When human numbers were small, use of the landscape to satisfy human needs could proceed without obvious global consequence. However, the expansion of the human enterprise has now produced increasingly competitive demands for food, water, energy, rich soil, clean air, and space for living and recreation. This transition is taking place on a planet whose forest resources, while nominally renewable, are finite and, under present conditions, rapidly diminishing.

There is a fundamental difference between a world that is empty and open to further exploitation in the face of expansion of the human presence, and a world that is full and running down (Daly, 1993). The difference lies in the progressive limitation of the options available for the support of people. We have now reached that critical stage where intensified use of forested landscapes is of increasing public consequence. As private interests progressively consume forests for land for agriculture and for timber, fibre and fuel, the interests of the public in the environmental services of forests become more important and more valuable relative to the common commercial values. Further net losses in forest area and function result in palpable, cumulative reductions in human welfare. Management of forests therefore needs to be imbued with a public purpose more closely allied to the long-term needs of a growing population and of future generations for a wholesome environment than to private interest. What is at stake now is the stability of the biosphere as a major element in human welfare.

1.2 Forests and the integrity of the human habitat

Forests are the planet's largest and most important terrestrial ecosystem. They have a profound influence on the structure and function of the human habitat locally and globally.

Forests are also the largest reservoir of plants and animals on land. They sustain much of the world's diversity of life with its body of genetic information, developed over evolutionary time, that defines survival of life itself.

Forests protect drainage basins and regulate local and distant water supplies. They create and retain soil. They affect productivity of fisheries and agriculture.

Forests provide living space for humans whose numbers measure in tens of millions. Forests provide the means for their livelihoods as well as succour to hundreds of millions more who live close to forest boundaries. Forests affect the colour of the earth and therefore its reflectivity and temperature, which in turn regulate global and local climate. The metabolism of forests affects the carbon dioxide, methane and nitrous oxide content of the atmosphere day by day, regulating the quality of the atmosphere, and the temperature of the earth and its climates.

Forests provide more than environmental and material services. They have spiritual, aesthetic and symbolic value for many.

They keep the human habitat.

current trends are toward an accelaration of the loss of forested area

1.3 Trends in forest area

The development of civilisation over the past 8,000 years, and especially the expansion and intensification of human activities over the past two centuries, have brought great changes in the area and character of forests globally. An approximation of the changes in area of forests over that time, and a measure of the contemporary potential in reforestation, are offered through a comparison of the maps of Figures 1.1 and 1.2, prepared for the Commission by the World Conservation Monitoring Centre. Over that period, and especially the last two centuries, waves of deforestation and reforestation have swept across regions and the status of forests at any time is but a momentary glimpse of landscapes in transition. Nevertheless, there has been a clear global trend toward a massive loss of forested area. When primary forest alone is considered (Figure 1.3), the transition is even more clear. The current trends are toward an acceleration of the loss of forested area, the loss of residual primary forests, and progressive reduction in the internal quality of residual forest stands.

Measures of total forest area do not reveal forest quality. For example, in the FAO's forest assessment, logging is not counted as deforestation, since forests of logged areas can be restored to forest in time (WRI, 1998). The assumption is misleading in that high latitude forests regenerate so slowly that recovery requires a century or more, a period that assures that recovery will be of little interest to current generations. Nor do statistics on reforestation reflect the reduced ecological and aesthetic values of the plantations that may replace natural forests in some areas.

The world's remaining forested areas are approximately evenly divided between non-tropical (boreal and temperate zone forests) and tropical (Figure 1.2). Their total area globally is variously estimated. The highest current estimate is about 3.60 billion hectares from an originally forested area of more than 6.0 billion hectares (Sharma, 1992). This latter figure is taken by the Commission to be a fair appraisal of the potential area for forests in the world

The largest forested area is the boreal forest zone of the northern hemisphere. The forest is circumpolar, primarily coniferous, and extends southward to mix with the deciduous broad-leaved forests and steppes of the temperate zone. The deciduous forests of the temperate zone were originally particularly well developed in North America, Europe and central China. This forest yields southward to the arid zone of the lower middle latitudes

Figure 1.1 Original global distribution of forests (8,000 years ago)

Source: compiled by World Conservation Monitoring Centre for WCFSD, 1998

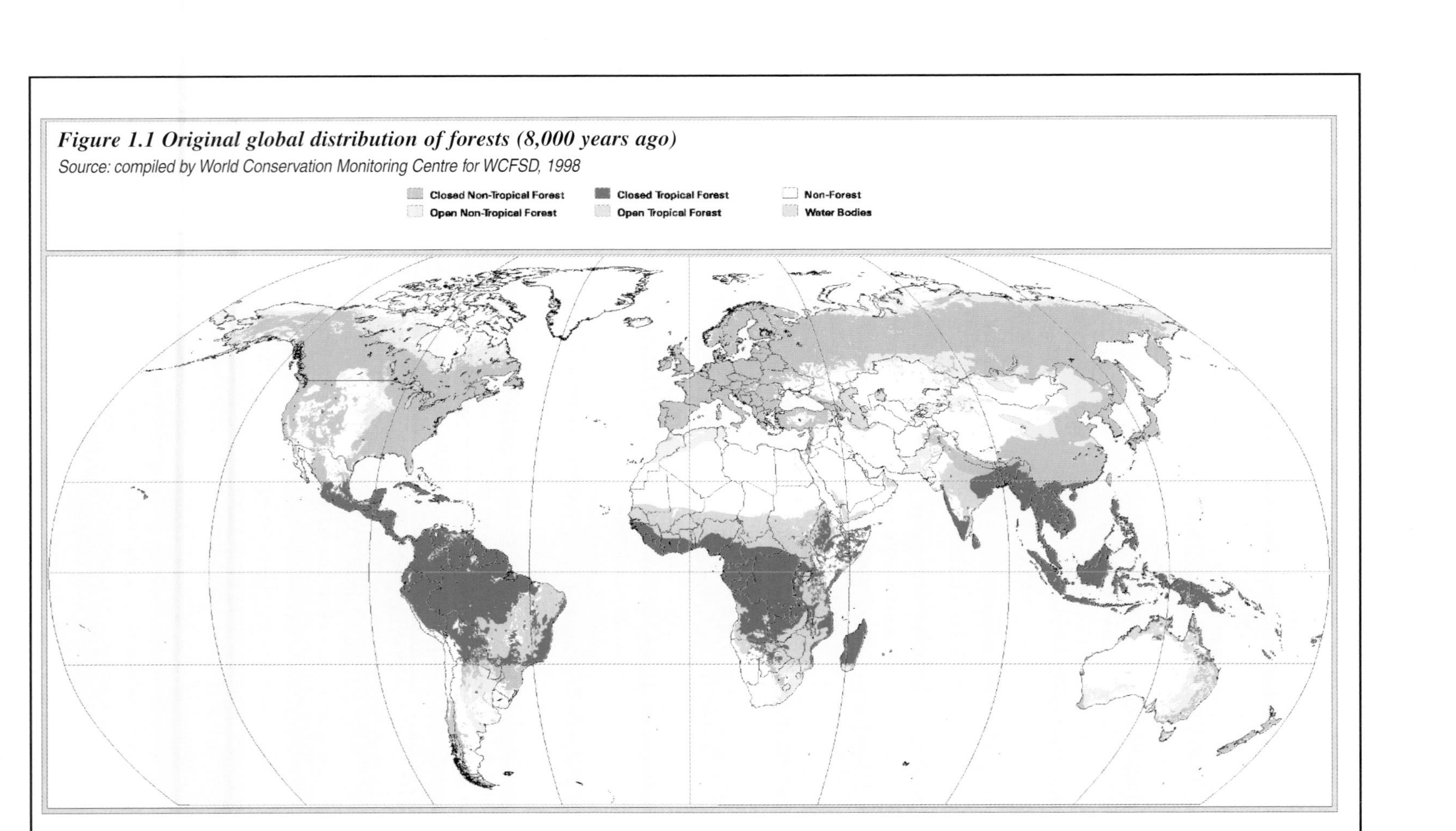

Figure 1.2 Present global distribution of forests

Source: compiled by World Conservation Monitoring Centre for WCFSD, 1998

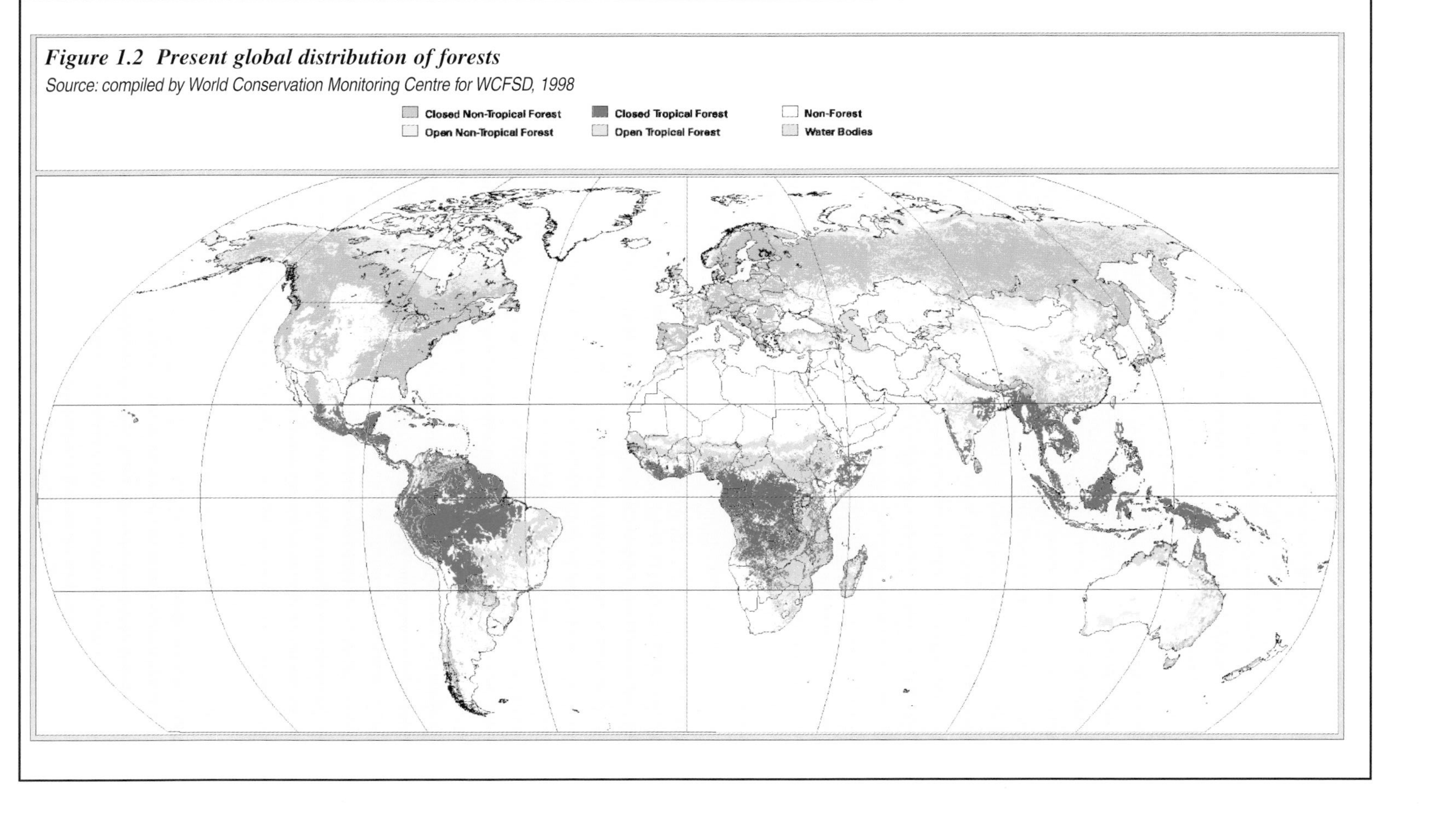

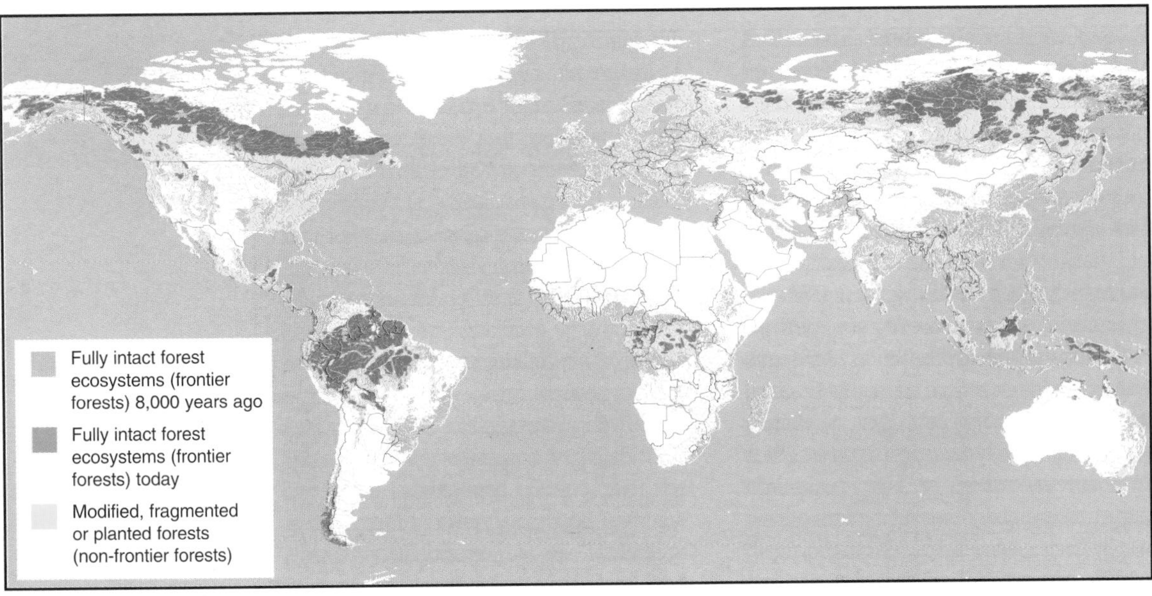

Figure 1.3 Fully intact forest ecosystems (frontier forests) today (shown in green)

Source: WRI, 1997

around the world. The deciduous forest zone includes the complex of pine forests that are in many cases fire-resistant, such as those of the extensive southeastern coastal plain of North America. It includes the *Araucaria* and *Nothofagus* forests of the southern hemisphere.

The moist tropics contain what many consider to be the world's most magnificent array of life. The largest moist tropical forest region is in the Amazon Basin, but the forests extend northward through the Isthmus of Panama into Mexico. In Africa moist tropical forests still dominate the Congo Basin and once reached to the Sahel. In Southeast Asia they extended throughout the islands, the Malay Peninsula, north through the Mekong drainage basin to southern China and eastward to the Indian Peninsula.

the moist tropics contain the world's most magnificent array of life

In the higher latitudes of the southern hemisphere forests are of limited extent because land is limited.

Some forested areas, especially the temperate and boreal forests of Europe and North America, have expanded over several decades as agricultural land has been abandoned in favour of richer lands more amenable to industrial agriculture elsewhere. There has been a net increase (by 0.1%) in forest cover in developed countries from 1980 mainly due to tree plantations (FAO, 1997). Between 1980 and 1995, forest plantations in developed countries increased from approximately 45–60 million hectares to about 80–100 million hectares (WRI, 1992).

Tropical forests have declined sharply in area and, over large areas, internal vigour and integrity over recent decades. It is estimated that about 14 million hectares of tropical forests have been lost each year since 1980 as a result of changes in landuse from forest to agriculture (FAO, 1997).

For the tropics as a whole, deforestation has increased steadily over the period 1960–90 (Singh and Marzoli, 1995), but deforestation rates differ among the regions. The rate of deforestation has continued to increase in South America, it has declined recently in Asia and appears to have stabilised in Africa as forested land useful in agriculture has become progressively limited. Remaining forests, however, are subject to 'high grading' wherever forests have become accessible and, almost universally, to degradation from the effects of mechanical disturbance, pollution, the introduction of exotics, and climatic disruption.

Forest decline threatens the genetic diversity of the world's plants and animals, particularly in the tropical zone where the diversity of plants and animals is greater than anywhere else. IUCN – The World Conservation Union recently calculated that about 12.5% of the world's 270,000 species of plants, and about 75% of the world's mammals are threatened by forest decline and the progressive erosion of other natural habitat (Figure 1.4).

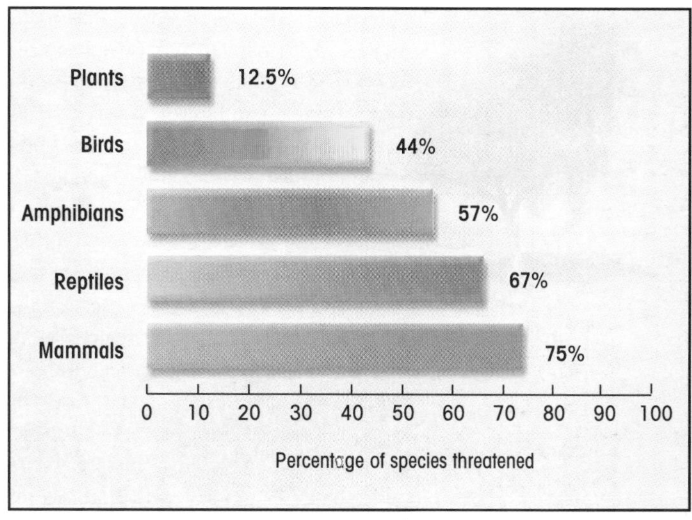

Figure 1.4 Species threatened by the decline of forests and other natural habitat

Source: IUCN, 1996; IUCN, 1997

1.4 The earth is the sum of its parts

The issues in conservation and management of forests differ between the developed and developing regions. In the less developed world, which is largely but not exclusively tropical, the major transition in forests is a rapid reduction in area (deforestation) as a result of the conversion of forested land to other uses (WRI, 1996). To a lesser extent there is a pervasive series of changes in the integrity of internal forest structure (forest degradation or impoverishment) through selective harvest of giant trees and chronic disturbance including climatic change and toxification. The leading causes of deforestation are the extension of subsistence farming (Africa), estate crops such as rubber and oil palm (Asia), and government-backed conversion of forests to other land uses such as large-scale ranching (Latin America) (FAO, 1997). Poverty, unemployment, and inequitable land distribution continue to drive forest clearance for subsistence farming in the tropics.

In the developed world of eastern North America lands abandoned from agriculture as farming moved westward to richer soils during the latter half of the 19th century and the first half of the 20th century have been reforested. In recent decades, however, this reforestation has been more than balanced by extensive harvest of trees from high latitude forests where regrowth is so slow that the harvest is the equivalent of deforestation in any time of human interest. The systematic impoverishment of forests throughout the region is almost universal as a result of chronic disturbance through heavy harvest for timber in some places such as eastern Canada, through toxification, accelerated climatic change, and fire. Primary forests are under great pressure in this entire region and have disappeared from very large sections of it. Table 1.1 summarises forest decline in different regions.

A small number of countries at present dominate the world's remaining forested area, production and export of woodpulp, and production, import and export of wood (FAO, 1995; FAO, 1997) (see Figures 6.1 to 6.6). These countries hold disproportionate power over the global biophysical and economic transitions involving forests. The importance of the direction of these transitions cannot be over-emphasised. Continuing in the same direction, with continued decline in the global forest capital, will speed the disruption of climate and increase the morbidity and mortality of trees globally. While there is no question that the stabilisation of the heat-trapping gas content of the atmosphere as called for under the Framework Convention on Climate Change will require a reduction in use of fossil fuels, there is also no question that the stabilisation cannot be realised without limiting emissions of heat trapping gases from deforestation and from the rapid cutting of trees of the carbon-rich primary forests globally. Failure to stabilise climates globally will lead to a differential warming in the high latitudes of the northern hemisphere and to additional releases of carbon from forests and soils that will only increase the rate of climatic warming globally.

Efforts at restabilising forests will contribute significantly to the restabilisation of climate and other essential attributes of environment, including precipitation, water supplies, and the improvement of the quality and productivity of streams, lakes and coastal waters, not to speak of the contributions to the security of the lives of forest-dwellers and rural communities around the world.

Forests exist within different geographical and ecological zones, and within various political, economic and social arrangements and traditions. The countries in which they exist experience different levels of economic welfare. As a result, the precise stresses to which forests are subject, and the nature and extent of forest decline, vary from region to region. So do the natural and human responses to forest decline. Thus the challenge in management differs regionally in nature and intensity, but is everywhere acute.

Much hinges on the fact that forests are important for more than just economic reasons to individual countries, but also for the common, global services from which all human societies and regions benefit. While contributions to sustaining these services may be analysed and approximated by region or country, the benefits of forests as well as the effects of forest decline are clearly transnational and are shared by all. The fires of 1997–8 in the moist tropical forest of the Amazon Basin, in Mexico, and in Indonesia have sent smoke far and wide to affect the health of tens of millions as though to confirm the regional and international implications of forest management. Seemingly local occurrences have more widespread impacts, and all societies are vulnerable to the consequences of forest decline.

1.5 Temperate boreal forests

Europe and Asia

Sprawling over 11 time zones from the Baltic Sea to the Pacific Ocean, the Commonwealth of Independent States (CIS) embraces the single largest forested area in the world (Figure 1.5), dwarfing the forests of China and Europe. It contains more than 70% of the world's remaining boreal forest.

The future of this vast forest resource of the CIS is threatened by industrial emissions, by the prospect of massive cutting particularly in Siberia and European Russia and by illegal activities and ineffectual government policies. For the time being at least, forest exploitation is out of control in the region. About 10,000 km^2 of forests are estimated to have been lost due to air pollution alone, while large areas appear degraded. Air contamination from nickel smelters of Norlisk has killed 3,500 km^2 and damaged trees over an additional 1,400 km^2 of forests. The Chernobyl

Table 1.1 Regional forest decline

Source: based on work by WCMC, WRI and FAO

Region	Reduction in forest cover during the past 8,000 years (all forests)* %	Reduction in forest cover during the past 8,000 years (intact closed forests)** %	Annual rate of deforestation 1990–1995*** %
CIS	25	70	n.s.
Europe	60	.100	n.s.
Asia[1]	70	95	high, esp. in tropics
Oceania	40	80	high, esp. in tropics
Africa	50	90	high, esp. in tropics mod. in non-tropics
Latin America	40[2]	60[3]	high in tropics very high in C. Am. low in non-tropics
Caribbean	70	90	very high
North America	25[3]	55[2]	high in tropics n.s. in non-tropics

Legend: n.s. (not significant): below 0.1% p.a.
low: 0.1% to below 0.35% p.a.
moderate: 0.35% to below 0.6% p.a.
high: 0.6% to below 1.0% p.a.
very high: above 1.0% p.a.

[1] does not include Japan, where deforestation is n.s.
[2] not including Mexico
[3] including Mexico

* Based on a reconstruction by WCMC for WCFSD (1998). 'All forests' include closed forests (minimum 30% tree canopy cover) and open forests (between 10 and 30% tree canopy cover).

** Based on reconstruction by WRI (1997). CIS figure includes Russia only. Mexico included under Latin America rather than North America. Figure used for Caribbean is same as WRI figure for Central America.

*** Based on FAO's statistics of forest cover which exclude various categories of open woodland, forest fallow and scrub, shrub and brushland.

nuclear disaster of 1987 is thought to have contaminated 7 million hectares of forest and other wooded land in Russia, Belarus and Ukraine. Furthermore, in areas with developed infrastructure, severe local over-harvesting has taken place, along with removal of the most highly valued species over huge areas. Ecologically fragile boreal forests in parts of the Siberian permafrost zone are undergoing severe disturbances from logging, and it is not clear how much they will recover (Shvidenko and Nilsson, 1996).

Europe has been through a cycle of deforestation and reforestation. In 1995 about 40% of the potentially forested land supported forest and there was virtually no primary forest remaining. Deteriorating forest vigour is a matter of major concern. While progressive deforestation is not significant and in most of contemporary Europe forest area may even be increasing at a modest rate, forest degradation remains a considerable threat. For example, FAO reported that though forest cover in Europe (excluding the former

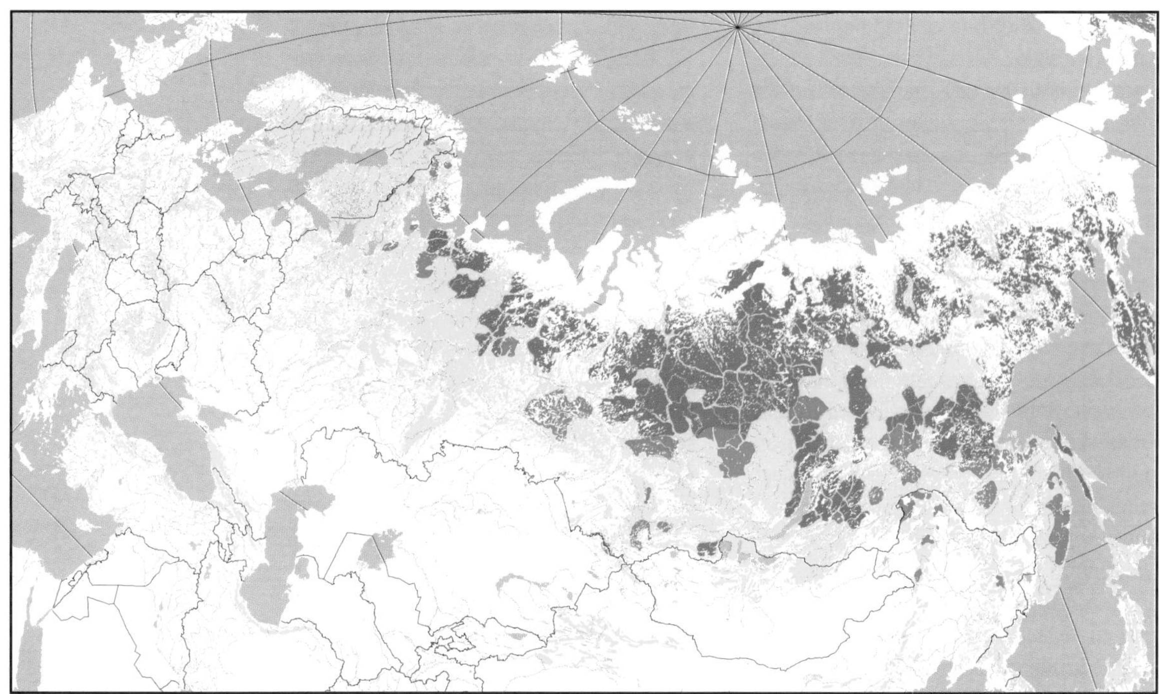

Figure 1.5
CIS and Europe: forests under threat

Fully intact forest ecosystems (frontier forests) under medium or high threat

Fully intact forest ecosystems (frontier forests) unassessed for threat

Fully intact forest ecosystems (frontier forests) under low or no threat

Modified, fragmented or planted forests (non-frontier forests)

Source: WRI, 1997

USSR) increased by more than 4% between 1980 and 1994, forest quality worsened (FAO, 1996). A study carried out in 1995 by the European Commission and the United Nations Economic Commission for Europe (EC-UN/ECE) suggests that the direct causes for decline in forest quality in Europe are drought, heat, pests, and a legacy of silvicultural errors. Air pollution from industrial sources and from other chronic disturbances is identified as an indirect cause of forest decline (FAO, 1997). All of these factors predispose forests to disease.

As a result, more than one-quarter of Europe's trees show signs of significant leaf-loss.[1] A 1997 EC-UN/ECE study classified more than half of Europe's forests as 'damaged'. Forests in north central Europe were especially heavily affected, along with forests in Luxembourg and The Netherlands (Figure 1.6). While improvements in forest condition have been noted in certain locations, overall forest damage seems to be increasing on a regional level. In some parts of north-central Europe (most notably Poland, the Czech Republic and eastern Germany) at least 100,000 hectares of forests have died in the last 20 years (FAO, 1997). Forest damage is severe in some parts of central and Eastern Europe (EC-UN/ECE, 1996). More than 25% of trees assessed in a survey of forest conditions in Europe were suffering significant defoliation. Annual European survey results show the number of completely healthy trees falling from 69% in 1988 to 39% in 1995 (EC-UN/ECE, 1996).

The general pattern now is to conserve what little is left of the primary forests and to manage secondary forests for long-term use. All forests, however, are vulnerable to the ravages of pollution, pests, diseases, and to climatic disruption.

North America

North American forests account for about 13% of the world total (457 million hectares) and cover about 75% of their potentially forested area (Figure 1.7) (FAO, 1997).[2] While primary forests may cover as much as 46% of the potentially forested area (Table 1.1), much of that forest is high latitude boreal forest of low productivity. The highly productive primary forests of giant trees of the Sierra Nevada and other more accessible regions have been reduced in area far more extensively. While net deforestation rates are not significant in temperate North America, they remain high in the sub-tropics of Mexico. In the temperate and boreal regions, forest degradation has come to replace deforestation as the primary concern.

After two centuries of decline following European settlement, the forests of eastern USA and sections of eastern Canada that expanded into land abandoned from agriculture during the 20th century, have fallen victim to a variety of new challenges. Air pollution including acid rain plays a key role in the decline of various forest species, such as the sugar maple (*Acer saccharum*) in eastern Canada and the high elevation forests of red spruce (*Picea rubens*) in the eastern USA (FAO, 1997).

The preservation of primary forests is a matter of great concern in North America, which has some of the most remarkable tracts of giant trees anywhere in the world. These include the extraordinarily rich temperate zone rainforests of the Olympic Peninsula and the Canadian coast, as well as the Sitka spruce forests of the southeastern Alaskan archipelago and adjacent Canada. They include the coastal redwood groves, and the giant Douglas fir forests of the Sierra Nevada and the Cascades, and the complex of pine forests of California and Mexico. All are threatened in their last bastions by commercial interests in timber. The release early in 1998 by the US Forest Service of a management plan that allows large-scale clearcutting in Alaska's Tongass National Forest brings one such threat to reality. This 7 million hectare wilderness, in which some of the trees may be up to one thousand years old, is the largest remaining temperate zone rainforest in the world.

In Mexico, there has been a long history of forest loss due to clearing for land for agriculture. This process continues today, but new forces of industrialisation and pollution now contribute to forest decline.

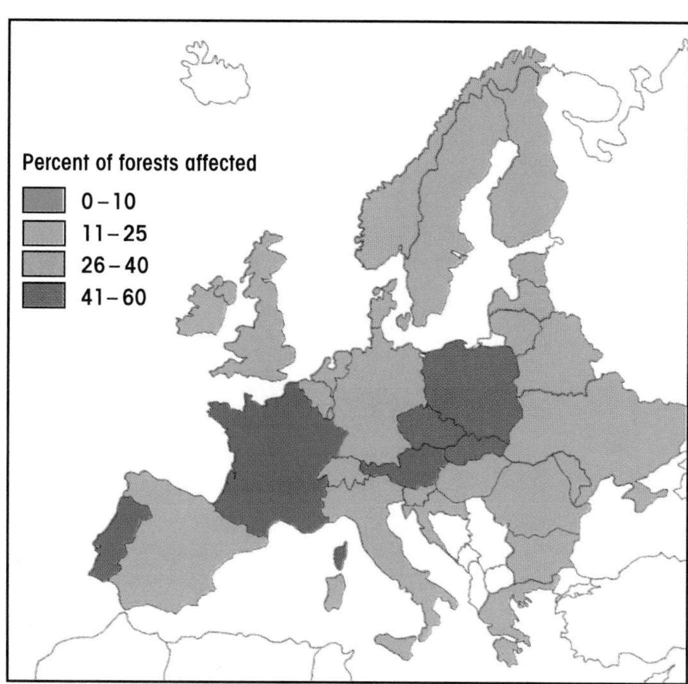

***Figure 1.6* European forests either moderately or severely defoliated or dead, by country, 1994**

Source: EC-UN/ECE, 1995

Figure 1.7
North America: forests under threat

Source: WRI, 1997

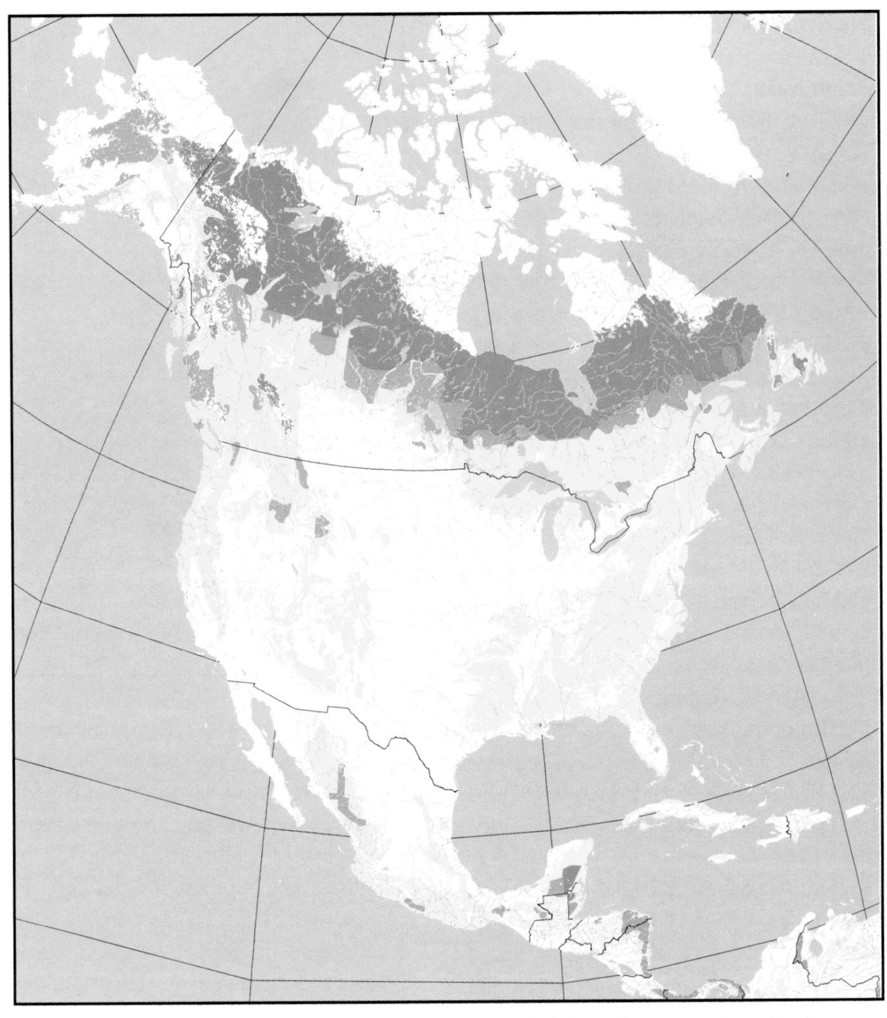

Fully intact forest ecosystems (frontier forests) under medium or high threat

Fully intact forest ecosystems (frontier forests) under low or no threat

Fully intact forest ecosystems (frontier forests) unassessed for threat

Modified, fragmented or planted forests (non-frontier forests)

1.6 Tropical and sub-tropical forests

Asia and Oceania

Asia, the Indian sub-continent, Australia, and the island chain of the Southwestern Pacific, collectively, despite their great land area, are impoverished of forests (Figures 1.8 and 1.9). They contain about 16% (568 million hectares) of the world's residual forest. Under pressures of human expansion in Asia, about 32% of the region's potentially forested area remained in forest in the mid-1990s. Only 6% of the potentially forested land retains primary forest (Table 1.1). In Oceania the forest area is about 60% and primary forest exists over about 22% of the potentially forested region.

Between 1990 and 1995, Asia and Oceania suffered high rates of deforestation, concentrated in tropical areas. During this period, tropical Asian forests suffered from deforestation rates averaging 1.1% per year. Losses in Oceania were lower, at 0.4% per year, but still a cause for concern. Consider what this pattern has meant for some countries. For example, during the 1980s Thailand lost over 5 million hectares of forest, or almost one-third of its natural forest. Over the same period Indonesia lost over 12 million hectares, or 10% of its natural forests.

Forest decline in Asia and Oceania has occurred mainly through clearing for agriculture (both shifting cultivation and commercial farming) and timber (both harvesting and the conversion of biologically diverse forests into plantations) (Figure 1.10). High population densities have led to widespread forest degradation from fuelwood and fodder harvesting, cattle grazing, land invasion and shifting cultivation, and timber harvesting for local construction (FAO, 1997). Commercial timber harvesting has been more widespread (measured as a percentage of forest area) and intensive (timber volume removals per hectare) than in any other tropical region. Other activities implicated in the decline include mining, irrigation, hydroelectric projects and urban expansion (FAO, 1997).

Throughout Asia and Oceania there are many visible signs of land degradation associated with forest decline: reductions in agricultural productivity over large areas of land which was once productive forest, and high rates of soil erosion and sedimentation of dams, reservoirs and irrigation systems. These effects threaten the options for poor rural people in sustaining already precarious livelihoods. In the upland watersheds of

Figure 1.8 Asia: forests under threat

Source: WRI, 1997

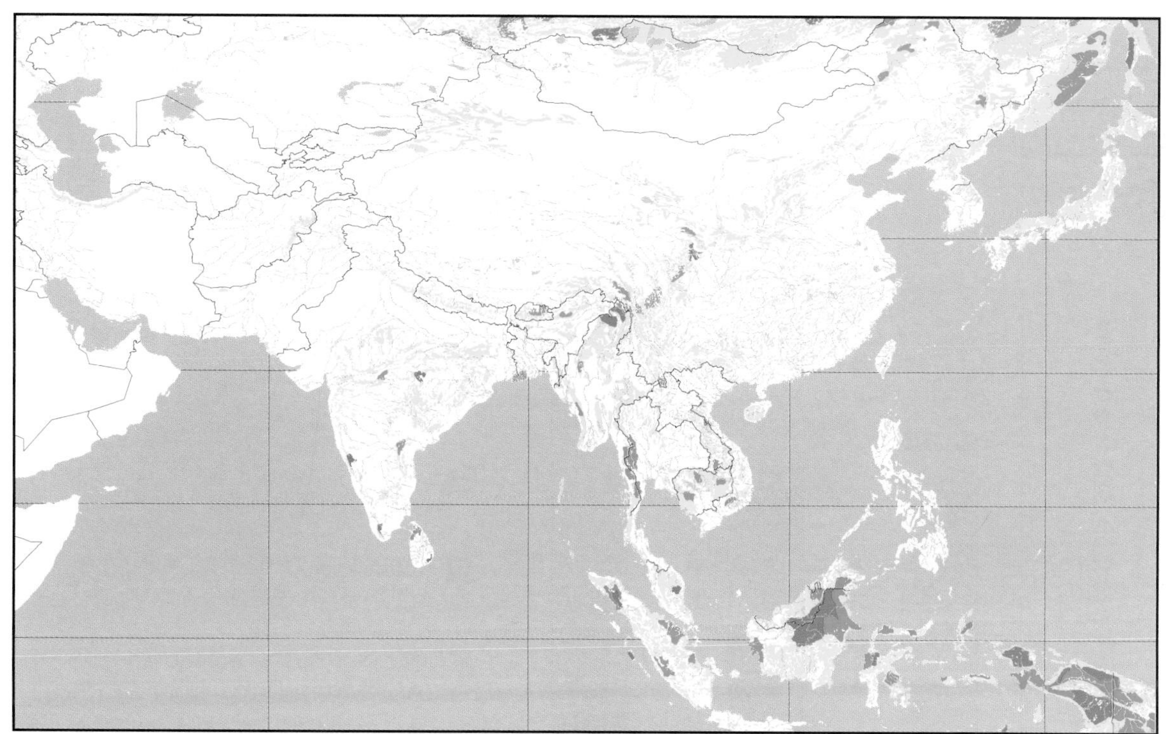

Fully intact forest ecosystems (frontier forests) under medium or high threat

Fully intact forest ecosystems (frontier forests) under low or no threat

Fully intact forest ecosystems (frontier forests) unassessed for threat

Modified, fragmented or planted forests (non-frontier forests)

Figure 1.9 Oceania: forests under threat

Source: WRI, 1997

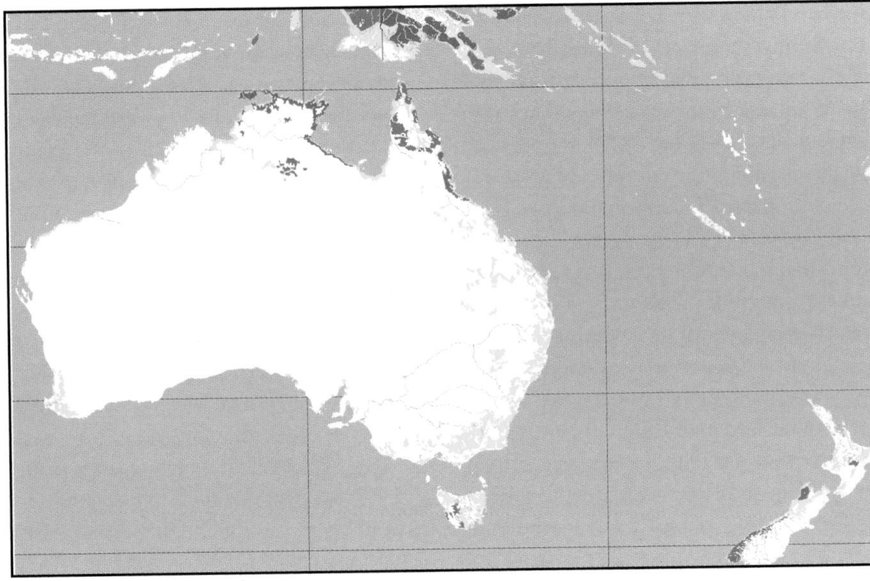

Fully intact forest ecosystems (frontier forests) under medium or high threat

Fully intact forest ecosystems (frontier forests) unassessed for threat

Fully intact forest ecosystems (frontier forests) under low or no threat

Modified, fragmented or planted forests (non-frontier forests)

Figure 1.10 Changes in forest land cover in tropical regions, 1980–1990

Source: based on FAO, 1996

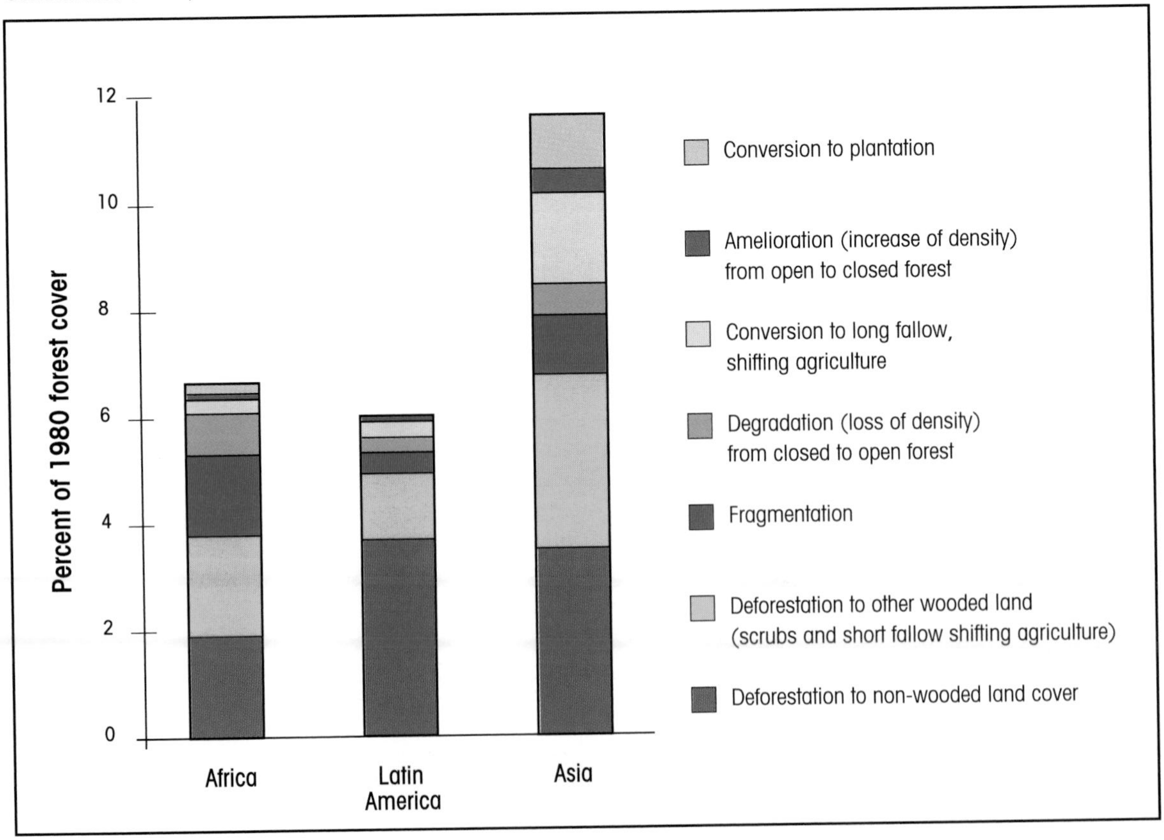

Percent of 1980 forest cover

0
2
4
6
8
10
12

Africa
Latin America
Asia

Conversion to plantation

Amelioration (increase of density) from open to closed forest

Conversion to long fallow, shifting agriculture

Degradation (loss of density) from closed to open forest

Fragmentation

Deforestation to other wooded land (scrubs and short fallow shifting agriculture)

Deforestation to non-wooded land cover

Nepal, Bhutan, China, India and Pakistan, for example, the hillsides are degraded as a result of wood removal. Once-forested parts of Thailand, Indonesia and the Philippines have been reduced to fire-prone scrub and grassland. During 1997–8 drought in Kalimantan Province of Indonesia opened normally moist primary forests dominated by giant Dipterocarps to fires that affected untold areas that will probably, when measured, come to millions of hectares. Recent floods in China have now been accepted by the government as being exacerbated by forest removal. Species such as Japan's *Cryptomeria japonica* are suffering from air pollution (FAO, 1997).

Africa

In 1995, African forests accounted for about 15% of the world total (520 million hectares) (FAO, 1997) (Figure 1.11). About 50% of the region's potential forest cover had been lost. Primary forest existed on 8% of the potential area of forest (Table 1.1). Meanwhile, net deforestation continues at a high rate, particularly

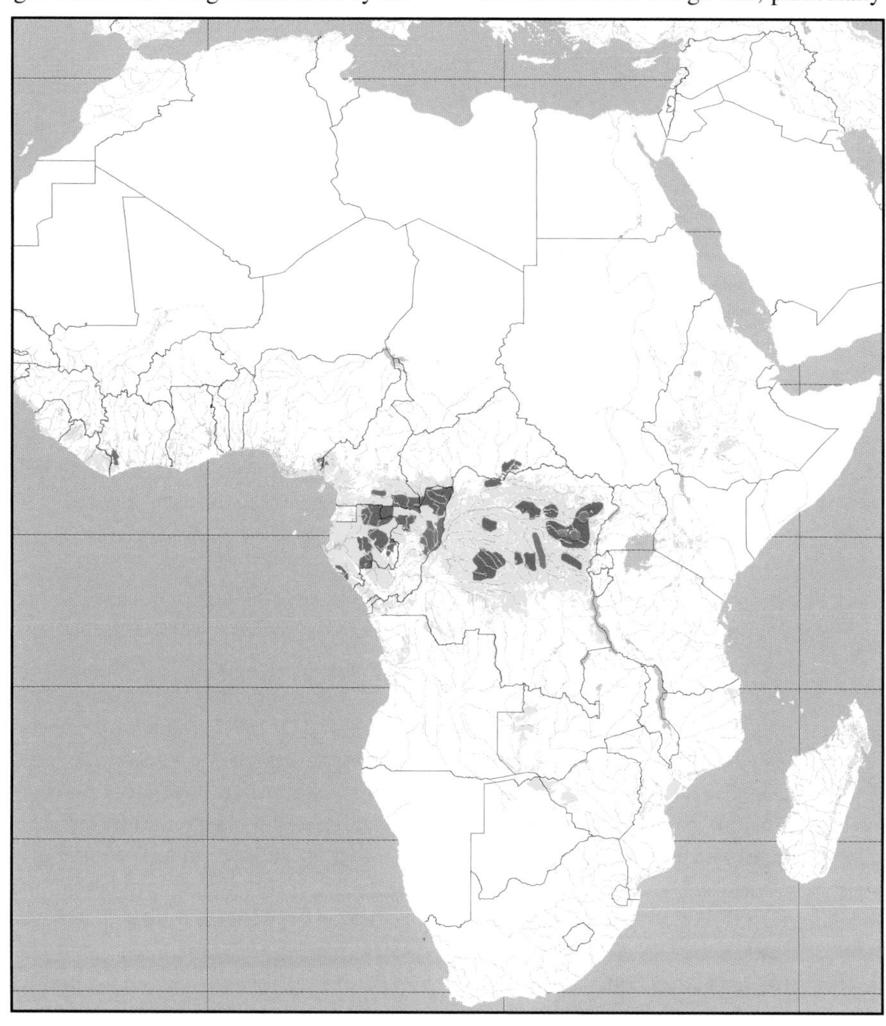

Figure 1.11* *Africa: forests under threat

Source: WRI, 1997

in tropical areas, though deforestation rates are more moderate in both the southern and northern reaches of Africa. Over the 1980–95 period, Africa experienced a greater percentage decrease in total forest area – 10.5% – than any other region (FAO, 1997). During the 1980s alone, Africa lost some 40 million hectares of natural forests.

Nearly three-quarters of the original tropical moist forest in West Africa have been lost over the past 50 years. Several countries (Burundi, Côte d'Ivoire, Kenya, Madagascar, Nigeria, Rwanda) lost more than 90% of their original forest cover in this short period as population exploded and the demand for agricultural land soared. Nigeria, a major timber exporter in the 1960s, now imports wood products valued in excess of US$100 million per year.

Much of the West African tropical humid forests, located mainly in lowland areas and accessible to the coast, has undergone substantial commercial harvesting. In many areas, these forests have been converted to agricultural uses. In Nigeria and Côte d'Ivoire, for example, primary forests were heavily logged in the 1970s and expansion of agriculture onto forest lands has occurred during the intervening period (FAO, 1997). Timber harvesting has intensified in some West African countries, and many timber companies are now operating in Central Africa, which contains more than 90% of the region's remaining rainforests. Political instability has enabled exploitative use to be made of timber resources in the Congo Basin. Pressure on Africa's extensive open forests is also heavy in many places due to agricultural expansion and increased fuelwood collection and livestock grazing (FAO, 1997).

Latin America and the Caribbean

The forests of this region include the extensive primary forests of the Amazon Basin, the largest contiguous area of tropical forest remaining in the world. This region is rapidly being opened to settlement to relieve population pressures in South America's giant cities such as Rio de Janeiro and São Paulo, and to feed the interests of commerce. In 1995, forests in Latin America and the Caribbean accounted for about 28% of the world's forests (950 million hectares) (Figure 1.12). In the mid-1990s, forests occupied about 62% of the potentially forested area and about 40% of the primary closed forest remained. The more densely occupied Caribbean islands retain about 28% of their potentially forested area in forests and about 10% of their original primary forests (Table 1.1).

The Latin America and Caribbean region suffers from some of the highest current-day rates of forest decline. Deforestation rates for the 1990–95 period were high throughout the tropical areas, and very high in Central America (2.2% per year) and the Caribbean (1.7% per year) (FAO, 1997). The region lost 9.7% of its forest area between 1980 and 1995 alone (FAO, 1997). Over the 1990 to 1995 period, this meant a loss of about 5.3 million hectares of forest each year.

This loss is largely due to the direct conversion of forests to non-forest uses, linked to large-scale projects to settle and develop the region: clearance for agriculture and stockfarming; construction of roads, dams and other infrastructure; and mining (FAO, 1997). Furthermore, forest decline is driven by inequitable land tenure systems that force large numbers of landless rural people to invade forests in order to survive. Forest decline also arises from fire, pest infestation and extraction of timber and fuelwood (FAO, 1997). Forest fires are a major contributing factor to forest decline especially in the arid and semi-arid zone. Fires are often lit to clear land for agriculture (FAO, 1997). A recent additional phenomenon is the arrival of transnational corpora-

Fully intact forest ecosystems (frontier forests) under medium or high threat

Fully intact forest ecosystems (frontier forests) unassessed for threat

Fully intact forest ecosystems (frontier forests) under low or no threat

Modified, fragmented or planted forests (non-frontier forests)

Figure 1.12 Latin America and the Caribbean: forests under threat

Source: WRI, 1997

tions, increasingly from other developing regions like Southeast Asia, interested in large logging operations, and with no commitment to long-term sustainability of the forests which they mine. Some cash-poor governments are willing to accept their operations because of the short-term economic opportunities they offer.

Fire-related deforestation increased sharply in Brazil in recent years. Official estimates of Amazon deforestation have not been released, but indications are that the deforestation rate increased significantly in 1997–8, primarily due to the spread of fires during the unusual drought of that period. Satellite data for the Amazon region show a 50% increase from 1996 to 1997 in the number of forest fires set by farmers to clear land for cultivation

Despite the significant decrease in area of primary forest, the region remains the repository of a very high proportion of the world's biotic wealth.

1.7 Importance of forests

forests have a great influence on the structure and functioning of the human habitat.

Despite the emphasis on the economic value of forests and their local economic and ecological importance, forests are universally significant for their planetary functions.[3] Forests contribute to the fundamental ecological processes which keep the planet in a state of quasi-equilibrium.[4] Forests have, apart from humans themselves, the greatest influence on the structure and functioning of the human habitat. Forests are fundamental to the maintenance of a habitable biosphere: they conserve biological diversity, shield the earth's landscape from abrupt change, bring order to the flow and quality of water, and help to stabilise climate regionally and globally. These are the common, global services from which all regions and human societies benefit. All societies are vulnerable to the global effects of massive losses of forests, as the continuity of forest functions touches everyone directly and indirectly. It is worth exploring some of these functions in detail.

Biodiversity

Forests contain at least two-thirds of the earth's terrestrial species. This wealth of species is heavily dependent for habitat on primary forests in all regions, although the greatest diversity occurs in the tropics. Plant diversity ensures a sufficiently wide range of tree species to buffer forests and their function in regulating landscapes from disruption by pests, disease, and the normal vagaries of climate. The biotic diversity of forests is used as building blocks for selection and breeding of plants and animals to a range of environments and human uses. This genetic bank is also drawn upon to strengthen the yield and resistance of domesticated and commercial food crops and for materials of medicinal, pharmaceutical and industrial value. The evidence is that we have tapped but a fraction of the potential of this genetic resource. At the same time, that genetic resource base is constantly under threat: for example, it is reported that 10% of the world's tree species (more than 8,750 of the 80,000 to 100,000 species known to science) is threatened with extinction (WCMC/IUCN/WWF, 1998).

Landscapes and water

In their natural state, not disrupted by human incursions, forests stabilise the landscape. The binding action of tree roots slows erosion, reducing sedimentation, protecting rivers, coastlines and fisheries. They control the chemistry of water in groundwater and in streams and lakes, thereby protecting fish and fisheries. Forests make rain locally and keep landscapes moist in periods of drought. They prevent desertification and natural disasters caused by flooding and landslides. All forests play a central role in the nutrient cycles of elements including nitrogen, phosphorus, and potassium as well as calcium, magnesium, and iron and the trace elements. Trees absorb and store the nutrients, preventing them from being leached away to cause pollution of waterways as well as impoverishment of the land.

Forests regulate water supplies. They collect, store, filter, and re-circulate the water so essential for all life. On a global level, forests contribute to the integrity and stability of the hydrological cycle and ensure the proper stability of the circulation of water from land to atmosphere and, through precipitation, back to the land. As much as half the precipitation in the Amazon Basin arises as evapo-transpiration from forests within the Basin. The latent heat of evaporation is the major source of energy driving climates globally and forests have a major influence on that part of the global hydrologic cycle.

Climate

The role of forests in climate is complex, large and important, but difficult to define in detail. Forests, on the one hand, are said to cause precipitation and to assure an equable climate. On the other hand, climatologists have long believed that climate determines the vegetation which then influences climate only to the extent of local microclimate.

There is little question, however, as to the influence of forests on reflectivity of the planetary surface. Forests are a black body in contrast to non-forest and the removal of forest cools the lower atmosphere while warming the ground surface, which becomes more reflective. The removal also reduces evapo-transpiration and the energy transferred to the atmosphere in latent heat, thereby affecting not only the amount of water and energy transferred, say, from the tropics to the higher latitudes, but also affecting the energy content of the atmosphere and its distribution. The magnitude of these disruptions through deforestation or simple transformation of forests through harvest of timber is potentially large. It is a topic of intensive contemporary study.

The issue is the more complicated because of the warming of the earth, now under way. Forests loom large in this set of considerations because they both fix carbon and metabolise carbon compounds. Forests, with their soils, contain two to three times the amount of carbon currently held in the atmosphere. They process each year through photosynthesis and respiration an amount of carbon equivalent to 15–20% of that total. The most serious threat is the possibility that the warming will tip the balance towards accelerated metabolism, releasing additional carbon dioxide and methane into the atmosphere. If so, we shall be faced with a significant feedback that speeds the warming and might put realisation of the objectives of the Framework Convention on Climate Change beyond reach (Houghton, 1998).

In contrast to that possibility is the potential of forests for absorbing carbon into plants and soil, thereby reducing the accumulation in the atmosphere. This absorption is continuous in the contemporary world. But the potential for absorbing carbon is reduced when deforestation or forest impoverishment occurs. The circumstance provides one further reason for protecting the remaining primary forests globally and avoiding a further net release of carbon into the atmosphere.

the role of forests in climate is complex, large and important

Commercial products

The production of wood and the manufacture of wood products contribute about US$400 billion to the world market economy (about 2% of total GDP). Over US$100 billion is traded internationally and accounts for about 3% of world merchandise trade. Commercial wood production occupies a central economic position in Scandinavian countries, Canada, USA, Indonesia and Malaysia, among other countries, generating valuable export revenue for national development and improving their balance of payments. A growing range of non-wood forest products, from rattans and rubber to fruits, nuts and nature-based medicine and recreational services, also enter into commercial transactions. There is a rising demand for these products based on a desire to use natural materials, and their economic importance appears vigorous enough to continue to grow in the coming years.

Rural livelihoods

Forests are a major factor in contributing directly to the livelihoods and independence of hundreds of millions, many of whom may be but marginal participants in national or regional economic systems. Much of the economic importance of forests is not reflected in financial transactions at all. Forests provide a wide range of other wood and non-wood products which are not reflected in national income accounts but which remain critical to large numbers of poor people. These products include wood, vines and other materials for building homes, tools and other everyday implements; fruits, nuts, roots, meat and other food; herbal medicines for curing ailments and improving health, and much more besides. Forests and farm trees thus act as a buffer against poverty. Forests provide opportunities to the poorest and least educated members of the community for small-scale processing and trading activities which require little financial capital or skill. Forests contribute to food security of poor rural communities by providing a wide range of foodstuffs to supplement their small-scale agricultural production. Forests contribute to small-scale agricultural productivity by maintaining soil fertility, by providing fodder and shade for livestock, and by protecting watersheds and regulating water flow and quality.

forests and farm trees act as a buffer against poverty

Energy security

Two billion people in developing countries still rely on traditional fuels as their principal source of energy. Biomass accounts for 15% of the world's total energy consumption. Fuelwood accounts for 5% of total energy consumption and represents half of all wood consumption (or about 1.9 billion cubic metres per year). Fuelwood is used for 58% of all the energy used in Africa, 15% in Latin America and 11% in Asia. In some 40 developing countries (many of them amongst the least developed), fuelwood accounts for more than 70% of all energy use. Used wisely, fuelwood offers a potentially renewable source of energy for future generations.

Women and children

Because of traditional division of labour, women and their children have specific needs and interests in forests compared with men. In many societies, it is women and children who collect and transport the household's fuelwood for cooking and heating, who gather wild fruit, nuts, fodder, medicines and other materials, and who engage in small-scale, forest-based enterprises as a source of income. As a result, forests often have special importance for women and family welfare.

Cultural and recreational value

Forests are an intrinsic part of all cultures with a forest heritage. Forests occupy a central position in the daily lives of many people, most notably for many indigenous and rural communities. Others still find the roots of their modern cultural identity in the forest, whether as formerly forest-worshipping Scandinavians or Japanese, as Canadians with their maple leaf flag, or as new urbanites from Jakarta to São Paulo. Everywhere, even people without obviously forest-defined cultures go to forests to enjoy their special aesthetic and recreational qualities.

1.8 Forests and sustainable development

The phrase 'sustainable development' gained international prominence in 1980 when the International Union for the Conservation of Nature published the World Conservation Strategy (WCS). The WCS had "the overall aim of achieving sustainable development through the conservation of living resources" (IUCN, 1980). According to the WCS, development could be sustained only if human activities operate within the reality of resource limitations and carrying capacities of ecosystems. The WCS thus emphasised the biophysical sustainability of ecosystems. It was thought that human well-being would automatically follow from efforts to maintain ecosystem health. However, the WCS failed to recognise the political nature of the development process as it assumed that the benefits from conservation could bypass structures of inequality in society and reach the poor. It ignored structures of inequality in society which prevented the flow of benefits from conservation to the poor (Adams, 1990).

Some development thinkers notably Sachs (1979) and Glaeser (1984) sought to rectify this shortcoming through the introduction of the concept of 'ecodevelopment' (Adams, 1990). Ecodevelopment focused on the satisfaction of basic human needs while maintaining ecological health (Sachs, 1979; Glaeser and Vyasulu, 1984). In contrast to the physical sustainability approach of the WCS, ecodevelopment concentrated on need fulfilment at the local level. In its early phase of conceptualisation, ecodevelopment was influenced by the neo-populist approach to development thinking in the 1970s (Adams, 1990). Kitching (1982) has defined neo-populism as a "pattern of development based on small scale individual enterprise both in industry and agriculture". Neo-populism emphasised basic needs, decentralisation, community participation, use of indigenous knowledge, and the adoption of appropriate technology.

Ecodevelopment remained marginal to the development debate as it limited itself to development at the local scale and neglected larger issues of national economic management (Adams, 1990). However the basic needs approach of neo-populism and ecodevelopment was instrumental in shaping present thinking on sustainable development as laid out in the 1987 report of the World Commission on Environment and Development. This report, popularly known as the Brundtland Report, defined sustainable development as "development that meets the needs of the present without compromising the ability of future generations to meet their own needs" (WCED, 1987). This definition and the approach of the Brundtland Report moved the debate beyond the goal of achieving physical sustainability by advocating 'critical objectives' of sustainable development as the satisfaction of basic needs and conserving and enhancing the resource base of the poor (WCED, 1987), with emphasis on both inter-generational and intra-generational equity.

the Brundtland Report moved the debate beyond the goal of achieving physical sustainability

The June 1992 United Nations Conference on Environment and Development (UNCED) at Rio recognised that problems of poverty and food security were linked to deforestation and that external indebtedness of developing countries had reduced their capacity to manage forests sustainably. Countering the effects of deforestation became a major component of sustainable development efforts aimed at poverty elimination, as deforestation had impoverished a large number of forest-dependent communities in developing countries.

It is the linkage between forests and sustainable development which motivated the Commission and those who contributed to its public hearings. There is a high level of understanding that forest decline threatens all of its functions and services. It impairs the functional integrity of forests globally, contributes to economic insecurity for the world community, and undermines social stability and cultural diversity locally. The effects on environment, economy, and society interconnect and affect one another, compounding cause and effect, transcending national boundaries, and undermining our ability to sustain forests and development. Impairing the capacity of forests to sus-

the linkage between forests and sustainable development motivated the Commission

tain these functions imperils not just the welfare of this generation but others to come. People understand these issues, worry about them, and are increasingly willing to change the way things are done. This report is about why such change needs to take place, and with urgency.

Current interest in the fate of forests has been enhanced by the concern about global warming. The role of forests as cause of, and as potential cure for, global warming has brought new attention to retaining sufficient forests globally to protect the public interest in a habitable earth. The quality and continuity of the human habitat is now equated with the continuity of forests globally. Reducing, or stopping, the transfers of forested land to other uses, and stopping the further degradation or impoverishment of existing forests, are essential, early steps in stabilising the atmosphere.

developing countries lose US$45 billion each year because of poor forest management

But at the same time forests are in demand for more conventional purposes – to satisfy the needs of forest dwellers and others who rely on forest resources for their food, fuel and fibre. The fuel, even today, for about one billion people in the world, is wood. Forest decline threatens their source of these staples for subsistence.

There are also less visible relationships. Forest decline leads to loss of biological resources and their diversity, which threatens humanity's food and wood supplies, and the availability of medicinal elements. It leads to loss of economic and recreational opportunity. It disrupts essential ecological functions such as the regulation of water runoff, the control of erosion, the assimilation of wastes and purification of water, cycling of carbon and nutrients, and climate stability (Heywood, 1995).

Figure 1.13
World population, 1950–2050, with three projections of growth

Source: United Nations, 1998

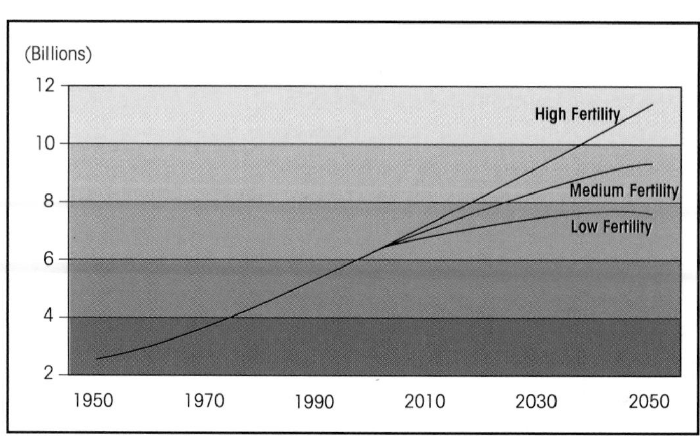

Human demands on the landscape are set not only to continue but to increase exponentially in the foreseeable future, due to the increase in human numbers that is already in train and irreversible (Figure 1.13); to consumption patterns, levels, and aspirations; and to further increases in wealth among those who already consume disproportionately. Interpret all of these into the demand for food, energy, living space, and other amenities of modern living in the decades ahead, and the prospects for satisfying these increased demands from the finite space of the planet are not encouraging. If everything remains unchanged, and unless human society radically changes the way that the overall landscape is used and managed, the implications for forests are that their decline will continue, further eroding the capital resources of the earth, further reducing the capacity of countries to meet their development needs in a sustained way, and exacerbating social and political unrest.

In developing countries alone, it is calculated that approximately US$45 billion are lost each year because of poor forest management (Chandrasekharan 1996). The most significant losses are often not recorded in the money economy or in national and corporate accounts: the extinction of species, the loss of topsoil, the sedimentation of reservoirs, and the loss of productive fisheries (MacNeill, 1996). The irony is that it is precisely these countries which need to maximise the contribution of forests to their economic development. Rural poverty and forest degradation are closely linked as a large number of people in developing countries depend on forest resources, mainly fuelwood, for their sustenance. Forest degradation increases poverty, as forest products become harder or costlier to obtain.

If forests were important only for supplying the material needs of human societies, then perhaps there would be no crisis. Human evolution has always involved making use of the world's natural resources for shelter, energy, tools and food. Human ingenuity would no doubt develop substitutes for meeting those needs when nature's sources expire. But forests are also important for meeting material needs of other species, non-material needs of the human species, and ecological needs of the planet. There is no substitute. The continued services must be assured through political choices and policy decisions; and they must be reflected in landscape planning and management that are intended to allow forests to endure.

1.9 Politics and policies for a new era

Some major issues are set to dominate politics and policies into the twenty-first century. These have appropriately been the subject of the major United Nations Conferences during this decade: stabilisation of the human habitat, population and development, poverty eradication, gender equity, food security, social infrastructure. They have all generated their respective programmes of action as roadmaps to guide policy and action towards the objectives which they enshrine. Many of these imperatives are now reflected in the continuing work programme of the United Nations Commission on Sustainable Development.

The most fundamental and urgent among them, from the perspective of this Commission, are the needs to stabilise the human habitat and to ameliorate the condition of poverty in which the majority of the world's people live. With the demands on the landscape that the expansion of human numbers will create, these issues are set to dominate the politics of development into the 21st century. Given the preceding discussion, the fate of forests will be a key element in that political process, within countries and among them.

The majority of those who live outside the money economy and pass for 'poor' live in rural areas, depend on locally available natural resources, and are knowledgeable about the environment on which they depend. This recognition echoed throughout the public hearings of the Commission. The subjects of forests and poverty are closely linked. But the linkage goes well beyond the contribution of forests and trees to food security and fuelwood: it embraces issues of population growth, governance, empowerment, equity, consumption, and public versus private interests. Neither restoring forests nor tackling poverty can be divorced from these issues.

Improved forest management arrangements and practices are needed to sustain forests indefinitely and to contribute to more equity in the distribution of benefits from their use. However, the analysis of forest decline, and the commensurate responses which are called for, go well beyond the forestry sector. Thus the Commission addresses causes of forest decline which derive from current policies and from economic and political arrangements. The Commission believes that there is scope for short-term improvement in some aspects of these, for example, removal of perverse subsidies, increased transparency in decision-making about forest concessions, improvement in community and civil society participation.

greater participation in decision-making and management by communities is needed

Undoubtedly some causes will require solutions that are only possible in the long term, for example, creation of market mechanisms which can allow the wide range of values placed on forests to be reflected in the economic sphere. Human beings have designed these systems, based on different imperatives, informed by different concerns, guided by different values. They are not immutable. They need to be changed in keeping with the requirements of a new era. Resource problems are, after all, human problems that are generated through economic and political systems which humans design (Ludwig *et al.*, 1993).

Choices are made in contemporary societies through the operation of political and economic forces. The weak and disempowered segments of society are destined to become more so, unless the politics of countries makes space for them at the decision-making table. Private interests will always find ways of overriding the public interest, unless governance arrangements force openness and transparency and equity into the public's business regarding forests, and unless civil society is vigilant about the discharge of a responsibility to hold forests in trust. Here lies a major challenge for governments as well as civil society in the new era.

The Commission presents some examples of the positive contribution which civil society organisations and communities are making, drawn from, among other sources, the public hearings of the Commission. If only their full potential could be liberated through policies and measures that would remove obstacles in their way! The Commission argues for greater participation in decision-making and management by communities who closely depend on forest resources, and by civil society generally. While the Commission recognises that simply opening up decision-making and management to participation will not by itself reverse the decline of forests, given that many of the causes of decline originate outside forestry operations, it is advocated as a necessary means of achieving greater social equity, which is so essential to sustaining human societies and to achieving sustainable development. New forms of governance and institutions to permit wider and more nearly equitable participation therefore have to be high on the political and social agenda in the new millennium. Radical changes are required in the objectives of forest management: from sustaining timber yields to sustaining forests, from securing private interests to assuring the public interest.

The Commission accordingly explores the role of government in creating a governance framework that would be conducive to such empowerment, as well as its role in representing and securing the public interest. Similarly, the Commission argues for mechanisms to encourage, catalyse and support a larger public role in discharging the public trust in forests.

Some controversial practices are at the centre of forest management debates. Scientists and foresters advise that we are able to manage forests sustainably. This would secure products for human use, assure the required threshold of environmental services, contribute to more equity in use of and benefits from forest resources, conserve forest capital for future generations and maintain economic viability. Present scientific knowledge and understanding of forest ecology are not perfect but progressing. The Commission found an impressive and increasing body of analysis and policies which can be put into effect immediately to overcome some of the root causes of forest decline, as well as many initiatives aimed at sustainable forest management now in train. Much of this becomes possible when science is brought together with local knowledge and stewardship of forest resources. The Commission asserts that human societies, and especially their political leadership, can no longer hide under cover of not enough information or understanding, although it is acknowledged that there are many areas in which further research is required and that there is need for continuous learning.

While management of forests and operations of the forestry industry do need to improve by integrating economic needs with environmental imperatives and social objectives, that is not a sufficient response to the forces which underlie forest decline. Many of these forces originate in non-forest sectors, associated with the need for agriculture, energy, transportation, and human settlements. So it is not simply the decisions that are made about forests alone that would sustain them or not. The Commission discusses projected demand in several of these sectors, and the implications for forests. It advocates that we must reach beyond forestry, into more holistic landscape planning, land and resource management, if the whole is to work to a common purpose. Thus the Commission encourages the adoption of landscape planning, in the context of widespread participation, as the approach to resource use that would sustain both forests and development.

Of course many issues relating to sustaining forests and development still need to be worked out. This is especially true of the international dimensions of the forest debate in an economically interdependent but unequal world. It is unfortunate but true that much of the debate on environmental issues since UNCED has been frustrated by a North–South, developed–developing, rich–poor divide, which has created a 'fault-line' throughout intergovernmental processes, including the Intergovernmental Panel on Forests and the Intergovernmental Forum on Forests. The desire of the developed world to impose environmental rectitude on governments in developing countries struggling with massive debt burdens and huge social demands, while continuing with its own conspicuous pattern and wasteful level of consumption, has not made a message of sustainable use or conservation acceptable to those with very little to consume. This has led to frustration and slow progress within intergovernmental processes. It is therefore inescapable that what has been referred to as the 'ecological footprints' of developed countries will need to be faced, otherwise any messages of prudent or wise use of resources will only be seen as posturing of the rich nations.

This inequity underlies many facets of international and intergovernmental discussion: whether about economic globalisation, liberalised trade, or technology cooperation. Traditional financial transfers through development aid have proved inadequate as a way of reducing that inequity and are no longer regarded as compensating for it. New financial transfer mechanisms are required. If forests are so vital to planetary stability which benefits all societies, then the services which forests provide ought to be recognised and valued.

The Commission discusses some of the issues which preoccupy but still divide the international community, and puts forward ideas which could span that divide. Perhaps the most intractable of these is the question of who bears the opportunity costs of conserving forests. The Commission proposes development of an index of the 'forest capital' of all countries, that would create the possibility for new financial mechanisms to compensate for forest services. The Commission has considered the value of all governments embarking on negotiations for a convention on forests at this time, and is convinced that more urgency is now required than such a process would engender. Moreover, more effective implementation of existing related treaties, as well as more committed pursuit of recommendations arising from the Intergovernmental Panel on Forests and the ongoing Intergovernmental Forum on Forests, would significantly address major issues. The Commission's overriding concern is for rapid and constructive attention to the forest crisis.

Forests have virtually disappeared in twenty-five countries; eighteen have lost more than 95% of their forests and another eleven have lost 90%. Ultimately, the implications of present rates of forest decline go far beyond individual societies: they affect all of humankind, all other species, and the planet as a whole. What the Commission advocates are conscientious political leadership, innovative processes for collaborative policies and actions, unifying of relevant expertise, and responding with a sense of urgency. It is this sense of urgency that has led the Commission to feel that at the present time negotiating an international convention on forests may not be the most effective response to the crisis. The Commission therefore calls on a select group of countries – given the forest resources which they command, their production, trade and consumption – to provide that political leadership, to inject a sense of urgency, and to accelerate the pace of searching for the solutions to the global forest crisis. The situation that they share should impel them towards full commitment and to collaborate more effectively in this endeavour.

The forest crisis presents us with a stark choice: whether to continue with approaches to economic development that threaten the health and survival of forests directly and assure the erosion of the human habitat, or to limit further intrusions into forest capital now to ensure the functioning of the human habitat into the future. During the life of this Commission there has been a recommitment by governments, international cooperation agencies, and societies generally to eliminate poverty. This will require many of the changes advocated in this report. It is not too late to choose a path which respects and reflects the many values of forests while still recognising their role in raising material standards of living – sustaining both forests and development. Switching to that sustainable path will become more and more costly the longer the decision is delayed. For the moment, that choice is still open, and it is in the hands of this present generation.

Endnotes

1 The UN-ECE and the European Union classify degrees of defoliation on the basis of the proportion of needle and leaf loss from 0 to 100%. Only three classes of defoliation (moderate (25 to 60% loss), severe (60 to 100% loss) and dead (100% loss) are included here. In Ireland and Sweden, only conifers were assessed. In Moldova, only broad-leaved trees were assessed. No data are available for Liechtenstein, the Russian Federation, Turkey, and the former Yugoslavia.

2 When other wooded lands are included, forests cover approximately 850 million ha, or slightly more than 40% of the total North American land area. Of this, closed forests account for about 500 million ha or 25% of the land area.

3 The biophysical role of forests has been explored in detail for the purposes of the Commission by a Scientific Advisory Committee, which has prepared a report,

Forests in a Full World, edited by G.M. Woodwell, which is being prepared for publication. For details of the following discussion this report should be consulted.

[4] Costanza *et al.* (1997) have estimated that ecosystems provide at least US$33 trillion worth of services annually, of which about 38% comes from terrestrial systems, mainly forests and wetlands.

Only when the last tree has died...

... will we realise that we cannot eat money
(19th century Cree Native American)

2

ROOTS OF THE CRISIS

Resource problems are, after all,
human problems that are generated
through economic and political
systems which humans design
(Ludwig *et al.*, 1993)

2.1 Roots are broad and deep

the economic forces which induce forest decline range from the local to the global

A complex set of forces combines to directly or indirectly cause forests to decline. Some of these are very readily visible, like the ways in which timber is over-harvested or forest land is converted to agricultural use. Others are less easily perceptible – underlying or root causes – but their effects on forests and how we manage them are no less real.

These forces originate in the basic economic, political and social systems and underpin the values and decisions relating to use of forest lands and forest resources. They influence one another in a dynamic process. Some are of a generic nature, affecting the way in which forests everywhere are used; some are of a specific nature, unique to a particular region or country. Some of these forces are entirely local in origin; others derive from international relationships, such as trade or multinational investments. Ultimately, the interplay among them determines how people – be they farmers or miners, policy makers or consumers, fuelwood gatherers or timber corporations – make decisions about how to use forest lands and products.

From place to place the causes vary, as was evident in the regional discussion in Chapter 1. The broad discussion which follows should be seen in this light. Most of these forces are extensively discussed in the literature relating to forest decline. They range from poor forest practices and land conversion, to consumption patterns and population growth, to debt and price imbalances, to world markets and unsustainable trade practices. It is not intended to review them all in this chapter; some are discussed elsewhere in the report.

Based on submissions to its public hearings, however, the Commission places special emphasis on the economic forces which lead to forest loss and degradation, as well as some factors of a political and social nature which are not normally associated with forest decline. Within the framework of sustainable development, which requires integration of social and political with economic and environmental considerations, the Commission considers these to be of immense importance, including the governance arrangements – or their absence – which determine how societies make decisions about forests, and the very ethics which underpin those decisions.

The individuals, communities, corporations and governments who are responsible for the depletion and destruction of the world's forests do so for the same basic reason – they find it beneficial from their own point of view. Presumably these decision-makers have compared the options open to them and concluded that depleting the forest resource, rather than using it in a sustainable manner, is their most advantageous course of action.

The economic forces which induce forest decline range from the local to the global. This chapter focuses on the local, and leaves the discussion of global aspects like multinational investment and trade to Chapter 6. Almost invariably, economic distortions tilt the balance against sustainable use of forest resources. These certainly occur in the forestry sector itself, but may also originate in other sectors.

2.2 Economic forces which lead to forest decline

Missing markets

A large part of the value of the world's ecosystem services and of its natural capital accrue directly to human benefit without passing through the money economy at all. In many cases people are not even aware of them (Constanza *et al.*, 1997). These include many of those services of forests discussed in Chapter 1.[1]

Much of the real value of forests is not normally reflected in the calculations which govern investment and management decisions about forests, either in national income accounting or in the balance sheet of an industrial firm. For example, many non-timber products and services which forests provide do not enter a commercial or market transaction. It is the failure of institutional, political and economic structures to reflect those values in prices that accounts substantially for the loss of the world's forest cover.

Although significant economic value resides in the world's forests, typically the main economic value assigned to forests is the value of the timber produced. Even then, the full and true costs of generating that timber product are not calculated. The dual effect of this approach is to undervalue and under-price both timber and forests in the larger sense.

Equally, market mechanisms today do not value the environmental and ecological services which forests provide to maintain a stable landscape and atmosphere. These markets are usually absent at the local or country level, and almost always at the international level. As a result markets do not provide signals conducive to forest conservation – in the language of economists, markets rarely capture the 'public good' aspects of forests.

A landowner in an upper watershed does not get paid for the protection against soil erosion or sedimentation that his forest provides for farmers or urban dwellers located downstream. Nor does the forest landowner profit from capturing carbon from the atmosphere that helps to arrest global climate change, from maintaining scenic beauty in the landscape, or from providing a natural habitat for endangered species.

markets rarely capture the 'public good' aspects of forests

Lacking economic incentives to keep forest lands forested, landowners usually prefer to dedicate their lands to more financially rewarding uses. Because markets do not reflect the wider values of forest resources, moreover, consumers use larger quantities of forest products than they would if higher prices reflected their full value.

Conversely, the structure of today's marketplace does not oblige those who destroy forests and convert them to other uses such as agriculture, mining or oil exploration, to compensate those whose lives have been adversely affected. Neither the owners of sulphur-spewing factories, nor the millions of motorists who pollute the air, have to pay for consequential damage to forests.

Forests in conservation use appear to produce lower returns than alternative

Small-scale farmers flooded out due to widespread clearing of forests

uses of the land. Thus, financial regimes offer the landowner less profit for sustainable timber management than unsustainable logging practices; agroforestry offers lower returns than slash-and-burn; sustainable timber and other forest products offer less than using the land for livestock; forests 'mined' for fuelwood are more lucrative than forests managed for sustainable fuelwood consumption, and so on.

It is this 'basic economic equation' that determines what actually happens to forests. Yet it is the same equation that can be used to change the economic forces that lead to forest destruction: if sustainably managed and conserved forest land would yield higher returns than unsustainable forestry and forest clearance, then there would be incentive to conserve forests.

Since the timber and agricultural benefits of forest land use generally have markets, the effect is an uneven playing field in which conservation cannot compete with those uses of forest land. If, say, the biodiversity value of a forest has no market, that value is effectively recorded at zero in the market place. Individuals may in principle be willing to pay for the conservation of forests, but there are no obvious markets in which the conservation values are expressed.

Further, very short-term outlooks of those who own or use forest lands operate against conservation. They bias decisions in favour of those that yield high, short-term gains regardless of the effect on long-

Box 2.1 Forest economic values

What economic value lies in the forest? Unfortunately, decades of popular and poorly researched literature have tended to produce exaggerated answers. Foremost among these is the view that the forests are repositories of immense economic wealth based on pharmaceutical products and other non-timber products. For some areas it is true that these forest products are valuable, but this is not generally the case. However, other values are also important and, most notably, the value of forests as a store of carbon.

The figures below illustrate the possible magnitudes involved for tropical and temperate forests in US$ per hectare per year:

Type of value	Tropical forests	Temperate forests (UK only)
Non-timber extractive values:	$0–50	$ 0
Non-extractive values:		
recreation	$5–10	$5–45[1]
		$75–630[2]
ecological	$30	not estimated
carbon	$600–4400[3]	$200–375[4]
Non-use values:	$2–27	not estimated

[1] uplands; [2] lowlands; [3] based on stock; [4] sequestration

Experts rightly note that even these values will be subject to substantial variation, depending on site conditions, nearness to markets, etc. Nonetheless, some of the values are substantial and, if suitable markets are developed, could compete with many logging operations.

Sources: Pearce, 1998; Pearce, 1994. On the variability of results see Chomitz and Kumari, 1996

term gains. For example, agroforestry may yield lower initial but sustained long-term returns compared to immediate logging or clearance for agriculture or ranching.

Absence of markets for conservation values combined with short-term outlooks go a long way to explain why conservation uses of forest land often appear to be less valuable than unsustainable uses. But markets do not exist independently of human values; rather, they reflect human values in monetary transactions and exchanges. In a full world of increasingly scarce natural resources, in which forests have been declining to the point where their functions, so important for the habitability of the earth, are under threat, forests have an increasingly obvious value to human societies. If in the future the many goods and services which forests provide become incorporated into market mechanisms, the prospects of conserving forests in a world that is predominantly economically motivated will be increased.

There is much work in train by economists to ascribe economic values to forest products other than timber[1] (see Box 2.1). This work is now beginning to influence policies of governments. Such work needs to be supported so that it is accelerated and consolidated in ways that can generate mechanisms through which all direct uses of forests are valued in economic decision-making.

More efforts are urgently required to value all forest functions and to create market mechanisms for them, if the desired change of behaviour is to come about among those who decide about forest land use. Proposals towards this end are discussed in Chapter 6.

Divergence between private values and public values

Markets do not exist independently of human values; rather, they serve to reflect human values in monetary transactions and exchanges. In a world of increasingly scarce natural resources and where the forest potential has declined so significantly (see Table 1.1), forests have an ever-more-obvious and increasing value to human societies. Forest sustainability has thus become a public value that now needs to be reflected in market mechanisms.

Many forest policies induce short-term exploitation of forests with little regard for future returns

Many argue that forests are too important to allow current market mechanisms alone to determine land use. In fact, economic value embraces all values, from intrinsic value – the value of forest in and of itself – to financial value at the other end of the spectrum. Market mechanisms need to be broadened to capture the full economic value of forests.

Many argue that governments should override economic failures through a variety of regulatory means. But the basic problem is that such an approach can leave the underlying economic incentives in place. Without a major monitoring and policing effort, regulations can easily be breached.

markets do not exist independently of human values

The evidence suggests that regulatory approaches only work sometimes, usually when sufficient resources are allocated to monitoring and policing. Regulations tend to work best in richer and well organised countries and worst in the poorest countries with weak and sometimes totally powerless institutions. Besides, there is the ethical difficulty in poor countries of regulating forest conversion by low-income cultivators who may well have no obvious alternative means of securing a livelihood. In any case, it is rarely a good idea for governments to 'micro-legislate'; it is usually more effective to try to address the larger forces at play.

A distinction needs to be made between economic values accruing to the land user (who may or may not be the owner) and those accruing to society generally. Society here may be the nation, the region or the world as a whole. Private and public economic values do differ because many of the economic benefits of conservation do not accrue to the land owner or user, but to others.

Societies often do override individual perceptions of gains and losses in the interests of the population at large. If public and private values diverge, then, it is important to change the economic signals so that the land user operates in the interests of society.

The Commission argues in Chapter 3 that the interests of society must become vested interests and that it is the primary role of governments to secure those interests. Governments should formulate policies that compensate for missing markets and that bridge the gap between private economic values of forest land users and public economic values such as conservation. In doing so, however, they should be mindful not to replace one set of bad policies with another. The next section provides a number of cautionary examples.

Limitations of government policies

A nation's forests are often one of its largest natural assets and the forest sector can be a significant contributor to the national economy. This is hardly a trivial matter in a world already lacking the necessary market signals for managing forests with the objective of sustaining them. It would seem reasonable to expect governments to try to correct this abysmal failure of the market, a mechanism which lies at the core of the dominant model of economic development.

Governments have indeed tended to make up for the absence or imperfection of markets by intervening in the economic parameters surrounding forest operations. But the results have not been good.

Governments exercise enormous influence over how societies treat their forests simply by virtue of the national regulatory and budgetary frameworks they control. Government policies set the broad rules of the economic game, determining the structure of financial incentives and disincentives for managing forests in a sustainable way. Unfortunately, many forest sector policies, as well as some originating in other sectors, have the opposite effect and induce short-term exploitation of the forest with little regard for future returns.

The public hearings of the Commission revealed a wide range of policies applied by governments which in fact contribute to forest decline (see Box 2.2). Given their contrary effects, it is clear that they are designed without systematic analysis of potential consequences. According to one expert, "Governments, many of which are committed in principle to conservation and wise resource use, are aggravating the loss of the forests under their stewardship through mistaken policies. Such policies, by and large, were adopted for worthy objectives: industrial or agricultural growth, regional development, job creation or poverty alleviation. But such objectives typically have not been realised or have been attained only at excessive cost" (Repetto, 1993).

What was also evident in the public hearings is that such policies are often negotiated between powerful companies and government officials and totally exclude participation by different interest groups directly engaged in or affected by their implementation.

Thus, one participant from East Kalimantan province of Indonesia described his situation this way: "Dayak people have lost access to lands that have been part of our livelihood for thousands of years. We have lost access to woods, to rattans and to many other forest products. It is not fair if the government decides that only timber concession companies can cut trees and trade the wood. Rights should also be given to the local community. If we had kept access to the land I think our Dayak people of East Kalimantan would not be as poor as they are today."

In Chapter 3 the Commission advocates that broader participation in policy making would help to avoid conflicts among groups. It would no doubt also operate to anticipate how a given policy measure would work in practice.

The Commission advocates urgent review of policies which, if corrected, can in the short term bring forest management more in line with the ultimate objective of sustaining forests indefinitely. These are timber concession policies, subsidies to forestry and other sectors, and land ownership and tenure policies. They are explored further below.

Timber concession policies and subsidies

There is nothing inherently bad about subsidies. They can accelerate the adoption of low-impact harvesting and less polluting technologies by industry and efficiently direct benefits to society's poorest. Subsidies can be particularly beneficial if they are limited in duration and sharply focused on specific economic, social or environmental goals which cannot be achieved by other means (Earth Council, 1996). Subsidies can, in effect, play a crucial role in helping development become more sustainable.

But largely they don't. Many of today's subsidies encourage practices that are economically perverse, trade-distorting, ecologically destructive or socially inequitable. Sometimes several of these harmful things occur at the same time. The problem lies in how subsidies are established – without adequate forethought and planning with respect to their social, environmental and economic consequences.

Timber concessions are contracts which define property rights and rules for forest exploitation. The terms of these concessions have considerable impact on how the forest will be used by logging

Box 2.2 Examples of policies which contribute to forest decline

- Timber concession terms which under-price wood, encourage waste or condone poor forestry practices
- Subsidies that encourage destructive forestry or forest land conversion to other uses
- Policies that require forest land clearing as a condition for obtaining legal titles to land ownership
- Road construction into forest areas
- Resettlement programmes in forest areas
- In some cases, log export bans that may reduce domestic prices of wood, and therefore reduce incentives to plant trees and also lead to conversion of natural forest lands to other uses
- Subsidies to industrial wood processing that lead to economic inefficiency
- Plantation subsidies that may induce natural forest conversion
- Price controls and taxes that discourage investment in forest planting or conservation
- Policies to boost mining without simultaneously enforcing strict environmental safeguards

companies. Where concessions are of short duration or insecure tenure, logging companies do not consider the long-term benefits of second cuts or sustainable management programmes. Forests are damaged as concessionaires with short time horizons harvest the existing stand without regard for the future possibilities of the residual stand.

stumpage rates and concession fees are routinely set at unrealistically low levels

Government timber concession terms routinely set stumpage prices and other concession fees at unrealistically low levels. The revenues forgone are often several times higher than the actual fees charged. Timber concession policies represent the classic case of few private interests benefiting from a profligate use of public resources (see Box 2.3).

Box 2.3 Private gains at public expense

- In 1996, the US government spent nearly US$15 million more on logging operations than private timber companies paid to purchase the wood.
- In 1994, the Russian government collected only from 3–20% of estimated potential revenues from stumpage fees – that is, only US$184 million instead of between US$0.9 and $5.5 billion.
- In Indonesia, it is estimated that the government loses between US$1 billion and $3 billion in potential revenues from its forest concessions each year.
- In Cambodia, revenues forgone from timber concessions are estimated at an incredible 63% of the government's entire revenues each year.
- In Vietnam, uncollected revenues were estimated at 17% of government revenues in 1992.
- In the mid-1980s, the government of British Columbia, Canada collected between US$1.1 and $1.4 billion of stumpage fees a year – but the potential revenues were still several times higher.
- In the 1970s and 1980s in Gabon, Indonesia, Malaysia and the Philippines, government revenues from timber concessions were in all cases less than 20% of their estimated recoverable value.

But governments in cash-strapped countries are often no match for powerful commercial interests in search of resources. In South America and Central Africa, for example, government leaders allocate large timber concessions in hopes of generating substantial export earnings, making deals with companies that employ crude logging methods and heavily damage the forest. In such countries, debt pressures also relate closely to forest decisions.

Large powerful companies exploit desperate economic conditions to extort very favourable terms. Consider this example described in the State of the World Report (Worldwatch Institute, 1998): "In the Solomon Islands, landowners were paid US$2.70 per cubic metre for timber that foreign companies then sold for US$350 per cubic metre. In Suriname, companies from Indonesia, Malaysia, and China proposed investments of more than US$500 million – an amount nearly the size of that nation's annual economic output. Yet what may appear to be a short-term boost to the national economy (and to the few individuals who benefit legally or illegally) often turns out to be both an economic and an ecological loss long after the logging operators have departed."

One expert (Vincent, 1990) argues that "timber producing countries often complain that they cannot afford the additional costs required for programmes to monitor and protect forests and promote their sustainable management unless the prices of timber and processed wood products can be increased. But if those same governments captured the full market value of timber concessions through stumpage fees they would have sufficient resources to enforce logging regulations fully and to administer programs to address other causes of deforestation."

This is one of the most important economic issues in the forestry sector – one that undermines good intentions of sustaining the forest. Undercharging for the value of the timber:

- creates windfall profits for a few private corporations at public expense
- encourages logging companies to rush to mine forests to reap these bonanza payoffs
- spurs companies to put intense pressure on forest owners to make forest lands available for logging
- enables inefficient logging companies to operate
- reduces the potential revenues, and therefore development opportunities, possible from sustainable use of a country's forests
- makes forest products too cheap and leads to wastage and wanton consumption of a vital resource.

There is no doubt that prevailing terms of timber concessions squander forest resources. Moreover, they are decided without transparency and operate inequitably. The need for urgent revision based on these economic and social grounds could not be clearer. The recent experience of Cameroon in reforming its timber concession policy provides new hope, though other policy incentives for forest decline still need to be resolved in that country (see Box 2.4).

The Commission advocates that all governments review their timber concession policies as a matter of urgency in the battle to save the forest capital of the world. The review should seek to ensure that public timber resources are properly priced to reflect their full timber and non-timber value.

governments should review their timber concession policies as a matter of urgency

The Commission advocates that concessions should as a matter of public policy be allocated through competitive auction. This would extend logging companies to their maximum willingness to pay for a concession. Forest owners – government or private citizens – would more likely capture the full economic rent and loggers would more likely adopt efficient logging practices to secure desired returns on investment. Together these would alter economic forces so that they operate to enhance the long-term sustainability of the forest.

Timber allocation procedures should also be reformed to involve local communities fully in the negotiation process. Together with public auctions of concessions, this would ensure transparency in

Box 2.4 Cameroon's recent successes in timber concession reform

A recent example of positive action by a government to raise concession prices comes from Cameroon. A series of 1995 reforms to timber allocation procedures have already resulted in improved forestry practices. Timber concessions used to be allocated for a period of only 5 years at a time, providing scant tenure security to concession-holders and encouraging ecologically-destructive harvesting practices. Concessions are now awarded for renewable 15-year periods as long as satisfactory forestry performance is achieved. An auctioning system was also adopted for timber concessions, replacing the previous standard government fee.

As a result of the new timber concession bidding system, annual government revenues have more than quadrupled. Thus while in 1993–94 they stood at 6 billion FCFA, only two years later they increased to 25 billion FCFA.
Source: Day, 1997

government administration of a public asset, especially given the corrupt practices which seem to surround forest operations, discussed later in this Chapter. Mechanisms for public vigilance about forest operations, such as those proposed in Chapter 3, are required to preclude attempts to rig public auctions and other timber allocation procedures.

Further, timber concession licences should be made strictly conditional upon sound forest management practices consistent with sustainability. Use of 'performance bonds' should be adopted that require companies to place a substantial sum in escrow, to be forfeited in case of failure by the company to adhere to satisfactory harvesting and management practices. This presupposes mandatory criteria for management and indicators for performance.

Market limitations and short-term outlooks, combined with the undervaluing of forest resources, may be made worse if the economic system distorts the playing field further by inflating the profits from unsustainable uses by giving subsides to them. Such subsidies may be explicit, in the case of payments for forest clearance, or subtle and hidden, in the case of some forms of tax concession.

A recent report from the Earth Council (1996) laid out the many types of subsidies which can have an impact on development. These include:

- direct grants or payments from governments
- favourable tax policies
- provision of goods and services by governments below cost
- concessions which reduce the cost of loans and liabilities
- other domestic and trade-oriented policies that favour some sectors, countries or interests with transfers through the market mechanism.

That report estimated that subsidies in only four sectors – agriculture, energy, road transport and water – add up to at least US$700 billion each year (Earth Council, 1996). Estimates for subsidies to forestry are awaited from continuing work by the study team.

A subsidy is often granted for one or

Box 2.5 Who benefits from subsidies?

The Earth Council report explains that often subsidies are defended for the wrong reasons – "because they help the poor (not as much as the well-off), because their removal would hinder economic growth (not demonstrated in theory or practice); because certain domestic industries would suffer (guess where their lobbying money comes from)" (Earth Council, 1996).

Subsidies can make some commodities too cheap, leading to wasteful consumption patterns. A recent report on the global energy situation, for example, points out how energy subsidies reduce economic efficiency in addition to creating extra fiscal burdens for governments (UNDP, 1997b).

Those who consume the lion's share of the world's economic production are often subsidised by others, sometimes from distant and poor countries. Subsidies in OECD countries are often two or three times as high as in the poorer non-OECD countries. Yet privileged OECD consumers often benefit further from the subsidies in export-dependent non-OECD countries, where consumption levels are lower (Earth Council, 1996).

The pattern also holds true at the domestic level. In India, for example, an official study by the National Institute of Public Finance and Policy in New Delhi found that national and state governments together were spending about US$40 billion, or 14.4% of the country's gross domestic product, on subsidies (Government of India, 1997). It was found that the rich, not the poor, more often benefited from subsidies, because the rich were in a position to buy and use subsidised commodities and services. This has led to a national questioning of the argument that cutting subsidies hurts primarily the poor.

more of the following reasons:

- to stimulate economic development or growth
- to protect employment or investment
- to safeguard domestic supply and reduce external dependency
- to reduce poverty or support the poor
- to provide the basics of life (Earth Council, 1996).

While no global assessment has yet been carried out of the impact of forestry subsidies on forest decline, indications are that forestry subsidies are large – and, in their current form, often harmful. Worldwatch Institute (1997) estimates that more than US$500 billion per year of consumers' and taxpayers' money is spent by governments to subsidise deforestation and other environmentally destructive activities. The low concession fees discussed earlier, for example, constitute an indirect subsidy to forest decline. And ongoing government spending on outdated and destructive forestry practices just adds to its magnitude. Apart from not fulfilling the objectives for which they are offered, subsidies in different sectors like agriculture, transport, energy and mining often contribute to forest decline.

Other subsidies affecting forests

Agriculture

Agriculture and livestock are often in competition with forests for use of land. If the returns to agriculture increase, so do the incentives for forest land to be replaced by agricultural land. Therefore, policies designed to encourage agricultural activities may well also stimulate deforestation. This can, however, be avoided provided agricultural policies emphasise enhancement of productivity rather than expansion of area. While increasing productivity is not a risk-free option, managed wisely it seems the best hope today. The Commission also argues in Chapter 4 that a similar 'intensification' of productivity in the forest sector is needed to produce any given quantity of forest products more efficiently – that is, using less land and other inputs, and avoiding further encroachment on remaining primary forests.

In Latin America large areas of forest are cleared for cattle ranching

Agricultural subsidies are estimated at about US$335 billion in the OECD countries and US$10 billion in the non-OECD countries each year. In countries including Mexico, Brazil and South Korea, the subsidies were equivalent to more than 50% of the total value of agricultural production during the mid-1980s (Earth Council, 1996)

Sometimes agricultural income is either taxed at very low rates or not taxed at all, while 'unutilised' forest lands are taxed at higher rates. This encourages the conversion of forests to agricultural production, sometimes on lands wholly unsuitable for pasture or cropping.

The Commission learned in its public hearing that in Panama and other parts of Latin America, deforestation is directly linked to subsidies for promoting cattle ranching in 'unproductive' wilderness areas. Also in Latin America, individuals and corporations are encouraged to convert forests to agricultural production because of generous tax incentives and other capital cost concessions.

Transport

Transport subsidies for roads alone amount to between US$85 and $200 billion in the OECD countries and US$15 billion in the non-OECD countries each year. When rail and other modes of transport are considered, the extent to which governments subsidise transport is even more pronounced (Earth Council, 1996).

While transport subsidies are often intended to stimulate industrial development in forest areas, all too frequently they encourage wasteful harvesting and poorly planned population incursions. In poor countries especially, roads leading into remote forest areas attract landless peasants who often practice slash-and-burn agriculture on the newly accessible lands. Road construction is one of the main facilitators of forest decline. A landscape management approach to decision-making about location of infrastructure, discussed in Chapter 5, would help to avoid such consequences.

Energy and mining

In the mid-1990s, global energy subsidies amounted to between US$70 and $80 billion in the OECD countries, and US$150–200 billion in the non-OECD countries each year. Among the non-OECD countries, most of the subsidies occurred in the transition economies (Earth Council, 1996). According to submissions to the Commission by MINEWATCH, mining subsidies add billions more. A significant proportion of these subsidies contributes to forest decline through direct impacts on forests during oil exploration and other mining activities, and through indirect impacts on climate change.

During its public hearings, the Commission heard much about the negative impacts of large-scale mining and exploration for petroleum and natural gas (developments which also bring new roads and settlements into once-inaccessible forests. Damming rivers for hydroelectric power can flood millions of hectares of forest and disrupt freshwater ecosystems; energy emissions contribute to air pollution that hurts forests in less direct but no less tangible ways.

While technologies and other mitigating measures are available to reduce the negative environmental and social impacts of energy and mining activities, these are frequently not adopted. As we now know, the effects on forests can be devastating.

'Reform the best, remove the rest'

In the face of such evidence, why do such subsidies persist? Subsidies are difficult to abolish because of the vested interests they engender. MINEWATCH contends that

Box 2.6 Roads to deforestation

Direct investment by the Brazilian government in roads into forest areas, including the Trans-Amazon highway, have contributed to deforestation and forest degradation. The policy objective was to develop new areas and to provide lands for the landless and the rural poor. In practice, however, these policies led to environmental deterioration and did not solve the problem of rural poverty. Road building may be the single most powerful element in the deforestation of frontier areas throughout the Brazilian Amazon and the rest of Latin America, as between 400 and 2000 hectares may be deforested by each kilometre of new road built into forest areas. An example of this is in the Brazilian state of Para, where deforestation as a consequence of road construction increased from 0.6% to 17.3% of the state's area between 1972 and 1985.

According to the State of the World Report (Worldwatch Institute, 1998), in federally managed US national forests, there are more than 600,000 kilometres of roads – enough to circle the globe nearly 15 times, and 2.4 times the length of the national highway system; and in one large timber concession in Indonesia, building 500 km of logging roads cleared 40,000 ha more than was directly logged.

many subsidies are kept in place through political pressure, campaign donations or even corruption. Governments also make use of subsidies to win votes.

Yet societies must find the will to act against the sort of blatantly harmful subsidies outlined above. While the goals which underlie many economic subsidies remain valid (for example, to support the production of forest products, food, energy and other vital commodities, and to reduce poverty and improve standards of living), these must now be achieved by more balanced and thoughtful means. As the Earth Council (1996) report put it, 'reform the best, remove the rest'.

The Commission advocates that it is urgent for governments to assess the full

Box 2.7 Adverse effects of mining and oil exploration on forests

Consider these submissions from MINEWATCH to the Commission's public hearing in Latin America and the Caribbean:

- In 1996 alone, foreign mining investments in Latin America reached almost US$1 billion, signalling the development of vast stretches of forest lands in the region for mining purposes.
- In Venezuela's Bolivar State, which has a size roughly that of the United Kingdom, more than 400 mining concessions are plying their trade. Gold exploration and extraction have caused both substantial forest and other environmental damage and the violent displacement of local populations. The extent of the damage is estimated at about 4 million hectares.
- Mining and oil exploration are devastating many indigenous territories including the traditional lands of the Kapon and Pemon Indians, who have been forced to migrate to other forest areas for survival. Substantial forest degradation and contamination are being caused by mercury pollution.
- One company alone, Zamuteba Mining from Brazil, secured a concession from the Guyana government to mine over half a million hectares of the central forested Potaro-Siparuni region.

The Network of Black Community Organizations of Colombia reported that up to 80,000 hectares of Colombia's rainforests alone are being destroyed every year due to industrial gold mining. Other submissions received relating to the impact of inappropriate oil exploration operations on forests in the Ecuadorian Amazon contained horrifying accounts of their effect on the health of local communities and on surrounding forests.

The danger from reckless mining and oil exploration extends well beyond Latin America. In North America, a US$25 billion 'oil sands' project – the biggest oil development on the continent – is planned for Alberta, Canada. The region, which encompasses a vast area of boreal forest about the size of the province of New Brunswick, may contain one-third of the world's oil resources - more even than Saudi Arabia's mighty reserves.

If oil exploitation proceeds without careful environmental and social safeguards, major damage could be done to both the forest ecosystems and the communities which inhabit them. In Africa, local communities in the Niger delta region have been forced to endure the negative effects of oil development on their health and that of the surrounding forests. In Asia, villagers in Papua New Guinea sued an Australian multinational for US$2.8 billion in 1994 for the destruction of a 200 kilometre river polluted by waste products from copper mining. The corporation faced charges in Australia and was forced to pay US$90 million to local communities for the negative impacts of the mine.

Sources: Submissions to the WCFSD's regional public hearings

Box 2.8 Subsidising conservation not exploitation

Land use in Brazil

When Brazil's National Space Research Institute released data showing that deforestation in its Amazon region had increased by almost 35% over the 1991–94 period, the government responded quickly with a package of new policy measures. Signs are that the reforms are already having a positive impact on the land-use practices of many forest farmers and land speculators. Reforms introduced in July, 1996 included:

- Removal of financial support for the development of private farm lands if there is less than 80% forest cover (up from just 50% previously)
- A ban on further forest clearance of already degraded forest lands
- A legal obligation to practice sustainable forest management in all primary forests.

Land taxes in France

In the 1980s, the French Government began the overhaul of a long-standing tax on undeveloped land to remove the incentive to destroy natural forests and other ecosystems. Ever since the early 19th century, tax authorities in France have levied a Tax on Undeveloped Land which essentially penalises commercially unproductive rural land. The tax was designed to encourage landholders to convert wilderness areas over to more profitable uses, and so stimulate rural development. In doing so, however, important environmental and recreational needs were ignored. Reforms initiated in 1990 have since begun to reduce the tax in order better to reflect environmental values. This has already had a positive impact by reducing agricultural pressures in marginal and forest lands (Hansen, 1994).

Transport subsidies in Russia

In 1995, as a consequence of internal government decisions to stabilise the economy, the Russian government took the decision to reduce transportation subsidies. The immediate result was to drastically reduce the viable economic haulage distance for logs and forest products. The net effect has been a significant reduction in the area under logging, as huge areas of forest that were earlier being exploited are no longer economically accessible (Day, 1997).

Subsidies in the USA

Subsidy reform has made unlikely bedfellows of deficit hawks, environmentalists, and neo-conservatives in the USA. They are united in agreement that Americans should not borrow from the future, either fiscally or environmentally. Beginning in 1993, this unlikely coalition has published a 'Green Scissors' report every year spotlighting wasteful and ecologically destructive subsidies that are in need of serious rethinking. Another report, called 'Dirty Little Secrets', concentrates on inequitable tax breaks, mostly to major polluters. Both campaigns have captured US media attention and are also showing concrete results. The Green Scissors Coalition has identified nine projects and programmes cancelled after being spotlighted, with projected savings of roughly US$22 billion (Friends of the Earth, 1997).

Agricultural subsidies in New Zealand

In 1984, New Zealand decided to pursue a drastic reform of its agricultural sector and abolish many support programmes which had become a drain on tax-payers and the national treasury. Land was being cleared for agricultural production and many marginal areas were being over-exploited. The results have been impressive: subsidies were eliminated almost completely. Farmers have become more diversified and competitive domestically and in the international marketplace, and the number of farms has even increased somewhat. Farm output initially declined somewhat but quickly recovered. And pressures to convert forests and other marginal lands to agriculture have been reduced.

range of subsidies in place to be sure that they do not have unintended negative consequences for forest lands. Transparency is required around the way in which subsidies are decided, and their costs, benefits, impacts and rationale should be kept under continual review. Alternative tools, including new economic instruments, should be developed to better target the same economic objectives, and address the needs of those who lose out financially. These should be accompanied by policy and fiscal supports that would positively contribute to conservation as distinct from exploitation. Correcting for the limitations of markets and the failure of policies (especially timber concession policies and subsidy policies) will not by itself remove all pressures on forests. But at least where such economic deficiencies and distortions are reduced, decisions can be made that will more closely reflect the long-term interests of society.

Land ownership and tenure

Land ownership and tenure help explain why some land uses appear to have economic values and others do not.

The spiritual values of the forest to indigenous peoples, for example, do not enter into the basic equation if indigenous people do not have rights to the land in question. In the same way, if the forest is essential to the well-being of a group of people on the forest frontier, but those people have no access or entitlement to the services of the forest, then their opinions will also not count in the way decisions are actually made. Insecure rights of tenure by existing occupants of forest land helps to explain reduced resistance to rival claims from those who wish to clear the land, and also encourage 'mining' of forest resources by timber concession-holders and other resource developers. Forest users who are uncertain whether they will have access to forests over the long-term tend to maximise their immediate returns at the expense of the long-term benefits that might arise from more sustainable uses.

In a number of countries establishment of property rights over forest land has even required proof of 'improvement': that is, forest clearance. The land user is thus given a further incentive to clear the land. For example, only 11% of Brazilian Amazon land was titled in the early 1980s, creating an essentially 'open access' resource. In the early 1990s, the land settlement agency still determined the spatial extent of settlement rights by multiplying the cleared area by a factor of three.

Clearly defined, secure and enforceable property rights are a fundamental requirement for encouraging sustainable use of forests. Recent studies in Africa indicate a positive relationship between secure tenure and tree-planting on farm (ICRAF, 1998) (see Figure 2.1). A high degree of local or individual control will not by itself arrest forest decline. Yet a well-structured land tenure system remains important to forms of management and participation which, in combination with government regulations, can contribute to sustainable use. Combined with the con-

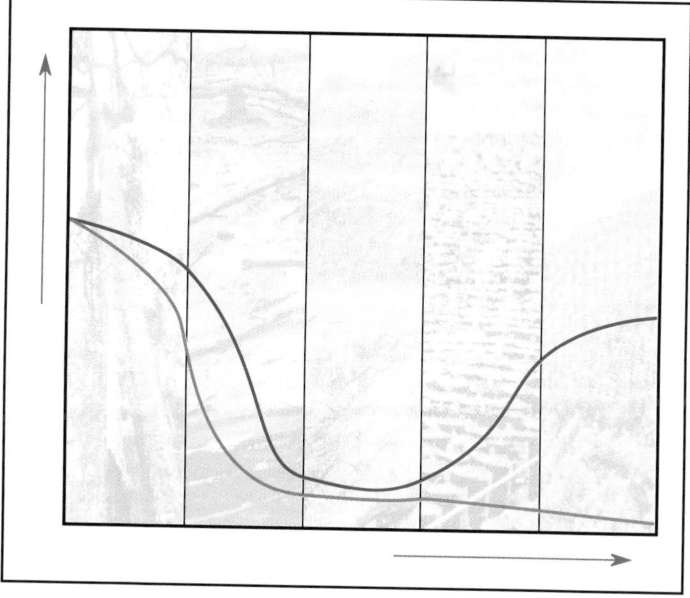

Figure 2.1 Effect of tenure on net primary productivity

Source: ICRAF, 1998

cern for empowerment discussed in the next chapter, the Commission considers that it is imperative to review how land ownership and tenure in any country affects conservation of forest lands.

2.3 Governance failure

some of the best protectors of the forest, the indigenous populations, are being destroyed

Concern about governance has been central to debates within development circles during the decade of the 1990s. Increasingly, this concept is becoming a focus of expanded analysis both within countries and in world affairs. (See Report of the recent Commission on Global Governance (1995) for a full discussion.) The concern of the Commission here is to examine aspects of governance which have implications for the world's forests.

Governance relates to the systems and processes, the legal framework and institutions through which decisions are made in a society, the ways in which these interrelate, and their relevance and relationship to the various constituent parts of the nation. In Chapter 3 the Commission draws attention to the way in which communities directly dependent on and actively involved in managing forests are excluded from decision-making about forest use and disposition of the benefits which forests generate. The Commission advocates there that societies should establish processes for participation and conflict resolution, which would become part of their governance arrangements.

Governance arrangements – or their absence – in societies can result in abuse of authority and power by those who enjoy high status, official authority, or economic and political power, leading to social insecurity and inequity for those who do not enjoy those privileges. It is evident in the relations between governments and people, between corporations and people, and increasingly between governments and corporations. Such abuse creates some of the conflicts illustrated in Chapter 3. Governance arrangements in a society also explain the existence – or absence – of social security for the nation as a whole, or for its constituent parts. This relationship is particularly evident in the affairs and situation of the most disadvantaged groups.

In relation to the use of forest lands and the distribution of the benefits which they generate, 'social insecurity' arises from and is manifested in the following dimensions of governance in a society: the character of land ownership and land tenure, the distribution of the benefits from the exploitation of the forest resources, the inequality between males and females, and the displacement of communities and groups.

Land hunger and lack of tenure

It was discussed earlier how insecure and inequitable land ownership discourages conservation of forests for future use by promoting rapid and unsustainable rates of harvesting.

In developing countries, for want of other options, economically marginalised and displaced communities often invade such public lands in order to survive. With no ownership or secure tenure, they have no incentive to care for the land or sustain the forests.

Many governments do not acknowledge traditional land ownership rights. As a participant in the public hearing for Latin America and the Caribbean expressed it: "The lack of respect for traditional land ownership rights is destroying some of the best protectors of the forest, the indigenous populations. The whites that invade our traditional lands to exploit our resources use force and threats, sometimes burning our homes, to impose their will. The government does not protect the weaker indigenous populations against the much larger commercial power of the invaders. Our traditional indigenous lands have no legal status, except that of public lands."

Lack of ownership and tenure can be overcome by policies which confer some measure of reward or security, but most often those responsible for planning in the relevant sectors (forests, agriculture, housing and settlements) are insensitive to the influence on forests which they and their policies have. Even those public agencies that manifest some concern regularly make forest-related decisions without involving and consulting with those groups in society who stand to be most affected by their actions.

Failure to share benefits

Given the experience of the most economically disadvantaged groups having a direct relationship with forests, it is obvious that the significant levels of income and benefits gained from exploitation of forests are not enjoyed by many. Some of the evidence of this presented in the Commission's public hearings is presented in Chapter 3. The co-existence of a high incidence of poverty with large endowments of forest capital, in some countries, is remarkable. It is also, in the opinion of this Commission, indefensible.

As Chapter 1 indicated, forests are the main terrestrial reservoir of biological diversity on the planet. The custodial services of indigenous and local communities towards conserving biological diversity have at least been recognised in the Convention on Biological Diversity (CBD). That treaty, to which 171 states are Parties, reflects the conclusion among governments that such services should be recognised. It also commits the world community to seek ways for more equitable sharing of the benefits to be derived from the use of biological resources. To date, no progress has been made in giving effect to these provisions, if viewed from the perspective of governance arrangements. There is no evidence of governments actually responding to this specific commitment through national systems for involving such communities in the decision-making for and benefit-sharing from forest resources. However, the recent decision of the World Intellectual Property Organisation to examine how indigenous peoples' knowledge can be reflected in its arrangements is a significant step that could enable societies to advance these provisions of the CBD.

Gender inequity

Gender roles define how women and men perform different tasks for the household, earn income in different ways, have different levels of control over their respective incomes, allocate time differently, have different legal and traditional rights, and possess different types of knowledge.

While women normally have multiple, often disproportionate responsibilities, they have little ownership or control over productive resources. This imbalance in the ownership and control over resources vis-à-vis gendered responsibilities places women in a subordinate and

women normally have multiple responsibilities but little ownership or control over productive resources

The burden falls heavily on women

disempowered position relative to men as they are forever dependent and run a greater risk of being excluded from their homes and livelihoods. As a consequence women and men have different perceptions, priorities and goals and development interventions affect them differently.

The Commission is of the view that gender equity is fundamentally an issue of governance. It is a requirement of the governance arrangements in any society to ensure attention to the situation of all the constituent communities which make up its polity. It is incumbent on governments, whose quintessential function is to secure the public interest, that they put in place the arrangements – constitutional provisions, legal frameworks, equitable policies, sensitive programmes, and even-handed administrations – that would meet that requirement.

What is the situation with respect to forests? As the Beijing Conference on Women of 1995 made clear, in many societies females are constitutionally debarred from owning land. Frequently they are not accorded tenurial rights. Where they exist those rights are in a formal sense often secondary to the rights of males, and in practical arrangements regarding disposition of land titles and access to resources including capital and credit, they tend to be subordinated to the claims or interests of males.

The direct and active involvement of women in primary environment care, especially in planting and nurturing trees and managing other forest resources, is not normally recognised, let alone rewarded. If they are rewarded in a contractual situation it is more than likely at a lower level than is offered to males.

Moreover, their potential intellectual contribution to the management of forests is not acknowledged: in many societies women make use of forest products for diverse household uses; they are thus likely to have a deep knowledge of the

Box 2.9 Gender equity initiatives in joint forest management in India

Lobbying for making the State Joint Forest Management (JFM) order more gender sensitive has resulted in the majority of State governments amending their earlier orders to make at least one man and one woman eligible for village institutional membership. Some States have now provided for at least one-third of the managing committee members being women. Such changes in the policy framework have started bringing more women into the JFM process and they have begun to make clear their priorities.

Some NGOs as well as some Forest Departments have started experimenting with various strategies for increasing women's participation in village institution decision-making. These have included:

- holding separate meetings with homogeneous groups of women to better understand their needs and priorities
- undertaking separate participatory appraisals with women and men and then facilitating negotiations between them to finalise the village plan
- promoting separate women's groups or organisations as a mechanism to increase their self-confidence and empowerment
- facilitating federations of such women's groups to increase their collective voice for influencing government and forest department policies
- motivating progressive local leaders to advocate women's equal rights and participation through emerging federations of grassroots groups.

medicinal and sustenance value of many forest plants and products; yet, they seldom have a voice in decisions about how forest resources are managed.

Because women have negligible ownership of private resources, poor rural women have a much greater dependence on common pool resources for meeting survival needs. The Commission is of the view that the participatory forest management mechanisms advocated in Chapter 3 would go a long way to meeting the need for empowerment of women, and for ensuring that their particular situation is taken into account. Unless this is done, poor forest-dependent women may be left worse off than before by losing even their customarily respected access to common pool resources.

The Commission advocates that the constitutional commitment of a society to gender equality should be reflected in the arrangements for participation, decision-making and management of forests. These arrangements should be based on male and female adults and not on the basis of head of household, and they should be supported by a range of enabling measures such as:

- silviculture and management options responsive to meeting diverse livelihood needs, instead of maximising timber production, need to be developed in order to be more sensitive to the interests of women
- strategies for increasing self-confidence and empowerment of women and marginalised groups need to be developed to increase the voice of the voiceless
- disaggregation of forest-based needs and usage by gender and socio-economic status must be incorporated in the participatory planning and implementation processes
- organisational change and improved gender balance within forest departments need to be pursued to make their functioning more conducive to gender-sensitive, participatory forest management
- education in support of gender equity goals
- creation of a gender ombudsman, as has been done in Sweden, to watch over such arrangements.

A travesty of justice: forest dwellers displaced by timber companies, farmers, ranchers and miners

Displacement of communities

It is equally a governance issue that so many communities are displaced by timber companies and other powerful interests. This reflects total disregard for their rights to possession of land, their historical custodial functions, their living space and livelihoods, and their culture and values. Evidence of such disregard is presented in Chapter 3, which has led the Commission to recommend that conflict resolution mechanisms be put in place in all societies to respond to such concerns.

2.4 Ethical failure

Underpinning governance failure is an ethical system that is contrary to underlying precepts of sustainable development. Some of the most important reasons for forest decline have ethical roots. Excessive concentration of wealth and power, both within countries and internationally, patterns of corruption, of consumption, of inequity, and of cultural discrimination which can be detrimental to the sustainability of forests, demonstrate that economic and other pursuits cannot be separated from ethical concerns.

there are too many opportunities for corruption in timber allocation processes

Corrupt practices

A principal ethical failure is the prevalence of illegal practices and corruption at all levels of forest-related decision-making. The Commission found that the most readily perceived problem in the forest sector – most prevalent and most blatant – but the one least discussed in the literature and in national or international fora on forests is the existence of corrupt practices.

The corruption that is most damaging to forest resources is not so much the petty bribery affecting low-ranking officials as it is the large-scale misuse of public resources for private gain by top-level political elites. Corruption encourages 'get-rich-quick' approaches, deprives governments and local communities of resources that could be used for development or improved forest management, and siphons scarce public resources into private pockets.

Common corrupt practices affecting forests include the concealed or secret sale of harvesting permits, negotiated timber agreements frequently involving large-scale corruption between government officials and private sector executives, illegal under-pricing of wood by companies (a practice called 'transfer pricing'), false certification of species or volumes cut in public forests, illegal logging, and trafficking in sensitive government information related to forests. These unethical practices cumulatively result in the loss of millions of dollars from the public purse that could be used for forest conservation and other social purposes.

Knowing that government mechanisms and capacity for supervision and scrutiny of their operations are often nonexistent or limited due to weak government institutions, firms often unconscionably contravene the terms and conditions of their concessions.

At all levels of prevailing timber allocation processes, there are opportunities for corruption sometimes on a very large scale. 'Sweetheart' deals between corrupt political leaders and incoming foreign industrialists or large local companies benefit the rich, the powerful, the elite, among them political leaders and public officials. 'Kickbacks' are a common part of the negotiating process in countries of both North and South.

These unethical practices have long been recognised. Recommendations for their reform can be found in many reports by FAO, the World Bank and other bodies over the last twenty years. But their adoption has been consistently blocked by industrialists and government politicians who stand to gain from such negotiated deals.

Forest corruption also involves manipulation of landless peasants. As the Commission learnt in its public hearing for Latin America and the Caribbean: "In the State of Barinas in Venezuela, 'mercenaries of the land' trade and distribute parcels covered by forests with absolute impunity. These parcels are meant for conversion to agriculture, often located inside forest reserves, a national patrimony. The front line 'invaders', mostly landless peasants, are frequently manipulated to trespass public land into private ownership. Affected forests are first creamed of their most valuable timbers. They are then burned. After a few years of agricultural activity, no matter how superficial or precarious it may be, the property of the land is transferred to the 'invading' peasants by application of the 'agrarian reform' law. The land is then sold, at meagre or symbolic prices, to the land-holders, politicians, cattle ranchers or local caudillos who incited and supported the original invasions."

Corrupt practices are often portrayed as a developing country problem. This is misleading. In 1994 the European Union charged several corporations for corrupt practices. A decade earlier, the EU fined 40 major pulp and paper producers for similar reasons.

The Commission was encouraged to learn about several non-governmental initiatives to combat corruption. Transparency International, Oilwatch, Minewatch, Environmental Investigation Agency and Global Witness – all independent international institutions created with the specific objective of attacking corruption; Skephi in Indonesia, the Junglees Project in India – community-based organisations uncovering corrupt practices, while defending the interests of disadvantaged communities and representing neglected values. They all need to be encouraged and supported in their efforts, and to have access to mechanisms for exposing and redressing corrupt practices in the forestry industry. The Commission argues in Chapter 3 for the creation of more and new mechanisms that would encourage and catalyse other similar community-based activities.

International financing institutions could be more active in addressing flagrant cases of malpractice and corruption. In 1996 the Government of Papua New Guinea, for example, saw its Structural Adjustment Programme loan suspended by the World Bank because of nonfulfilment of conditions related to forest sustainable development that *inter alia* would have addressed corruption. The power of commercial concerns and their influence on the government was behind the reluctance of senior government officials to fulfil those conditions.

The Commission noted some official attempts being made to combat corruption generally (see Box 2.10). Such mechanisms and regulations need to be harnessed for tackling cases of malpractice and corruption specifically related to the forestry industry.

international financing institutions should be more active in addressing flagrant cases of malpractice and corruption

The Commission sees the scale of corruption in the forest industry as one of the most intractable problems which societies have to face. Putting an end to corrupt and illegal practices will enable forests to contribute far more than at present towards reduction of poverty in societies. Such underhand transactions further exclude the interests of communities and forest-dwelling peoples, exacerbating the inequities that already result from the power relationships.

Radical and swift reforms are required. Such reforms will not come about unless the whole process of agreeing and allocating forest lands is opened up to permit scrutiny by civil society. The proposal of the Commission to subject the award of timber concession to public auction, as well as the proposals presented in Chapter 3, represent steps towards bringing transparency to the way in which the public patrimony is parcelled out. It will also lead to mechanisms through which decisive action can be taken to expose cases of corruption and to penalise offending corporations and individuals.

Inequity

Large-scale corporate exploitation of forests, which in some parts of the world has become the dominant pattern of forest management, ignores both public values and community needs. This leads to inequitable consequences such as insecurity of rights of relatively powerless

Box 2.10 The cost to the public purse

Transfer pricing by foreign companies was so prevalent in Papua New Guinea that until 1986 not a single company had declared a profit despite the booming timber trade (Barnett Commission, 1989).

WWF told the Commission that virtually all timber exports from Cambodia, Thailand and The Philippines are illegal, that a third of those from Malaysia may also be illegal, and as much as 95% of exports from Indonesia are not completely legal.

The Commission also learnt that:

- in Indonesia, by 1992, about 500,000 hectares of tropical forests were being illegally logged every year
- in the 1980s The Philippines lost about US$1.8 billion per year from illegal logging
- in Malaysia log exports to Japan in 1993 were under-declared by as much as 40%
- in Ghana, 11 foreign companies were implicated in fraud and other malpractices, costing the economy about US$50 million
- in 1994 the Indonesian Department of Forestry itself estimated that the country was losing US$3.5 billion per year, or a third of its potential revenue, because of illegal logging.

Box 2.11 Illegal and unethical practices in the forestry sector

Illegal logging

- logging timber species protected by national or international law, such as the Convention on International Trade in Endangered Species of Fauna and Flora (CITES)
- contracting with local entrepreneurs to buy logs from protected areas outside the concession
- logging outside concession boundaries
- contracting with local forest owners to harvest in their land but then cutting trees from neighbouring public lands instead
- logging in protected areas such as forest reserves
- logging in prohibited areas such as steep slopes, river banks and water catchment areas
- removing under/oversised trees
- extracting more timber than authorised
- logging without authorisation
- logging when in breach of contractual obligation
- obtaining timber concessions illegally.

Timber smuggling

- export/import of tree species banned under national or international law
- illegal log export/import in contravention of national bans
- obtaining declarations of lower volume exported.

Transfer pricing and other corrupt accounting practices

- declaring selling forest products at prices below prevailing market prices to reduce
- declared profits and corporate and income taxes
- declaring buying inputs at prices above the prevailing market price to reduce declared profits and taxes
- declaring lower-priced species exported
- manipulation of debt cash flows (transferring money to subsidiaries or parent company where debt repayment is freer than the export of profits; inflating repayments allowing untaxed larger repatriation of profits, reducing the level of declared profits and, therefore, of taxes)
- under-grading, under-measuring and under-valuing of timber and mis-classification of species
- avoiding royalties and duties by declaring a lower value of timber extracted from timber concessions
- logging in prohibited areas such as steep slopes, river banks and water catchment areas.

Box 2.12 Putting an end to corrupt practices

Under the 1977 Foreign Corrupt Practices Act, US firms are prohibited from bribing foreign officials. The US Export-Import Bank and the Overseas Private Investment Corporation and USAID have introduced regulations to deal with corruption.

In 1996, 23 member countries of the Organization of American States signed an Inter-American Convention Against Corruption, the first anti-corruption treaty which requires signatories to criminalise bribery of foreign officials. Signatories must update their legislation to criminalise a number of specific corrupt acts. Cooperation among signatories is strengthened on extradition, mutual legal assistance and asset forfeiture for corruption-related crimes.

In 1995, the World Bank revised procurement rules to strengthen transparency, mandate the use of Standard Bidding Documents and make explicit the Bank's policy to combat corruption on Bank financed contracts. The Bank will reject proposals for contract award or cancel a portion of the loan if the bidder or the borrower has engaged in fraud or corruption. Companies determined by the Bank to have engaged in corrupt practices will be blacklisted from participation in Bank-financed contracts.

Recently the OECD Development Assistance Committee Members adopted a statement of principle to include anti-corruption provisions in bilaterally-funded procurement contracts. Initiatives to fight corruption have been introduced at the World Trade Organization, the UN Economic and Social Council, the UN Commission on International Trade Law, Regional Development Banks and in the North American Free Trade Agreement.

groups, particularly collective rights and female rights. Moreover, these groups have differential access to the legal system, to government facilities and to justice. In many cases, the more disadvantaged groups in society are ignorant of their legal rights or the institutional options available to them to redress their grievances. The elites meanwhile not only have access to these, but influence the policies and priorities of the institutions which are associated with forest governance. Skewed patterns of land ownership in many countries, particularly in the developing world, relegate the landless to miserable conditions. On top of all this, consumption of forest products is very skewed, within societies and among them, with the wealthy imposing heavy demands on scarce resources that poor people need for subsistence.

The root causes of such inequity lie in the underlying economic and political systems, which create and contribute to such concentrations of power. The Commission considers such gross imbalance of power among the interest groups associated with forests as an ethical failure. That imbalance can be compensated by democratic participatory governance mechanisms which operate transparently and honourably. The Commission asserts that it is the responsibility of governments to create such mechanisms for more equitable representation of all interest groups associated with forests, and to ensure that public values and the public interest become central to the decision-making about how forests are managed.

Cultural discrimination

Underlying the processes leading to deforestation is a model of development which is overly reductionist and directed at maximisation of economic returns to the exclusion of other values stressing caring and concern. One expression of this approach is the denial of the value of other cultures and societies and the imposition of universal solutions that deny or undermine local cultural diversity. A narrow scientific vision of the management of forests is another manifestation of this approach.

the roots of the crisis are embedded in economics, politics, governance and ethics

Displacement of local communities and violation of their historical and accumulated rights in favour of economically and politically powerful elites also manifest the seeds of cultural discrimination. Cultural values simply do not appear to enter the equation: their erosion is contributing to decline of forests.

Valuable traditional forest-related knowledge is also being eroded. The effect is equivalent to destroying the libraries of entire nations – an extremely short-sighted act given the ecological wisdom contained therein, and the fact that this knowledge has evolved in application over generations.

Is it just coincidence that we have witnessed in this decade a rise in ethnic consciousness and conflagration? Anthropologists of the future may well illuminate the relationship between globalisation and cultural diversity and ethnic conflicts. Should our political and moral leaders of the present not take care to nurture cultural distinctions, just in case they are what will give us individual and social stability in the period ahead?

In a world of globalising economic relations, the individual and community may come to rely more heavily on the specificities of place and of culture to sustain their sense of being, their sense of self-worth, and their individual and group confidence. Cultural diversity may come to exist as a welcome relief in a world of a single economy.

The economic phenomenon of the 1990s – liberalisation of trade and globalisation of the factors of production – is leading to dominance of western values, including consumption patterns and models of development. Recent setbacks in Asian economies have at least led to renewed questioning of these models. This dominance, if unchecked, will exacerbate market limitations to adequately reflect the range of values associated with forest products and services.

The roots of the crisis about forests are indeed broad and deep, and are embedded in economics, politics, governance and ethics. Far more attention is required in these spheres if the solutions to arrest the decline of forests are to be found.

Endnote

[1] Much of this literature has been analysed for the Commission by the Centre for Social and Economic Research on the Global Environment, University College, London in internal papers for the Commission.

3

PRIVATE AND PUBLIC INTEREST

Many problems of resource depletion and environmental stress arise from disparities in economic and political power.
(WCED – The Brundtland Commission, 1987)

lands of forest dwellers are being taken over by governments and large timber companies

In Chapter 2 the Commission discussed roots of the forest crisis that go well beyond the forest sector. Underlying those forces are sharply contrasting values which different sections of society place on forests. These values are manifested in different interests, which compete for the use of and benefits from forest lands (see Box 3.1). Often such competition in demand leads to conflicts between individuals and groups. As individuals we often experience similar conflict within ourselves, as each of us values forests for many different things.

At the same time, all of humankind share in the environmental benefits which forests provide. Many species of wildlife also depend on forests for habitat and food. And sustainable development requires that resources are used in ways that ensure their continuity and integrity for benefit by future generations. All of these comprise a public interest in forests that must be secured.

In this Chapter the Commission reflects the range of private interests which are enjoined in the forest issues and which require mechanisms for managing them in an equitable way. It explores the nature of the public interest in forests, and asserts that the public interest should be paramount and be secured through appropriate governance and management mechanisms. The Commission also discusses the roles of government and civil society in discharging what it regards as a public trust in forests, and proposes mechanisms that could assist societies in the discharge of that responsibility.

3.1 A web of interests

The full gamut of needs, interests, concerns and expectations in forests was reflected in the submissions in the five regional public hearings of the Commission. Large numbers of people are directly involved in competing for some part of the economic benefits which forests provide, whether as forest-dwelling and other rural communities, timber logging companies, ranchers, and ecotourism companies, to name a few. The public hearings of the Commission gave opportunity for all of these interests to be represented, as well as the views of government officials or others representing the public interest. The Commission benefited from their submissions and from numerous technical papers from scientists, economists, environmentalists, foresters, and public officials.

Indigenous peoples and other forest dwellers explained how their lands had been taken over by governments or by large national and multinational timber companies. In some situations forest-dwelling communities had been subjected to human rights abuses, especially in areas being taken over by mining, timber, oil exploration or other industrial interests. Representatives of logging communities indicated how their livelihoods had either already been affected or were threatened by growing pressures from conservation groups to stop logging of old-growth forests and to modify their forest management practices. Executives and union members from forest industrial corporations voiced their concerns about environmental pressures that are making it increasingly difficult to carry out logging operations, timber production, and trade.

The Commission also heard from environmental advocacy groups, some of which had resorted to militant and sometimes life-threatening measures aimed at immobilising logging trucks and halting saw-milling and other industrial operations. It also received submissions from many international non-governmental organisations that are involved in promoting forest conservation.

The conflicts were conspicuous: between rich and poor, between forest dwellers and corporations, between politically strong and weak groups, between economic needs and environmental functions; between private interests and the public interest.

These conflicts – examples of which are presented in this Chapter – reflect imbalance in political power (see Boxes 3.2 to 3.6). They confirm the inadequacy of current policies and the need for a new

Box 3.1 Same forest, different uses

The same piece of forest land may be viewed by different persons as any, and by the same person as many, of the following:

- a source of foreign exchange
- a place to hunt wild animals for food
- a site for recreation and education
- space for a large plantation
- protection for watershed
- site for new settlements
- forest reserve for natural regeneration
- potential ranch for grazing animals
- a place to find new species
- a source of raw materials for industry
- a source of firewood, forage, medicines, building materials, food
- a place to live
- a sink for carbon sequestration
- large-scale agriculture or small scale food production.

Source: adapted from FAO, 1995

Box 3.2 Forest conflicts: Asia and the Pacific

Papua New Guinea: private interests vs. public interest

In the late 1980s, concerns about apparent inefficiencies in the public administration of national forest resources and links between high government officials and logging companies led the then Prime Minister Paias Wingti to create a Commission of Inquiry into the Timber Industry.

The Commission exposed corruption, fraud and tax evasion, pointing the finger at top government officials and blaming the government for failing to police the timber industry. Its findings led to charges being laid against the Deputy Prime Minister for breaches of the Leadership Code, and his recommended dismissal from office by the Independent Tribunal. The Deputy Prime Minister chose to resign rather than being dismissed.

The president of the Commission of Inquiry, Judge Thomas Barnett, also lashed out at foreign logging companies for behaving in an exploitative manner. Of the situation in New Ireland province, for example, he wrote: "It would be fair to say of some of the companies that they are now roaming the countryside with the self-assurance of robber barons, bribing politicians and leaders, creating social disharmony and ignoring laws in order to gain access to, rip out, and export the last remnants of the province's valuable timber. ... It downgrades Papua New Guinea's sovereign status that such rapacious foreign exploitation has been allowed to continue with such devastating effects to the social and physical environment, and with so few positive benefits." (Barnett Commission, 1989)

Source: WCFSD Public Hearing, Jakarta; Barnett Commission,1989

Box 3.3 Forest conflicts: North America

Canada: government vs. community

One of the most infamous conflicts over forests in North America centres around the Temagami region of Northern Ontario, Canada, the traditional territory of the Teme-Augama Anishnabai people. The Commission visited Temagami as part of its North American Region hearing and found a community deeply divided over competing visions for its forests.

The Temagami region is rich in forests, including one of North America's last remaining stands of 'old-growth' or undisturbed red and white pine. Its beauty and rarity is outstanding, drawing an increasing number of nature-based tourists and environmentalists to the region in addition to the local population of native people and townsfolk, hunters and fisher-people, forest workers and miners. The broad diversity of people underscores a great range of competing interests in the land base – forestry versus tourism versus native land claims, for instance. It is these unresolved issues and priorities which have erupted in a steady stream of forest-related conflicts over recent years.

In an effort to bring the community closer together the provincial government, responsible for the management of the region's forests, invited key interest groups to enter into a 'multi-stakeholder dialogue' to advise the government on future forest management in Temagami. The aim was to create a unified vision which all interest groups would accept, thus building legitimacy for an agreed land use approach. Six long years of discussion and debate passed before the advisory body produced a hard-won set of recommendations. These comprised a mix of land-use priorities, from protected forest areas to managed forestry zones, the elements of which represented a delicate balance of many of the interests in the community (not including native groups, who withdrew over objections with the process). When the government finally received the recommendations, however, it substantially modified them, shifting some of the protection and production zones.

This rekindled the flames of discontent in Temagami, especially among environmentalists who felt that the government had favoured industry in its final decisions. By the time the Commissioners arrived in Temagami, the community was again up in arms – sometimes literally, in the case of a Native road blockade and mysterious bridge explosion in an area about to be logged. Many who met with the Commission blamed the provincial government for not showing greater respect for the outcome of the intensive public dialogue in which the Temagami community had been engaged.
Source: WCFSD Public Hearing, Winnipeg

Box 3.4 Forest conflicts: Europe and the CIS

Former USSR and Eastern Europe: economic development vs. resource conservation

As the Commission heard at its Public Hearing in St. Petersburg, Russia, basic measures for sound forest management must be put in place in the post-communist 'Wild East'. With the shift from planned to market-oriented economies went public ownership of forest capital, central planning of forest management, and the security of Soviet-era safety nets. Laws are now being rewritten to set new ground rules for forest ownership, production and protection, as well as social stability in the wider sense, but progress is slow and hard won.

Environmentalists concerned about safeguarding the region's forests are strongly arguing for a cautious approach to industrial development, and advocated more stringent controls on loggers and polluters. Industrialists argue that the region's forests are ripe for development – that Russia and its neighbours must cash in their vast forest capital in the hope of building a strong economic future.

Many participants in the Hearing are advocating that ecological stability must go hand in hand with human stability – and that a golden opportunity now exists for societies in the region to build approaches for sustainable forest management, even as they struggle to re-invent their economic and political systems.
Source: WCFSD Hearing, St Petersburg

Box 3.5 Forest conflicts: Latin America and the Caribbean

The Guyana Shield: economic realities vs. environmental and social needs

The Guyana Shield area of South America, comprising Guyana, Suriname, Venezuela and French Guiana, is rife with controversy over the development of its rich tropical forests. Economic pressures to exploit surface timber and sub-surface minerals, as well as to raise adequate government revenues to repay a soaring foreign debt, are blamed for deforestation in the area, which is happening about twice as fast as in neighbouring countries.

Economic development needs are being pitted against other social and environmental needs, raising questions about the future security of the region's forests and forest-dwelling communities. The conflicts have involved a host of actors, including transnational corporations, government officials, indigenous peoples, environmentalists, and international development agencies.

Environmentalists criticise loggers for adopting heavily mechanised and environmentally destructive logging methods, exploiting the forests as if they were mines, causing extensive and irretrievable damage to the resource base.

The human rights of indigenous peoples are another major point of contention. In Suriname, the human and land rights of indigenous peoples and Maroons still lack formal legal recognition. Throughout the region, logging and mining concessions are routinely granted without consulting or even notifying local indigenous and Maroon populations. Sometimes the costs are dire, including the forced relocation of entire communities, cyanide poisoning of local rivers, and jeopardising the livelihood base of the inhabitants.

Government policies routinely come under fire for favouring powerful commercial interests over weaker groups. In Guyana, the government has been criticised by environmental groups for circumventing its own logging moratorium – introduced in 1995 to allow time to strengthen the government forest department – by granting 'exploratory leases' of dubious legality to foreign logging interests.
Source: WCFSD Hearing, San José

Box 3.6 Forest conflicts: Africa

Nigeria: corporations vs. people

In the early 1950s corporate logging rights were granted to extract timber from prime forests in an area exceeding 50,000 hectares in the surrounding forests of Udo, Nikorawa, in Edo State. The lack of sustainable means of timber harvesting – such as seed trees retention, replanting and the involvement of local people – has led to the doom of today. The company has now left behind a denuded forest, a devastated and desolate village, and siltation of the local stream. The village is now a ghost of itself. Villagers helplessly watched the plundering of the resources in their traditional space, and have been left poorer.

In Nigeria, forests and lands are owned by the state. The way in which the government exercises those rights puts severe pressures on the land and further impoverishes the local people. The Land Use Act is elitist and takes away the rights of the local people in land and forest matters. The grievances of local people are many. The lack of direct consultation with them in the use or appropriation of their lands insults them and makes them helpless. Where destruction of forest lands and crops is involved, inadequate compensation is paid to farmers. Compensation rates in Nigeria are pitiable and laughable.
Source: WCFSD Hearing, Yaounde (paraphrased from A Shout from the Fringe of the Forest *by Godwin Uyi Ojo of the Nigerian non-governmental organisation Environmental Rights Action)*

departure in managing this public resource. Those with political and economic power monopolise decision-making and management, and their interests are secured at the expense of all. Those without are reduced to protest and are further marginalised. These same power relationships account for the unconscionable way in which benefits derived from use of forest resources are distributed.

communities and civil society organisations are responding to the challenge of restoring forests

Following on from the discussion in Chapter 2 about governance failure, and given the conflicts about use of forest resources which exist in all societies, the Commission advocates the creation in all societies of mechanisms that are participatory and transparent in their operation, to ensure that the interests of all affected groups are represented in decision-making about forests. Such mechanisms would operate to redress the imbalance of power among the various interest groups, and to reconcile conflicting needs and demands from a limited resource. It is also through such mechanisms that more equity in the sharing of benefits from use of forest resources can be achieved.

The Commission's public hearings also revealed encouraging efforts of communities and civil society organisations to respond to the challenge of restoring forests. The Commission strongly advocates the removal of obstacles to release the great potential of communities to make an even more significant contribution to planting new and rehabilitating degraded forest stands. The potential of local communities would be more fully realised if, in addition, responsibility for forest management were partly devolved to them. More participation and devolution of management would not by themselves arrest forest decline. But these are desirable in their own right, are consistent with the objectives of sustainable development, and could create the conditions for transparency in forest matters.

3.2 Forest-dependent communities

The Commission has been aware throughout its work of public commitment to reduce substantially the numbers of people living in extreme poverty by the year 2015. Many donors, for example, have specifically restated that their fundamental objective is to eliminate poverty. The majority of poor people are rural, and sustaining rural livelihoods can be achieved only if there is no further decline in environmental conditions. This will require many of the changes advocated in this report, including greater participation by rural communities in decision-making regarding their future, end to corruption, fostering public–private partnerships, rethinking of government's role in securing the public interest, more recognition for the contributions of civil society organisations, using more appropriate technologies, and making full use of the talents of women.

Altogether, some 350 million of the world's poorest people depend almost entirely for their subsistence and survival needs on forests. A further 1 billion poor people – about 20% of the world's population – depend on remnant woodlands, on homestead tree gardens, and on agroforestry systems for their essential fuelwood, food and fodder needs. They also derive from the forests home construction materials, medicines, employment and income opportunities. Among forest-dependent communities, the situation of rural communities, forest dwellers, and shifting cultivators is discussed below.

Rural communities

Rural communities include various groups who live in close physical proximity to forests, and who have direct, often total, reliance on forests for all or the majority of their household needs. They include those who live in the forest or on its fringes, those who own and maintain small expanses of forest lands, and farmers who convert and cultivate forested lands. In many cases, they tend their own lands, in some cases public lands. A sustainable livelihood for these people requires secure tenure and access to forests.

Their lives and livelihoods are directly affected by the existence or disappearance of forests. Equally, their own activities and relationship with those forests directly affect the condition of forests. They obtain a range of goods from forests, and their husbandry contributes to maintaining the micro-systems on which forests depend.

The trees which such communities plant and manage, while augmenting production of fruits, fuelwood and other products for home consumption or sale, help to protect the soil, slow wind velocity, and conserve moisture, thus increasing crop yields and agricultural productivity.

In India, some 275 million landless people and small farmers benefit from gathering resources they find within adjacent forests. A study carried out in a lowland village in The Philippines found that 73% of households surveyed collected forest products for supplementary and emergency income, with more than half depending on rattan collection. In the public hearing for Africa, the importance of hunting as an important source of cash income for many households and villages was evident.

Forest dwellers

Indigenous peoples and other communities living in forests and depending on them for subsistence number some 60 million people world-wide. Forests are their habitat and their entire means of survival. A range of non-traditional forest products – fruits, vegetables, bush meat, spices, bark and clothing material like animal fur and skins, oils, building materials, gums, dyes, medicinal plants – contribute to their daily needs.

For many forest-dwelling indigenous people, forests also have aesthetic and spiritual importance. Their traditional knowledge, acquired over centuries of interaction with forests and trees, generally leads such communities to relate to their forest habitat in ways that protect and sustain the forest as an ecosystem. For them, the forest is an extension of their temporal and spiritual lives. Their cultural security is bound up with the security of forest lands. Some of their perspectives are reflected in Box 3.7.

a sustainable livelihood requires secure tenure and access to forests

Such forest-dwelling communities can be found in all types of forests, in every geographic region of the world. Everywhere they are beset by similar forces: loggers, ranchers, and others moving on to their lands; erosion of their traditional rights of access and use; displacement of their homes; erosion of their livelihoods; ignorance of their values, their historical custodial functions, their accumulated intellectual property; disregard by the authorities; often persecuted by the powers that be and the politically strong.

These forces are likely to become intensified as the world gets more crowded, as the demands on forests increase, and as the forest capital further declines.

Yet there was no evidence in any region of a constructive and compassionate movement on the part of political leaders to prevent these abuses and protect the poor and politically weak, despite the fact that we are still in the United Nations Decade for Indigenous Peoples. Moreover, those organisations which champion the human rights of these communities, like COAMA, GAIA, and People's Forest Alliance, are fighting an uphill battle against the power and resources of powerful corporations and indifferent public officials. Box 3.8 on Mexico, where even previously hard-won rights are being eroded, illustrates this point.

It is a travesty of justice that the rights of such communities – communities which via their custodial services to forests subsidise the world – are not secured, while financial fortunes from exploitation of a country's forest capital accrue to private corporate interests and government treasuries, to merchants and middlemen.

Box 3.7 Perspectives of indigenous peoples

From North America:
(Asked of a First Nations leader during the Commission's North America Hearing)

Question: What is the Forest for you?
Answer: It is my life.

From Asia:
(Comment during the WCFSD Asia Hearing from the Head of an Irian Jaya Tribal Group living in a forest area taken over by a mining company)

"The government has taken away our spiritual home and destroyed the graves of our ancestors."

From Latin America and the Caribbean:
(Statement by a Colombian NGO)

"The Northwest Amazon has been inhabited by people for at least 8,000 years. The cultures indigenous to the region have developed ways of living in the rainforest that are based on centuries of experimenting with the balance between the needs of communities and the needs of local ecosystems."
Source: WCFSD Public Hearings

Box 3.8 Indigenous peoples and land insecurity in Mexico

In 1992 Article 27 of the Agrarian Code of Mexico was revised to reinstate previous legal limits on the size of landholdings and to redistribute huge landholdings. It created the 'ejido' system of communal landholding which could not be sold or forfeited for non-payment of debt. Its intent was to assure the Mexican people a secure livelihood.

However, Article 27 was revised again in April 1997. It has removed the limits to the size of landholdings, and has provided for the sale of communal ejido land. It does not adequately address the needs of communal landowners and indigenous people, who hold title to 80% of the nation's forested land.

By popular accounts, this revision was stimulated by the promises of one large multinational corporation to invest heavily in Mexico if the country created financial incentives and clarified confusing language in the Forestry Law.
Source: The News, Mexico City, 25 April 1997

The United Nations Intergovernmental Panel on Forests has focused attention on the traditional knowledge of indigenous peoples and associated intellectual property rights concerns. While these issues are important to indigenous peoples, progress in finding solutions here would come to nought if these peoples continue to be displaced from their traditional lands.

There are a number of issues which affect indigenous peoples. The issues are addressed in a scattered way across a range of United Nations agencies and intergovernmental processes. Clearly some systematic attention within a single forum dedicated to issues concerning indigenous peoples would be a more effective way of achieving comprehensive attention, and of seeking application of the UN Declaration on the Rights of Indigenous Peoples. For this purpose the Commission strongly supports the initiative of the Government of Denmark, along with some private foundations, to advocate the creation of an Indigenous Peoples' Forum within the UN system, and commends it for attention by the UN Commission on Sustainable Development and by the UN Commission on Human Rights.

Shifting cultivators

About 200–300 million of the rural poor who depend heavily on forest lands are landless shifting cultivators whose primary interest is access to land under the forest for food production rather than the forest itself. Forest lands represent their principal means of survival. They value forest lands as a resource for food production mainly for subsistence but, in some cases, also for commercial agricultural production for local markets.

Seasonal harvesting of forest products is critically important to many shifting cultivator households. This is especially so when families need income to buy food during the 'hungry' period between food harvests. For example, in Sierra Leone, researchers found that fuelwood selling provided the first cash income from forest land cleared by shifting cultivators for rice production; subsequently fuelwood collection for the market was concentrated during the off-peak agriculture period providing cash income in a period when food supplies were at their lowest (Carrere and Lohmann, 1996).

Together with forest dwellers, shifting cultivators are the most economically deprived, the politically weakest group, among interest groups competing for forest resources. What is striking is that such communities with close historical relationships with forests are living in abject poverty and economic insecurity. Forest decline has grave negative effects on their ability to survive: it reduces their already low material standard of living, renders their existence more precarious, increases their vulnerability, and cuts off their options.

Many rural communities have been acting within their means and independently of public policies or public supports, to conserve forests and spontaneously reforest their living space, their farms and villages. The Commission heard from representatives of communities from Nepal, the state of Wisconsin in the USA, from Tanzania, Bolivia, and many other countries, how rural communities, frustrated by archaic forest laws and restrictions that inhibit their access to public forest land, have been taking matters into their own hands and assuming responsibility for protection and management of local forests and remnant woodlands (see Box 3.9).

The Commission also heard during its Asia Public Hearing that grassroots efforts in parts of Asia are achieving results where millions of dollars of external funding along with the application of new technologies and policy instruments

for many forest-dwelling indigenous peoples the forest is an extension of their temporal and spiritual lives

many communities have been spontaneously reforesting their farms and villages

in Africa on-farm tree density is increasing as population density goes up

have failed to dent the problem; that 85% of local peoples' forest product needs in Bangladesh are derived from individual home gardens; and that millions of small farmers have been responsible for much of the reforestation programme that China has successfully implemented in recent decades.

Much of the spontaneous reforestation taking place, particularly in the tropics, is driven by individual household decisions, usually by women, to protect indigenous on-farm trees and to establish home gardens or to plant small woodlots either for meeting family needs or to supply commercial fuelwood, charcoal, building pole or timber markets. These households and communities could be further encouraged, for example, by bringing science to bear on the type of trees that would yield high value products while contributing to soil fertility.

Preliminary conclusions from a series of recent studies in Africa are that tree density on-farm is increasing, and increasing with rural population density (ICRAF, 1998). This is encouraging news in the light of population trends and the increased pressures anticipated on forest and agricultural lands. The observa-

Box 3.9 Communities in action (1)

Asia and the Pacific – from Nepal:

"When the forest started to vanish there were only two options, stay in the village or migrate. Because of that we needed to protect the existing forest." During the past 15 years a great many village communities have taken the situation into their own hands and put into place local institutional arrangements to ensure that many hill forests were given basic protection and that access and use rights were prescribed. It was after all in their best interests to do so. Many of these indigenous management systems have survived, often with modifications, for more than 35 years – not perfectly, but with outcomes better than could be achieved by a fledgling Forest Department.

During the past decade about 4,000 agreements covering almost 200,000 hectares of forest have been negotiated between local village user groups and the Forest Department, and formalised as Operational Plans. New government laws legitimise the authority of user groups to manage specified areas of forests and to retain revenues derived from forest harvesting for reinvestment in either forest conservation or other local needs.
Source: Submission to the Asia and the Pacific Public Hearing

North America – from the USA:

For the past 135 years, the Menominee have practised deliberate, sustained-yield forest management practices on 95,000 hectares of forested tracts in northeastern Wisconsin. Their conservation and management of their forest has not only benefited wildlife, streams, and biodiversity, but also has provided a steady income for many of the tribe's members. In spite of this, at one time their rights to the land were terminated. However, their rights were later reinstated because because they could demonstrate their intact community and traditions.

"The Menominee forest greatly surpasses, in terms of total productivity (measured in value of the products removed on a sustained yield basis), the adjacent Nicoet National Forest that has more than twice the acreage of commercial forest land. Recently, harvesting practices were certified by Scientific Certification Systems, helping the Menominee to gain wider recognition for other conservation practices."
Source: Submission to the North American Public Hearing

Box 3.9 Communities in action (2)

Latin America and the Caribbean – from Bolivia:

Within recent years local communities living in the municipalities of Santa Rosa and Yapacani in the department of Santa Cruz, and Rurrenabaque in the department of Beni have been increasingly pressuring municipal governments to let them take over the responsibility for management of local natural resources including forests. In 1994 the Bolivian Congress passed a 'Popular Participation' law which gave municipal governments broad jurisdiction over rural areas, guaranteed them 20% of the national budget, and gave them responsibility for local education, health, roads, urban infrastructure, and water supplies.

"Decentralisation has created new opportunities for previously marginalised groups such as indigenous people, small farmers, and small-scale timber extractors."
Source: Submission to the Latin American and Caribbean Public Hearing

Africa – from Tanzania:

In the Miombo forests of northern Tanzania, local communities have taken steps to assert their ownership and right to manage local forest resources. In Duru-Haitemba, eight village communities have secured ownership over the forest, thus establishing the first Village Forest Reserves in Tanzania. In Mgori Forest, a 40,000 ha Miombo woodland, the five managing communities operate under an institutional arrangement of collaborative decision-making with the local government authority.

"Our main message is that the critical issue to be addressed concerns not the sharing of use rights, but the sharing of power, and the mechanisms through which this is tied inextricably within a framework of rights and responsibilities."
Source: Submission to the African Public Hearing

Europe and the CIS – from Russia:

Non-timber products in the walnut-fruit forests of southern Kyrgyzstan are important economic resources, used both for subsistence and commercial purposes by the communities living in and adjacent to the forests. It is estimated that, on average, 600–800 tonnes of walnuts are harvested per year, although yields in a good season can reach 3,500–4,000 tonnes. About 60 tonnes of pistachios are also produced in an average year. Other products harvested include honey, wild apples, cherry plums, rose-hips, and a range of medicinal plants. In addition, much of the forest land is subject to grazing and hay making.

A number of different communities use forest products. The most important are those located inside the leshozes (forest farms). On average, there are about 2,500 people in each leshoz, often scattered in a number of villages. In each leshoz, there may be 200 employees, with many others employed on a casual basis during peak periods. Many people living outside leshozes, on the recently privatised farms, also use the forests for a range of purposes.

The social and institutional arrangements governing resource use and management are changing in Kyrgyzstan. Already State collective and cooperative farms have been privatised. However, it seems likely that forests will remain under State control, at least in the medium term, because of their national importance for both productive and protective purposes. Nevertheless, arrangements governing the access to and use of forest resources may change. Devolving responsibility and authority for resource management to local entities is clearly on Russia's national agenda.
Source: WCFSD Public Hearing, St Petersburg

tion is based on results of a series of studies in Kenya, Uganda, Burundi, and Nigeria. Farmers are motivated to plant more trees to satisfy their own needs, where they no longer have access to forests for fuelwood, poles, timber, fodder, fruits, medicines, etc. Key determinants of this positive relationship are secure long-term household tenure rights to land and its trees, or where the forest frontier is too far or legally inaccessible. The authors point out that the Kyoto Protocol essentially ignores trees on-farm, a potential source of carbon credits for African small farmers. Various policy measures are indicated to augment the contribution which can be made by on-farm tree cultivation. These include: facilitating tree planting through the removal of information and germplasm constraints; ensuring that tenure is secure; market development that will foster and promote tree planting; focusing forest development on those functions that cannot be met by agro-forestry; considering the use of trees on-farm in the Kyoto Protocol to benefit farmers.

Much spontaneous reforestation is taking place through efforts of individuals and households

Such spontaneous community efforts like those described above are not yet recognised in official statistics, nationally or globally. Yet such efforts constitute a positive response to the global forest crisis, and cumulatively account for much of the reforestation that is taking place. If such community forestry is supported by public policy it would contribute even more to poverty elimination and food security, to fuelwood and fodder, to crop protection, to soil and water conservation, to conserving biological diversity, to sustaining incomes and livelihoods, and to creating and sustaining forests.

Such support would involve removing the legal and institutional obstacles to community forestry and reinforcing local property and usufruct rights through land tenure reforms. In this context gender imbalances need to be addressed (discussed in Chapter 2 in the context of governance failure), and forest education and training strengthened to support agro-forestry farming systems outside forests. Creating assets for such groups and communities – credit schemes, technical assistance, marketing supports, etc. – would also increase efficiency in the use of forest resources while generating jobs and livelihoods, thereby contributing to poverty reduction.

There is a new willingness to tackle the scourge of poverty which besets many rural people. As already mentioned major donors are now aligned in accepting poverty reduction as the major goal of development assistance and ambitious targets have been set. It is inconceivable that these targets can be attained unless it is possible for rural livelihoods to be sustained without damage to the resource base including forests. The whole spectrum from natural forests, through woodland, and trees on farms, to plantations therefore become vital props to household food security, income generation, local employment and environmental protection. This is one way in which the rhetoric of poverty elimination needs to be underpinned by active engagement of rural people in resource management.

3.3 Private woodland owners

In several industrialised countries, it is private woodland owners who manage a substantial part of the national forest estate. In the USA, private forests grew by 4 million hectares from 1977 to 1992, exceeding the reforestation by state or federal agencies. In Sweden private woodland owners control more than 60% of the country's forests and produce more than 50% of its industrial wood supply. In Switzerland, many forests are owned and sustainably managed by villages. In Scandinavian countries, private forest owners are subject to strict national laws and regulations as to how their forests should be managed.

Ownership or other forms of security of tenure are the most direct incentive in enabling individuals, corporations and communities to take a long-term view of the value of the forest resources. However, security of tenure will not automatically lead to good husbandry: that depends upon the economic, social and political context, and especially on the package of rights and responsibilities which accompanies them.

secure tenure allows everyone to take a long-term view of the value of forests

Public policy is as relevant to privately owned forest lands as it is to the use and management of state-owned and controlled forest lands. Who owns the forests is not as such decisive for how forests are managed. Performance standards, management criteria and success indicators should apply to all forests, regardless of ownership structure.

3.4 Corporations, traders and forest industry workers

Timber corporations, groups who trade in non-timber forest products, and forest workers, value forests for the profit, income, and job opportunities they provide. Forests support a variety of activities ranging from logging to forest products processing and trading. Timber corporations represent a combination of private sector firms managing their own forests or forests they lease or license, multinational forest companies buying long-term concessions, and migratory logging companies which harvest in one region and then move on to another more profitable region.

Large companies reap the highest profits from timber activities. They produce 38% of the global yearly turnover of all forest products (Carrere and Lohmann, 1996). Just 40 corporations now control some 115 million hectares of the world's forests, through ownership, leases and licences. Their activities, especially large-scale felling of trees for timber or pulp, have contributed heavily to forest decline. At the same time, the security of the incomes, profits and jobs which they generate is threatened by that decline.

Migratory logging companies have contributed heavily to forest decline as they have no stake in the long-term productivity of the land. Thus they havest without contributing to its regeneration, until the land becomes unprofitable to harvest. Considerable ecological damage is also caused in the process.

Against this background, it is encouraging that some corporations are beginning to realise that long-term success depends upon effective performance in integrating profitability with environmental and social needs and standards (see Box 3.10). Such corporations need encouragement. The initiative of the World Bank in inviting a number of such corporations to work with it to deepen and expand corporate commitment to forest stewardship is a recognition of the important role the corporate sector has to play in achieving sustainable forest management.

All corporations need clear signals about which forests are 'out of bounds' for logging, and codes of conduct specifying appropriate management practices and performance criteria for lands on which logging is allowed. While there are stirrings within the global forest industry on this subject, public policy must insist on defining, applying and monitoring the required management practices and performance indicators.

One thousand years of growth – more than ten times that of a human lifespan – can be felled in as many seconds

Forest industrial workers are at the front line regarding the effects of industrial practice – or malpractice, as the case may be. In the Commission's public hearing for North America representatives of forest worker communities and associations were concerned about the disruption being caused by pressures from environmental organisations. Their concern is understandable, given their direct dependence on the continuity of forest industrial activity for their jobs and incomes. Environmental organisations argued, on the other hand, that it is use of modern technology that caused layoff of workers even as it ravaged the resource base (see Box 3.11).

Far more careful examination of this dilemma is required in a given situation than has been the pattern to date. It is necessary to distinguish between industrial layoffs that are the consequence of changing economic circumstances, industrial restructuring because of competition, or relocation of firms, technological change, and instances where there is a correlation between industrial layoffs and environmentally based decisions to withdraw some areas from logging.

The need to restructure industries occurs in other areas of the economy. Witness adjustments that have been made in textile, shipbuilding, coal and steel industries, for example. Jobs in the forest sector may sometimes have to be sacrificed for the sake of the public interest in protection of forests to sustain vital environmental services. For such situations, worker retraining to move away from dependence on a single extractive activity and to transform economic activities, nationally or locally, will be necessary to cushion the loss of employment and to assimilate their productive capacity elsewhere.

In this regard, it is encouraging to note the emergence of small and medium scale businesses associated with the timber industry, many of them built on materials that would previously have gone to

Box 3.10 Voluntary code of conduct?

The following proposed principles were developed by some representatives of the global forest industry. These principles are intended to be consistent with the Helsinki, Tarapoto and Montreal Processes to develop criteria and indicators.

Elements of sustainable forestry:

❑ **Compliance with Laws**

Forest management shall respect all applicable laws, including international treaties, of the country in which it occurs. Industry will participate actively in the development of national legislation and international treaties to ensure that all aspects of sustainable development are well expressed.

❑ **Tenure and Use Rights and Responsibilities**

Long-term tenure and use rights to the land and forest resources shall be clearly defined, documented, and legally established. The rights of private owners of forest land shall be respected and maintained.

❑ **Indigenous Peoples' Rights**

The rights of indigenous people to own, use, and manage their lands, territories, and resources shall be clearly defined, documented, and legally established.

❑ **Economic Viability**

Forest management should be economically viable in the long term.

❑ **Sustainable Yield of Products**

Forest management at a regional level shall seek to maintain or increase the long-term production of wood and other goods and services from forests.

❑ **Biological Diversity**

Forest management should enable and contribute towards the conservation of natural biological diversity at the national, regional, or landscape scale.

❑ **Soil and Water Quality**

Forest management shall conserve soil productivity and water quality.

❑ **Use of Chemical Products**

Chemical products will be used only in strict compliance with the laws of the country in which they are applied. Efforts will be made to use non-chemical economically efficient alternatives when appropriate.

❑ **Management Plan**

A management plan – appropriate to the scale and intensity of operations – shall be written, implemented, and kept up to date. The long-term objectives of management, and the means to achieving them, shall be clearly stated in the plan.

❑ **Monitoring and Assessment**

Monitoring shall be conducted – appropriate to scale and intensity of forest management – to assess the condition of the forest, yields of forest products, management activities and other environmental impacts.

❑ **Conservation of Special Areas**

Sites of major environmental, social, or cultural significance shall be adequately conserved.

❑ **Forest Protection**

Forests shall be managed to protect their health and productivity, specifically providing protection against wildfire, pests, and diseases.

❑ **Continuous Improvement**

Industry will work to continually improve the environmental performance of its forest management activities by integrating new and improved practices gained through research and experience.

Source: Third International Forestry Roundtable, 1997

waste. These create economic and job opportunities while contributing to efficiency in use of forest resources.

Balancing the needs for secure employment, acceptable profits of corporations, and environmental protection, is one of the most difficult challenges within the forest crisis. Technology choice is an important variable in this equation. In Canada, Sweden and Finland, for example, forest worker training puts strong emphasis on safety and use of equipment that minimises damage to forest soils, flora and fauna. In Brazil, private sector/ITTO supported experimental programmes being pursued by the Tropical Forest Foundation are focusing on training of forest workers in low impact harvesting practices.

worker organisations can help strike a balance between employment, profits, conservation and sustainable use

The Commission witnessed in East Kalimantan province in Indonesia the application of computer assisted harvesting methods which allowed rigorous tree selection, directional felling to minimise disruption to vegetation, and prescribed the gradients of access roads to reduce soil erosion. Such technology allows corporations to be sensitive to environmental considerations while not negatively affecting the employment potential of their operations. Regrettably, this example of careful low impact harvesting is the exception rather than the rule in Indonesia.

The role and effectiveness of worker organisations is vital in achieving the balance between employment, profitability, conservation and sustainable use. They need to forge strategic alliances to contribute to decision-making processes relating to use of forest lands and how they should be managed. They need to collaborate in designing and implementing training programmes, especially those relating to more efficient end use of forest raw materials and introduction of more environmentally acceptable harvesting and forest management practices. They need to work jointly with management in anticipating and planning for possible changes in the structure and geographic

Box 3.11 Environment and jobs: the case of British Columbia, Canada

"For too long the public has been led to believe that the entire economy of the Province is dependent on the forest industry and that for every forest industry job, two more jobs are created elsewhere in the province. A recent economic study commissioned by the David Suzuki Foundation found that the forest industry's contribution to the provincial Gross Domestic Product has actually declined from 15% in the 1960s to only 7.5% by 1994. And the number of jobs generated by the industry has declined by 15,000 since the 1980s, and the jobs per 1,000 metres^3 fell by over 30% since the 1960s. Most of this job loss is due to mechanisation and overcutting, rather than conservation. The study found that the claim of high numbers of indirect jobs tied to the forest industry is based on the use of 'multipliers' which are at best, only crude estimates that do not accurately take into account a host of other economic factors.

The public and the province should not continue to be pressured by threats of economic doom if annual allowable cuts are lowered to truly sustainable levels. Instead, we need to improve the effort to work towards solutions that include value-added manufacturing, commercial thinning of second growth stands and more labour-intensive, innovative logging practices. Also, communities need to recognise that ecosystem conservation can help to enhance rural economies by improving eco-tourism opportunities and providing a quality environment for urban and retiring seniors."

Source: 'British Columbia's Forest Crisis', a discussion paper by Jim Cooperman, Editor, BC Environmental Report

location of forest industries as a consequence of either changing economic circumstances or forest management policies. Workers themselves need to be encouraged to join with community organisations and the public in deciding the best use of forest lands. Governance mechanisms for reconciling demands and resolving conflicts would provide such opportunities.

3.5 Consumers

As a group consumers can be instrumental in bringing about a convergence between private interests and the public interest. Environmentally-aware citizens everywhere – urban and non-urban – have become increasingly concerned in recent years about the implications for human welfare, and that of the planet, from forest decline. They are reflecting this concern by forming consumers' associations, buyers' groups, pressure points, civil society organisations; and by engaging more actively in public debates about a future that depends on the fate of forests.

Increasingly consumers, especially in the industrialised North, manifest their interest in the ecological and aesthetic values of forests by insisting on purchasing forest products that are 'certified' as having been derived from sustainably managed forests. Alliances of 'Buyers Groups' are rapidly gaining ground in the United Kingdom and elsewhere in western Europe (see Box 3.12).

Similar initiatives are getting under way in the USA and Japan. Although the number of consumers involved in these initiatives is still relatively low, their ranks are growing rapidly and their voices are beginning to be heard. Increasingly, also, consumers in their capacity as investors are using social and environmental screens to ensure that their savings match their own values.

Those who are interested in forest conservation would do well to direct investments to support reforestation by small farmers and villages. Such consumer groups could become a significant driving force for sustainable management of forests particularly if mechanisms could be created for their participation in processes related to standard-setting, monitoring, and certification.

more consumers are showing an interest in the aesthetic and ecological values of forests

3.6 Civil Society

A wide range of non-governmental and civil-society organisations have been playing an increasingly proactive role in promoting conservation and sustainable management of forests. Their activities include:

- promoting transparent and democratic political and institutional arrangements for forest policy dialogue
- fostering public–private partnerships
- pressing for expansion of protected areas
- campaigning for protection of the property rights of forest-dwelling communities
- monitoring global forest developments
- participating actively in assessing whether there is need for a Global Forest Convention
- developing and insisting on responsible forest stewardship standards
- designing and testing innovative financing mechanisms
- exposing cases of corruption and malpractice and proposing remedial action.

This is part of a new and active role in which they engage in debate about power, responsibility, and accountability.

What is noticeable is that these organisations have taken up the challenge on behalf of civil society, as governments have become less able to regulate powerful international or domestic companies. They have been quite successful in raising the threshold of performance in the forest industry through their mechanisms for independent certification and labelling of forest products.

Given the crisis relating to the world's forests, it is very encouraging that responsible citizens are taking initiatives through non-governmental and civil society organisations to address some difficult aspects of forest policy, forest politics and forest practice. The Commission was impressed by the initiatives and potential for creating solutions which have been led by various national and international non-governmental organisations. It is convinced that such efforts would contribute even more effectively towards finding a balance among competing demands and objectives, and towards conservation and sustainable management of forests in general, if they were facilitated and supported. Support and facilitation are

Box 3.12 Signs of hope?

Converging public and private interests?
Around 7% of UK's top 250 companies are implementing or actively considering a social audit – a key indication of the extent to which business is reflecting the rise of public concern about business ethics. Social auditing has been around for many years; but it is only in the last five years that it has emerged as a tool for making organisations more accountable to stakeholders – particularly for those whose views and interests have traditionally been excluded.

Cause and effect?
86% of consumers in the UK are more likely to buy a product related to a cause: 93% of companies in the UK are now relating their marketing to a cause!

Corporate viability with environmental responsibility?
According to Fortune Magazine of the US, Britain's most admired company is British Petroleum because of its record in environmental responsibility. BP's return to shareholders was 330% over three years – nearly three times that of the average major corporation, indicating that environmental responsibility can go hand in hand with corporate viability.

Economics with ethics?
Social Accountability 8000 (SA8000) is a global standard for ethical sourcing now under development. It aims to provide a framework for the ethical sourcing and production of goods. Based on ISO 9000 and 14000, SA8000 is designed for independent verification by outside auditors.

Benefit not burden?
There has been a remarkable rise in the number of ethical and green businesses that have embraced a strong social or environmental agenda. Their relative success has been associated with the fact that they tend to have strong management capacity if they embrace social and environmental objectives successfully. Equally, the presence of a strong sense of purpose in a company, so that it tries to take care of its reputation rather than simply project an image, is central to long term business sustainability. A recent US survey showed that of the top 500 companies listed in 1956, two-thirds have disappeared, with those remaining tending to be those with 'a strong moral core'.
Source: New Economics Foundation, 1997

especially required in the countries of the developing world where, for obvious economic reasons, groups need financial and sometimes technical support to become independent and effective.

3.7 The general public

People living far from forests are not immune to the perils which beset forests or to the effects of their decline. The smoke from recent forest fires in Indonesia, for example, disrupted its entire national life as well as affecting that of neighbouring countries.

Almost half the world's population is now urban and by about 2015, according to UN projections, 5 billion people will live in urban settlements. The world over, many city-dwellers derive economic benefit from selling or trading in forest products. Many others for whom forests offer no financial return value them for aesthetic, spiritual and recreational purposes. All are consumers of forest products and services in one form or another. And all of them share in the public services which forests provide: ultimately, their quality of life depends on these services.

simply reconciling competing private interests will not address the causes of forest decline

3.8 The public interest

The Commission organised public hearings in order to talk to people living in and off the forests, who are otherwise directly dependent on forests, or who held strong views on forest issues. These are legitimate interests which cannot be ignored in any effort to reform forest policies and management. Where there is competition for the same resource, that must be resolved through public process. But simply reconciling competing private interests will not address the causes of forest decline as discussed in Chapter 2.

Ultimately everyone has an interest in the forest, whether as consumers of forest products, as beneficiaries of the general development which forests support, or for the environmental services which forests provide. What is essential is to safeguard the functions of forests, which requires an integration of the environmental, economic and social benefits which are derived from forests. Private interests may need to be reconsidered in the interest of all, that is, in the public interest. And, given globalisation, the public interest must be weighed in the balance with corporate interests.

The public interest goes beyond the material interests of a single group and it exceeds the sum of all group interests. The public interest involves securing all those environmental functions of forests presented in Chapter 1, which are essential for humankind as a whole. We share those benefits, collectively and indivisibly: going beyond individuals to communities, beyond communities to entire societies, beyond individual nations to all nations, beyond humankind to the wellbeing of all other species, and beyond present to future generations.

The role of government

What emerged clearly from the Commission's public hearings is the recognition that resolving these local conflicts and the forces that have provoked them is an essential part of the strategy that will need to be put in place to slow global forest decline. The Commission warns that the competing claims and competition, and the conflicts to which they give rise, are likely to get worse, given the multiple functions of forests and the multiplicity of human needs and interests to be met from a declining resource base.

To date, such conflicts have tended to be settled either by the exercise of the authority of the state or the exercise of power by corporations or individuals, acting to the exclusion of other interest groups. The needs and concerns of the politically weaker groups, and the public interest as a whole, have been ignored or subordinated.

governments have a responsibility to perceive articulate defend and secure the public interest

Civil society organisations and NGOs have been in the vanguard in either waging the battles on behalf of groups or in finding solutions to the conflicts on behalf of society. But, however energised, active and effective they have been in calling attention to the issues, this does not relieve governments of their duty and their responsibility to secure the public interest while reconciling the competing demands on forest lands and resources.

The Commission asserts that it is the responsibility of governments to perceive, articulate, defend and secure the public interest. The Barnett Report illustrated how bureaucratic inefficiency and political indifference resulted in an environment in Papua New Guinea in which powerful and unscrupulous corporations overrode other group interests as well as the public interest (see Box 3.2). The Commission advocates that governments must do much more than they have been doing to attack the root causes of forest decline. Among the imperatives for their action is to achieve a shift in the balance of political power among interest groups through appropriate governance mechanisms. This additional responsibility may require governments to assign values which do not necessarily please everyone, as the same good or service can be seen positively or negatively, depending on who is looking at it.

There are no standard formulae for reconciling competing needs and interests. That has to be a dynamic process, adaptable to a specific place at a point in time, to a given forest site, to the parties involved and the range of uses being proposed – hence the necessity for establishing mechanisms through which such a process of decision-making and balancing might take place. No outcome will ever satisfy all persons all the time on all issues, especially in a situation of scarcity. But interested groups should be able to anticipate how their competing needs will be addressed. Together with the transparency which should attend the process, the confidence of citizens in the

Box 3.13 Private values, public interest, and role of government

"For the slash and burn forest farmer, it may be rational from an economic point of view to move on and clear the next piece of forest. The farmer's family has no choice if they are to survive; and thus, the value they implicitly attach to cleared land (and the food produced on it) far exceeds any value they attach to the standing forest. For an environmentalist living comfortably in a city, a different point of view and set of values may hold, e.g. maintenance of virgin forest may take on much greater value than the meagre agricultural output of slash and burn farmers. However, the farmer is on the ground and makes the decision to clear the forest based on his or her individual point of view and set of values. The farmer is de facto the decision-maker in this case. A country can legislate against deforestation by forest farmers, and it can enforce such legislation – which essentially means that the country is imposing a different set of values than those held by the farmer. In this case the decision-making power has shifted from the farmer to the government; and what matters in terms of action is the valuation context and the point of view of the government."

Source: Gregerson et al., *1995*

decisions relating to forest use will gradually be built.

The Commission recognises that economic and social conditions vary from place to place. So too does the type of forest which occurs. These will combine with the political system and political traditions to determine the conditions and the processes for people's participation in decisions about forests. But whatever the context and culture, participatory decision-making and processes for conflict resolution are essential for arriving at appropriate solutions.

This is not to advocate that governments should limit their role to become merely arbiters of such conflicts. An important part of their role would be the creation of mechanisms for consultation, dialogue and debate in which all private interests contend, in which the poor and the politically weak are represented, and through which the public interest also becomes a vested interest. Sustainable forest management requires attention to political as much as to technical matters. In the same way that governments specify and administer the fiscal measures to govern the operation of firms in the forestry sector, so they need to establish the framework conditions within which the reconciliation of competing demands and divergent interests are worked out, and in which all segments of affected society are involved in decision-making about forest land use.

Such processes will need to be guided by persons with the right skills and experience. The role played by Judge Barnett in Papua New Guinea gives a good example of how persons with skills of inquiry, imbued with the precepts of justice and equity, and with experience in weighing and balancing conflicting points of view in order to serve the public interest, can be called upon for similar purposes. All societies have a corps of such expertise which can be used to guide such processes and support such policies. They must be so engaged.

However, as Reitbergen (1997) points out "achieving a 'balance of use' is not an easy task, even for the most well-intentioned authorities. Economically rational and socially fair decisions about forest management require not only political commitment, but also knowledge: about the various parties involved and their resource use and needs; the trade-offs and compatibilities between their interests; and the technical options available for managing forests for a variety of objectives. There is need for fora where local, national and international interests can be represented and management agreements negotiated, to make sure that they are acceptable to most if not all parties affected. And, last but not least, decisions need to be applied, and implementation and monitoring capacity established in the public agencies concerned."

sustainable forest management requires attention to political as much as to technical matters

Securing the public interest in forests indicates various types of functions for governments:

- a facilitative function in creating and administering mechanisms of public process
- a representative function in advancing and securing the public interest
- an executive function in ensuring that the outcomes of public process are reflected in policies, laws, regulations and management guidelines
- an administrative function in organising the public administration system to operate in conformity with the above.

Such functions for government in forest management are echoed in the requirements put forward by forest scientists and policy analysts: "These are at very least: a legal framework which is enforceable and enforced; stable policies which inspire confidence and are not changed arbitrarily; open and transparent processes for resource allocation and decision making; committed forest management staff; freedom from corruption; security of access to resources; adequate facilities for education, technical training and research; and adequate and freely available information about resources and their management." (World Bank, 1998).

The role of civil society

some states are creating governance mechanisms to facilitate the changing role of civil society

While the role of governments is essential in creating the mechanisms for such participation and contributions, there are things that citizens can and must do for themselves. Ultimately, it is we as citizens who hold in trust these vital resources for present and future generations. It is we therefore who need to be vigilant about that responsibility.

One of the impressive developments in the last two decades has been the active engagement of civil society in national and global affairs. This is particularly evident in environmental matters. There is indication of a changing role of civil society – from being the governed to active interest and involvement in governance. This provides much cause for hope. The Commission considers this indication an important beginning to what it feels will increasingly be recognised as a foundation of 21st century civilisation. It is encouraging to note that some states have recognised this changing role of civil society and, what is more important, are responding to create governance mechanisms that would facilitate that role (see Box 3.14).

The Commission's public hearings revealed an increasing consciousness among citizens of the public trust in forests. Citizens are becoming highly motivated to instil a sense of moral responsibility and ethical stewardship in the management of earth's natural resources. As discussed in Chapter 2 in the context of governance failure, mechanisms are required to permit citizens to have a more structured participation in the policy-making for and management of forests, and to allow widespread civic interest and energy to well up and be channeled into constructive and effective scrutiny of practices and performance in the forest. For example, the Commission has drawn attention to the corruption which pervades forest operations. The only way that corrupt practices will be exposed will be through the active and independent efforts of civil society in keeping forest operations under scrutiny.

The Commission takes the view that more, not fewer, mechanisms are necessary to make this possible. The Commission thus calls for new and different kinds of mechanisms: designed to address the

Box 3.14 Public participation given legal recognition

In June 1998 member states of the United Nations Economic Commission for Europe (UN-ECE) signed a Public Participation Convention to regulate relations between the public and governments in environmental matters. The Convention has three pillars:

- access to information: a general right for everyone to access environmental information held by public authorities
- public participation in environmental decision-making: through public participation mechanisms in a range of activities
- access to justice: judicial or administrative procedures to provide remedies that are fair and equitable.

Source: UN/ECE, 1998

specificities of the issues that need attention; predicated on the active involvement of local communities; with efforts that are localised to make possible direct and close vigilance of the actions where they take place; organised to operate independently of national governmental or global intergovernmental institutions; but which are interconnected nationally and globally for mutual support and interdependence.

The Commission has so far taken the following positions:

- that the ecological, economic and social significance of forests means that forests can no longer be managed primarily for supplying timber and pulp
- that private interests alone fail to manage forests in the public interest; that the public interest becomes more pressing as human demands increase while forests decrease
- that the public interest must be paramount in deciding on policies about forest lands and forest resources, and about other sectors which directly and indirectly have an impact on forests
- that forest policy-making and management can no longer be left to governments and private corporations only, though both of these have inescapable responsibilities in ensuring that forests are sustained
- that solutions have to be sought in land use and resource management, not just through the activities of the forest sector
- that mechanisms are required for civil society participation in policy making to enable the public interest in forests to be expressed.

We hold the forests in trust for the present generation and those to come

Indeed, enabling the public interest to be expressed is an important part of the reason for the Commission coming into being in the first place. In this report some examples of ordinary citizens spontaneously coming together in defence of their forests have been presented. The Commission has been gratified by the appreciation of and participation in its public hearings through which it has sought to give a voice to those who are directly affected by but not connected with the debates that are taking place about their lives and livelihoods. The Commission is therefore anxious to see that such opportunities for citizen involvement persist beyond its life.

The Commission places a high priority on the demands expressed for dialogue between governments and civil society at the international level beyond the limited opportunities accorded to industry and NGOs as observers to intergovernmental processes. The Commission joins with them in pressing:

- for dialogue between government and civil society at the national level
- for more objective data on what is happening within and to the world's forests and for civil society involvement in collecting and verifying those data

- for certified forest products domestically and internationally and for harmonised criteria and indicators for these
- for more transparency in decision-making about forest concessions, policies, and management
- for an end to corruption in the forest sector
- for recognition and support of the spontaneous efforts being made towards sustaining forests.

3.9 FORESTRUST INTERNATIONAL

Thus the Commission advocates the concept of a citizens' force for discharge of the public trust and defence of the public interest in forests, **FORESTRUST INTERNATIONAL**. This is envisaged as a set of arrangements that could find application at global, national and local levels, that would enable the world's citizens to help build the normative framework for forest management, and that would permit them to exercise their right to have oversight of how forests, which the present generation holds in trust for humankind and all other species, are being managed in their interest and for that of future generations.

The overall purpose is to catalyse, encourage, facilitate, and support communities in organising themselves in relevant localised activities. FORESTRUST INTERNATIONAL envisages four objectives, with corresponding activities, dedicated to:

- monitoring the forest situation **(FORESTWATCH)**
- investigating and publicising incidents of abuse of rights and power and passing critical judgements on policies pursued **(FOREST OMBUDSMAN)**
- encouraging coordinated approaches and harmonised provisions in management criteria and performance indicators **(FOREST MANAGEMENT COUNCIL)**
- recognising and rewarding exemplary practice by communities, corporations and countries in managing forests sustainably **(FOREST AWARD)**.

FORESTRUST INTERNATIONAL ***will catalyse facilitate and support communities in organising themselves***

The objectives of FORESTRUST INTERNATIONAL will be:

- to serve as an international consultative forum on forest-related issues between government and civil society
- to encourage establishment of national counterparts
- to work with them to conduct the Forestwatch, Forest Ombudsman, and Forest Award activities described below
- to assist in securing financing and technical support for the activities described.

FORESTRUST INTERNATIONAL will be an association open to interested governments, NGOs, and other civil society organisations, the business community, science and intergovernmental institutions. It will come into being by networking among all of those interested in joining their voices and resources for conserving and sustaining forests. It will be a vehicle for getting people involved, for keeping forest issues prominently and permanently on the agenda internationally and nationally, and for creating fora for dialogue on equal terms between governments and civil society, internationally and nationally. It will operate through a Council and standing committees for the major activities proposed.

It will encourage the creation of national and local counterpart groups and activities, comprised and carried out by national and local forest experts, individual citizens, and communities directly involved in and affected by forest issues. A national ForesTrust would basically serve the same purpose on the national level. Its organisational design, as well as that of the pillars on which it is based, would most likely differ from country to country depending on already existing organisations, traditions and political structures.

FORESTRUST INTERNATIONAL will be organised around the objectives and activity areas mentioned above. These objectives, activities and groups will be mutually dependent and reinforcing, locally, nationally and globally, and will operate to increase the momentum towards conservation and sustainable forest management.

FORESTWATCH

This is envisaged as a network for information gathering, analysis, and dissemination; connecting organisations at the national and global levels; connecting with local experts and communities everywhere who are on the spot and best placed to know what is happening in their backyards and feed data and observations into the national and global networks; bringing to public notice issues of actual or potential conflict, such as those described earlier, and instances of abuse of corporate power or official authority. FORESTWATCH will be a challenge to the unfettered corrupt activity of timber corporations, government officials, and individuals. The challenge will be posed by ordinary citizens working through their community and national organisations, and actively advocating and pressing for whatever the standard of management and business practice they wish to have in their back yards. FORESTWATCH would also allow communities to be vigilant about other development policies and decisions that could negatively affect forests.

Discussions during the time that the Commission engaged in its work elicited much enthusiasm for this proposal. Indeed, the Commission is gratified by the leadership which has already been given by the World Resources Institute in mobilising other key international non-governmental organisations in the catalytic work required to bring this concept into being.

FORESTWATCH at the national level would collect information for national purposes as well as feed into the international network. These activities would be essential to the monitoring and assessment required for application of management criteria and performance indicators.

FOREST OMBUDSMAN

An international FOREST OMBUDSMAN would represent an innovation among international institutions. Its purpose is to be an international watchdog on issues of discrimination, abuse, inequity, and corruption associated with forest operations. It will be informed on such issues and incidents through the operation of the national and international FORESTWATCH. Activities would be non-advocacy and non-partisan in character. If possible and so desired by the parties involved, it could also engage in conflict resolution.

As for the other pillars, FOREST OMBUDSMAN will be based on national chapters which carry out analagous functions guided by recognised and reputable nationals. A national FOREST OMBUDSMAN could be modelled on similar functions in other areas of national concern.

an international FOREST OMBUDSMAN would be an innovation among international institutions

An international FOREST OMBUDSMAN is not expected to have legal status or authority in any country. Its findings or 'rulings' would be non-punitive, as are decisions by a National Forest Ombudsman. Emphasis will be on the normative effect of their findings, which would thus serve as one of many building blocks for a comprehensive policy for sustaining forests and development. To be successful they will need to establish themselves as objective, non-advocacy organisations. The effect of their findings and statements would depend on their reputation as impartial authorities, and on their powers of moral suasion. They will need to have totally independent status. Financing will have to be without any ties.

Two options could be considered: as an independent UN body, similar to the Human Rights Committee; or as a creation of international NGOs active in forest conservation.

criteria and indicators certification and labelling need coordinating and harmonising

FOREST MANAGEMENT COUNCIL

The Commission has concluded that there is a need for coordinated efforts and harmonisation of criteria and indicators, certification and labeling initiatives (see discussion in Chapter 4). It thus proposes a Forest Management Council with objectives to:

- help build a normative framework for sustainable forest management and be supportive of intergovernmental negotiations in that area
- encourage the establishment of criteria and indicators, and certification systems for forest management based on up-to-date requirements at the national level
- encourage dialogue between ongoing processes to achieve coordinated approaches and harmonised provisions for internationally traded products
- promote improvement in aspects of these mechanisms which are still weak (i.e. in the social and participatory aspect of forest management)
- encourage internationally acceptable certification systems which allow for adjustments to local conditions.

National Forest Management Councils will provide the national and local underpinning for the above, will monitor the application of the provisions adopted by countries for forest management, and support buyers' groups and consumer organisations in discriminating in favour of sustainably produced forest products.

FOREST AWARD

This is envisaged as a mechanism for recognising and rewarding good practice and performance in conservation and towards sustainable forest management by communities, corporations and countries. It will rely on information and inputs generated through the operation of FORESTWATCH and on the outcome of the issues investigated by OMBUDSMAN.

The FOREST AWARD proposed by the Commission will be a mechanism for recognising and rewarding good achievements in conservation and in support of sustainable management of forests. The Commission has already embarked on development of stipulations and format for nomination, composition of the committee, administrative and financial matters, nature and level of award/s. FOREST AWARD committees at national level will make nominations under this scheme.

During a limited follow-up phase after the launching of this Report the Commission will be in active discussion with individuals, organisations and governments on the foregoing ideas and pillars that comprise FORESTRUST INTERNATIONAL. One of the immediate follow-up activities of the Commission is to bring these interested parties together to advance this discussion and to set the arrangements in motion. The Commission invites interested parties to convey their interest and wish to be involved in this process to the Commission's follow-up office.

4

MANAGING FORESTS SUSTAINABLY

Economies cannot remain healthy unless the resources on which they depend are sustainably managed. Economies that degrade their environments for short-term gain are rarely stable and never sustainable. Nowhere is this more obvious than in our mismanagement of the world's forests. Forests are often called the lungs of the world for their role in helping to regulate the exchange of oxygen and carbon dioxide. Yet everywhere we look, from the rain forests of the Amazon to the boreal forests of North America, the lungs are gasping

(Wolfensohn and Fuller, 1998)

4.1 Beyond forestry

whether forests renew themselves depends upon how we affect their resilience

Sustainable development requires integrating economic viability and human development with the necessity to protect the environment and sustain indefinitely the natural resource base. In Chapter 1 the Commission discussed the environmental, economic and social importance of forests. Sustainable forest management requires integration of these dimensions into the policies and practices for utilising and managing forests, so that economic and social needs are met while leaving forests capable of fulfilling their environmental functions and enduring. In Chapter 2 the Commission discussed some of the root causes of forest decline, and indicated that many of them originate outside forestry activities.

In Chapter 5, the Commission draws attention to the effect of population growth on the level of demand for key goods and services and to the consequent pressure for use of more forest lands and forest products. It is evident that solutions need to be sought in areas beyond the scope of forest management and forest sector operations, and throughout this Report the Commission makes proposals that could contribute to those solutions. Nevertheless, it is also necessary that approaches to forest management also adjust to the need to manage forests for a public purpose, in which the primary objective becomes sustainability of forests.

Forests have long been managed for generating a continuous stream of products, notably commercial timber and pulp, and to a lesser extent a range of non-timber products. Management objectives have been principally to satisfy private interests, therefore a profitable enterprise is the overriding factor. The discussion in Chapter 3 noted that some forest companies and communities are now actively pursuing the required changes. Some of this is undoubtedly influenced by the forestry profession as it responds to the imperatives of sustainable development to integrate economic, environmental and social needs within the forest sector; some of it as a result of pressure on forest companies by international non-governmental and civil society organisations.

Whatever the impetus for change, forest managers now have different responsibilities than in the past. Effective discharge of those responsibilities – by corporations, communities and foresters – will depend primarily on the responses that are made by governments to the economic, policy and ethical failures discussed in Chapter 2, as well as the macro-policies and planning approaches which are addressed to sustaining forests and development, discussed in Chapter 5. Together these responses will circumscribe how forests can be managed sustainably.

Much of the existing controversy about sustainable forest management derives from differing interpretations of the term 'sustainability'. At one time it was limited to ensuring sustainable timber yields. While the limitations of that definition are now widely recognised, a far more comprehensive approach is required to devise appropriate macro and micro-policies to be able to move from understanding those limitations to overcoming them in practice.

However, we need to be certain that within the forest sector itself, all the possibilities for sustainable forest management – and not just sustaining timber yields – are activated and reflected in management practices that would contribute to sustaining forests. Forests are renewable, and should be capable of providing their services in perpetuity. But forest lands are finite, and whether the forests renew themselves or not depends upon how we affect their resilience. Their management must address these factors. This chapter sets out some of the more important principles that the Commission believes should underlie forest management, and it reviews some controversial forest practices. It discusses the need for consolidating and accelerating research efforts for continuous learning about forests and forest management.

4.2 Objectives of sustainable forest management

Since the 1992 Rio Earth Summit, the term 'sustainable forest management' (SFM) has been widely used in forest policy circles. Several perspectives about SFM exist today: some view SFM as production of a continuous flow of desired forest products without loss in inherent productivity; others say that SFM does not entail production or extraction, but is all about maintaining and enhancing ecosystem functions; some say SFM is nothing but wise management. The term is variously used – in political, scientific, environmental and public relations contexts.

Traditional forest management was supposed to be based on managing forests for a combination of forest values, but timber and fibre production and profits derived from these have dominated. SFM reflects a shift towards forest practices that have a stronger ecological and social focus compared with the past. In other words, SFM requires integrating concerns for economic and ecological viability of forests, while ensuring that their use and management contribute to the social objectives of societies.

In order to secure this range of economic, ecological and social values, a strategy for SFM must reflect the following objectives:

- to indefinitely satisfy needs for timber, fibre and non-timber forest products
- to ensure conservation of soil and water
- to sustain the resilience and renewal capacity of forests
- to support the food security and livelihood needs of marginalised communities which are dependent on forests
- to conserve biological diversity
- to achieve all the above consistent with the incremental productive capacity of forests and the requirements of ecological security
- to realise a more equitable sharing of the benefits from the uses to which forests are put
- more organised management, cultivation, harvesting and utilisation of minor forest products as potential pillars of sustainable forestry to sustain livelihoods from dwindling resources
- reduction of industrial pollution which is inimical both to soil and atmosphere, affecting the forests and biodiversity
- better management of effluents which have serious degrading effects on soil and flora
- securing tenurial rights of the millions of people living in villages skirting forest areas as a means to promote conservation.

4.3 Principles for sustainable forest management

Landscape management

In Chapter 5 the Commission argues that in a full world, with escalating human demand on a shrinking natural resource base, it is vital that planning for meeting that demand takes all aspects of the landscape together as a totality.[1] Managing forests for sustainability must emerge from and fit within a broader approach to planning for and managing the overall landscape. A process of landscape planning should lead to identification of how the requirements for forests for conservation, for commerce, and for communities can be met. Moreover, management specifics will vary according to type of forest (temperate, boreal, tropical, peat swamp, mangrove, etc.).

Ecosystem-based management

Forestry practices have been evolving as scientific information and understanding grow, and as pressures are exerted by environmentalists to treat forests as more than sources of timber and fibre. For example, 'New Forestry' was a concept developed by a group of forest ecologists in the USA as a way of managing forest land to conserve a range of 'old-growth' values while at the same time allowing for the extraction of timber (Gillis, 1990). It was an attempt to move certain environmental groups away from their insistence on forest preservation (which seeks to limit wood harvesting over large areas), and to persuade timber production-oriented foresters to develop and use more ecologically-sensitive systems of silviculture and forest management. Management practices include retention of large decomposing logs as habitat for small mammals, amphibians, and other organisms; and removal of less wood per hectare at harvest time in order to maintain site organic matter resources and carbon storage. But New Forestry ran into resistance from commercial interests on the grounds that this system could lower the yield of logs from the forest, and that much of this loss would be in the more valuable large-diameter logs.

landscape planning should show how to conserve forests for commerce and communities

The debate on Sustainable Forest Management has led to the emergence of 'Ecosystem Management' (Forest Ecosystem Management Assessment Team, 1993; Overbay, 1992; Slocombe, 1993). Ecosystem Management involves ecological site classification that identifies ecologically significant variations in climate, soil, vegetation, and ecosystem function across the landscape. Site-specific management objectives and practices are then developed for the ecologically distinct portions of the landscape: objectives and practices consistent with both the ecology and the individual landscape units and the applicable forest management objectives. Ecosystem Management is also concerned with the rate and landscape pattern of forest harvesting, with watershed effects and impacts on fish and streams, and with wildlife habitat.

Many of the ideas of New Forestry are incorporated into Ecosystem Management, but the latter goes further. Although there is still much debate about Ecosystem Management, the concept is fast being accepted as the ecological foundation for sustainable forest management.

Experience has led to a better understanding of the ecological constraints to forest growth and regeneration, and therefore to a better appreciation that management specificities will vary according to type of forest. (See for example Box 4.1 on management of tropical moist forests and Box 4.2 on management of tropical dry forests.) Temperate, boreal, tropical, or peat swamp forests behave in different

Box 4.1 Tropical moist forest management

There has been increasing emphasis on management for preservation of non-timber forest products and services that are essential to the way of life of forest communities, and for preservation of the biodiversity, carbon sequestration, and watershed catchment protection benefits of tropical moist forests.

The fundamental difference between temperate and tropical forests lies in the much greater ecological complexity of the latter and also in the social and population pressures to which they are being subjected. About two-thirds of the world's approximately 250,000 species of flowering plants flourish in the humid tropics. Few of these species are common to all three main blocks of tropical moist forest. The immense richness of some tropical moist forest is also not uniform. Infertile soil, poor drainage, or difficult topography support forest ecosystems that may be poor in species. Some forests are adapted to disturbances such as hurricanes or cyclones or landslides. Salt-tolerant mangroves, for example, form on muddy tropical coasts. Increased seasonality of climate causes dramatic reductions in the numbers of species. There are notable examples of forests dominated by one or a few non-pioneer species in areas. Silviculture and management of these species-poor forests are relatively easy if regeneration of the dominant species is abundant (as in some *Mora excelsa* forests in Trinidad), or difficult when regeneration is usually absent (as in forests dominated by Meliaceae in West Africa or the *Shorea albida* peat-swamp forests in Borneo).

The trend toward multiple end-use management of tropical moist forests reflects recognition of the wide range of forest goods and services that they provide.

Box 4.2 Tropical dry forest management

The world's open forests include most dry forests. While much global attention has been focused on destruction of tropical rainforest and its consequences, less attention has been given to the tropical and sub-tropical dry forests. Yet dry forests are at least as problematic and are disappearing as fast. Because such forests occur in more densely populated regions than rainforests, their disappearance is likely to have a more severe impact on people living nearby. They are usually also major sources of fuelwood for rural and urban markets. Their disappearance will increase rural poverty and desertification (as it already does in parts of the Sahel region).

Tropical and sub-tropical dry forests are important for a variety of reasons. Like the rainforests, they protect and cool soil, directly affecting soil fertility and productivity. They also act as a store of carbon and are therefore relevant to dealing with climate change. While they contribute less moisture to the atmosphere than rainforests on a per hectare basis, their size and their presence in lower rainfall areas make their moisture contribution of very great importance. When they are removed, the increased albedo effect is marked. They support larger numbers of people and domesticated animals per hectare than do rainforests, though their carrying capacity is still relatively low. Humans have learned to live in symbiosis with these woodlands by relying both upon the milk and meat which animals produce from tree-browse, and upon the replenishment of soil fertility which the trees bring to agriculture. As a result, their disappearance will severely affect local people.

Dry forest management has also benefited from improved understanding of the social and ecological significance of such forests. From a technical perspective it has been recognised that earlier attempts to meet forest product needs by establishment of dry-zone tree plantations is not much of an answer. The emphasis has shifted to management practices aimed at sustainable harvesting of the slow-growing but ecologically robust indigenous tree species of open savannahs and desert margins. Requirements of pastoral communities have been recognised as important. Management techniques such as frequent light lopping of trees have been shown to produce more digestible fodder. Likewise, harvests of poles and fuelwood from multiple sprouts on coppiced or cut stumps may have more usable biomass than the large logs produced from timber-oriented management systems.

Source: Shepard et al., *1993*

ways and will respond differently to a particular use or threat. Thus no prescription of forest management practices will be appropriate to all contexts. Ecosystem-based forest management will involve site classification and characterisation, so that the management requirements, the techniques for harvesting, etc. can be informed by the successional sequences of that type of forest. This demands much from traditional foresters. Traditional silvicultural knowledge now needs to be fused with the new technologies of information capture, processing and analysis. The ability to communicate these ideas to non-technical audiences is also becoming a necessity.

no prescription of forest management practices will be appropriate to all contexts

Participatory decision-making

Managing forests sustainably involves more than technical matters. It must get to the human issues – betterment of the human condition, social equity, poverty reduction, power relations, gender roles – which lie at the heart of forest resource problems and conflicts. Embracing these human issues requires the participation of a broad cross-section of people in planning for and decisions about forest management.

The Commission has argued in Chapter 3 for governance mechanisms to be put in place to open up the decision-making process and involve civil society and especially groups directly affected by forest land use. In this way, accumulated community knowledge and experience of forests and trees can be drawn upon.

The Commission recognises that improved participation in decision-making regarding forest use (discussed further in Chapter 5 on participatory land use planning) will not by itself deliver societies to the 'promised land' of sustainable forests. But participation is one of the foundations for sustainable development, and is in turn a prerequisite for more community involvement in forest management.

An extensive review of community forestry projects has led to the identification of key principles to apply in a participatory approach to forest management (see Box 4.4).

Localised management

In many countries there is a history of community management of forests. It is true that much of that has been displaced through state acquisition and control of

Box 4.3 Communities can contribute: example from Cameroon

Cameroon's Community Forestry Development Project (CFDP) will help to establish effective community-based forest planning and management. The project will establish a Community Forestry Unit in the Forestry Department. It will define the legal and institutional framework. It will seek to improve understanding of traditional natural resource management systems. It will raise awareness of the implications of the new forest policy and law. It will pilot community-based planning and management. It will develop consultation procedures for the establishment of permanent forest reserves.

The project is accompanied by a land-use planning exercise within the Forestry Department, through which areas for inclusion in the Permanent Forest Estate will be identified. Active participation of local people in defining the boundaries, and incorporating within agreements their usufruct rights, would ultimately contribute to the protection of the Permanent Forest Estate. Since they are cognisant of the need to secure access for themselves, and their children, to the diverse products and services the forest provides, they would rather manage the forest sustainably than destroy it. Management would thus rest with those who have the greatest interest in preserving it as a national capital asset.

Source: WCFSD Public Hearing, Yaounde

Box 4.4 Policies that work for forests and people: suggested principles

1. Participation in policy and planning. There should be an independent forum at national and sub-national levels, to understand stakeholder views and needs, forge decisions and develop partnerships; this will require strong capacities for negotiation and conflict management.

2. Information, monitoring and research which is designed to deal better with change and actively feed into policy and management processes. Monitoring and information need to cover multiple aspects of forest assets, demand and use, and to involve stakeholders. Research should help to develop capacities to adapt to change.

3. Capabilities to address cross-sectoral influences on forest and people. Stakeholder analysis, impact assessment and valuation approaches may offer useful instruments for understanding.

4. Agreed national goals for forests – based on sustainability, productivity and equity. SFM may provide a compelling trajectory to help stakeholders to work together, but it will need translation into sub(national) standards. The concept of 'security of forest goods and services', to be met from forest and non-forest sources, may be more useful when it comes to negotiating trade-offs within and between local, national and global levels since its focus is on people and what they need from forests, rather than on forests *per se*. Tying forestry goals with poverty alleviation goals may assist an (often essential) focus on improving equity for SFM.

5. Policy instruments better geared to stakeholders and national goals. Informational and institutional instruments, to meet the incremental costs of improved management, can be more efficient than coercion. But regulations remain essential for non-substitutable forest services such as critical biodiversity, landscapes and watershed regulation.

6. Decentralisation, devolution and strengthening capacity as appropriate. In many countries this may now be the key issue. The challenge is to agree new roles between community, state, and private sector; to issue (and ensure the security of) adequate and equitable rights; and to build capacity. For multiple objectives and/or stakeholders, user rights and/or partnership approaches are promising. Fostering reflective processes within institutions, with external support where appropriate, is crucial for developing attitudinal change for such renegotiation.

7. Standards and codes of practice form improved accountability. Recognising inter-stakeholder dependencies, (sub)national principles, criteria and standards may help in providing practical benchmarks and checks and balances.

8. Spread of resource-conserving technology. A more critical look is needed at how current policies/incentives encourage inefficient technology; and imaginative approaches are required to encourage SFM (as SFM will be information-intensive).

9. Democracy of knowledge. Better awareness of aims and standards, and available technology, is needed at all 'levels' for empowering effective forest stewardship.

10. Framework for continuous policy improvement. The above elements of policy formulation, implementation and review require an equitable, participatory process; so far, the best option seems to be a partnership arrangement between stakeholder fora and government to organise this.

Source: Excerpt from Bass et al., *1997*

forest lands, through operations of large timber corporations, and through insecure land tenure. There appears to be, however, a renaissance of community involvement in forest management (see Chapter 3 and Boxes 4.5 and 4.6). The Commission has argued in Chapter 3 for removal of obstacles that prevent the full realisation of this capacity and capability. Localised management of forest resources is more likely to alleviate poverty by a more equitable sharing of the benefits from the use of this public resource than large-scale corporate exploitation of forests has done.

localised management of forest resources is more likely to alleviate poverty

Maximise agroforestry potential

Conversion of forest lands for agriculture and pasture for ranching has been a major reason for forest loss and degradation. Food will continue to be demanded, and in increasing quantity as population and incomes increase. Where forest lands become relatively scarce and public policy is pressured to preserve remaining undisturbed forest lands for their environmental value, increasing emphasis on improving agricultural productivity will be required. This needs to go hand in hand with efforts to regenerate forests.

There is encouraging evidence, despite some false starts, that agroforestry represents a solution. As common property resources disappear or are degraded, farmers have sought to shift the production of outputs of value into their own land by protecting, planting, and managing trees of selected species alongside their normal agricultural activities. Many farmers now depend on their own tree stocks and on agro-forestry systems for some products and on common property resources for others. Recently the process of adding trees to farming systems has been accelerated or transformed by the growing commoditisation of fuelwood and other tree products, and the consequent emergence of the growing of trees as a cash crop.

Improving agricultural productivity needs to go hand in hand with efforts to regenerate forests

The practice of agroforestry is widespread in the tropics. The types of systems used are consequently diverse and complex. The main agroforestry systems have been broadly classified as:

- agrosilvicultural (crops and trees)
- silvopastoral (trees and pasture /animals)
- agrosilvopastoral (crops, trees and pasture/animals).

Other specialised agroforestry systems can also be found (for example, apiculture with trees, aquaculture involving trees and shrubs, and multipurpose tree lots).

Agroforestry holds considerable potential as a major land-management alternative for conserving the soil and maintaining soil fertility and productivity in the tropics. This conclusion is based on scientific evidence as well as farmers' experience that trees and other vegetation can improve the soil beneath them and also the yields of associated crops. Farmers have long known that they will get a good crop by planting in forest clearances. Soils that develop under natural woodland and forests are known to be well structured, with good moisture-holding capacity and high organic matter content. The ability of trees to restore soil fertility is illustrated by experiences in many developing countries, which indicate that the best way to reclaim degraded land is through afforestation or a similar

Box 4.5 Localised forest management in India

Some of the most promising experiences of dryland forestry management come from India where Joint Forest Management (JFM) schemes have emerged as a highly influential force in restoring India's degraded forest lands (Poffenberger and McGean, 1994). JFM is a variant of community forestry widely adopted in India, in which responsibility and benefits are shared by local user groups with government forestry departments. As of now, 16 of 25 states in India have issued JFM agreements covering about 2 million hectares of forests. JFM agreements are an increasingly influential worldwide model in attempts to reverse deforestation trends and uplift disadvantaged rural groups (Jeffery, 1997).

In some regions of India self-initiated community efforts to manage forests have proved more effective at regenerating forests than government supported JFM programmes (Krishnaswamy, 1995). Without waiting for supportive policies and judicial decisions, through the 1980s and 1990s thousands of communities began protecting their degrading forests, primarily in eastern India's tribal forest tracts. Often with little or no outside help from government, NGOs, or donor programmes, village leaders began recognising the environmental crisis confronting them as their once densely forested hills were denuded. Communities formed hamlet-based forest protection groups and halted cutting and grazing, often initiating rapid regeneration of the natural forests.

Around Tangi and the Khurda Forest Division of eastern Orissa, in response to growing environmental problems, village leaders from five neighbouring communities began holding meetings in 1985 to discuss how to preserve and restore their natural forests. In 1987, the communities agreed to form the Five-Village Forest Protection Committee.

Over the past decade, 120 villages have joined the original five in the Kurdha Forest Division alone. Now in Orissa state, 4,000 communities protect over 250,000 ha of vigorously regenerating mixed *Shorea robusta* forests. In response to these growing political demands of village communities, a national policy breakthrough occurred with the passing by Government of a new National Forest Policy Act in 1988 that explicitly recognised the legal status of Joint Forest Management contracts. By 1996, between 10,000 and 15,000 communities across India joined this grassroots forest protection movement with minimal cost to the government. In many areas, flora and fauna that had been disappearing from these habitats have begun to return.

Much ground still remains to be covered, however. For example, the sharing of power between government forest agencies and local groups may still be far from satisfactory. Consider this statement from a woman in India: "I wish to demand a Joint Forestry model. But a model in which roles are reversed. So far the Governments owned the land and the poor toiled on it to plant and raise trees. I wish to change this role assignment. Let the rural poor women own the plots on the canal side or road side or other places. It may be their own private marginal plots. Let the Government's Forestry Departments provide their technical and professional services to these women on a demand basis. Let us move away from supply side forestry to demand driven forestry. But the demand addressed must be that of the poor women. In this way we will know if there is a market for the forest agencies and at what price." (Batt, 1997).

Box 4.6 Tree planting by rural poor people

Many of the world's one billion poorest people are highly dependent on management of remnant woodlands, on-farm trees and agroforestry farming both for subsistence needs (fruit, fuelwood, fodder, medicinal products) and income generation. There are many well-documented examples of how local communities and small farmers have been sustainably managing forest resources and on-farm trees based on traditional knowledge over long periods of time (Arnold, 1992; Barrow, 1986; King *et al.*, 1990). The development imperative of poverty reduction justifies special emphasis on local community efforts and on the major role they play in improving the welfare of local people – particularly the rural poor.

Spontaneous tree planting by local communities and small farmers outside closed forests are making a highly significant (but inadequately acknowledged) contribution to reforesting the tropics. For example, as a recent International Food Policy Research Institute (IFPRI, 1996) research study in Africa observed, "A picture is beginning to emerge of how deforested land is subsequently used. As it turns out, reestablishment of ground cover plays a major role in that picture. In parts of Africa over the decade from 1980–1990, for example, much of the land lost to open forest was not left barren, but rather converted to agriculture, including planting of trees. A 1985 aerial inventory of selected districts in Kenya, conducted for the Beijer Institute, revealed close to 20% of originally forested agricultural land to be under woody biomass; this despite a tripling of Kenya's population between 1966 and 1996! Evidence of such spontaneous 'reforestation' exists for Asia and Latin America as well."

In many situations spontaneous community forest management and on-farm tree planting far exceed the accomplishments of national forest agencies and at very much lower cost. The Commission heard during its Asia regional hearing that grassroots efforts by landowners and small farmers in parts of Asia are achieving results where millions of dollars of external funding along with the application of new technologies and policy instruments have failed to dent the problem.

type of tree-based land use. For example, the micro-site enrichment qualities of trees such as *Faidherbia albida* in West Africa and *Prosopis cineraria* in India have long been recognised. The conversion of natural ecosystems to arable farming systems often leads to a decline in soil fertility and a degradation of other soil properties unless appropriate, and often expensive, corrective measures are taken.

Such observations have led to a number of research studies on the role of trees in soil productivity and protection, especially in the context of agroforestry. There is now a substantial volume of scientific information available on the soil-improving and positive crop yield attributes of trees. There is a wealth of evidence to indicate that agroforestry farming systems incorporating trees and shrubs can make a significant contribution to maintaining and improving the fertility and overall productivity of the soil beneath them, to increasing the productivity of agriculture, to generation of rural incomes and other benefits, and to regeneration and maintenance of forest stock.

What is now required are concerted efforts to apply the body of rich experience and research results to accelerate development of agroforestry as a way of meeting food requirements while avoiding further indiscriminate conversion of forest lands.

4.4 Verifying sustainable forest management

Criteria and Indicators

There has been much effort to develop methods to measure and assess sustainable forest management (see Box 4.8). The most well-known mechanisms are those of the Forest Stewardship Council and the International Standards Organization. These processes have been useful in catalysing effort and commitment towards sustainable forest management. They seek to establish principles, criteria, and indicators for sustainable forest management and mechanisms for its certification.

Criteria and indicators are still evolving, very much along the same lines as forest management itself – beginning with the narrowly economic, moving on to incorporate the ecological, and now also grappling with how to incorporate the social dimension of sustainability. Generally speaking, it is the social issues including participatory management which have been most difficult, though essential, to capture. The measurement process also presents its own challenges: monitoring is closely dependent on local participation, as it requires in addition to technical expertise familiarity with the local context, with local issues and arrangements, and appreciation of the local culture.

It is clear that, as forest types vary, there can be no universally applicable body of criteria and indicators for sustainability. Further, criteria and indicators encompass both quantitative and qualitative aspects,

Box 4.7 Localising management through model forest alliances

Deep in the heart of Mexico's Yucatan Peninsula, 16,000 campesinos or subsistence farmers have joined together with the government, local foresters and conservationists to deal with issues of forestry and sustainable resource management. The fight for food security by developing new land use practices is a priority here. The area, prone to land degradation and periods of hunger, is now being introduced to activities such as agroforestry which can stabilise land use and make the best use of cleared land.

This practical alliance between community groups, non-government organisations and government agencies is just one of a number of partnership-based 'model forest' initiatives emerging around the world. What began as a largely Canadian initiative with model forest sites in all the Canadian provinces, is fast-becoming a priority among governments and communities in many countries, as far apart as Russia and Japan.

While the vast differences in geography, culture, politics and policies around the world preclude a single blueprint for all model forests, five attributes are common:

- partnerships between principal land users and other groups interested in forests
- a commitment to sustainable development and the sustainable management of forests
- a focus on the local community or landscape level
- governance structured toward consensus-building
- cooperation, sharing and networking with outside groups.

All model forests are managed to reflect local priorities. Work is under way to develop an international network of model forests. The Network will provide unique opportunities for transferring know-how and new technology between disparate regions of the world.

Source: International Model Forest Network Secretariat website

Box 4.8 Criteria and Indicators for SFM

Since the Earth Summit, there have been concerted intergovernmental efforts to develop standards and benchmarks of SFM. Initiated by the International Tropical Timber Organization (ITTO) in 1992, approximately 110 countries have since participated in eight intergovernmental processes to discuss the scientific and policy aspects of SFM. Each is applicable to the forests of a specific region of the world. These processes have resulted in the development of the following eight sets of criteria and indicators for sustainable forest management:

The eight intergovernmental processes for the development of SFM C&I are:

International Tropical Timber Organization covering most forested countries in the tropics – 27 producer countries
The Helsinki Process – 39 European countries
The Montreal Process – 12 non-European countries with boreal and temperate forests
The Tarapoto Proposal – 8 countries in the Amazonian Cooperation Treaty
Lepateriqui – 7 Central American nations
Sub-Sahel Dry Zone Africa – 28 sub-Saharan countries
North Africa and Near East – 20 countries stretching from Morocco to Afghanistan
Central Africa – 13 countries of the African Timber Organization

Many nations are using international sets of criteria and indicators to develop a more detailed set that is specific to their forests and situation. Some governments are writing these criteria and indicators into national and sub-national forest legislation. The profusion of national and international efforts to develop criteria and indicators has now led to a need for their harmonisation.

The questions of definition of criteria and indicators and minimum acceptable standards of logging were extensively debated by the Intergovernmental Panel on Forests which recommended *inter alia* the need for a broad spectrum of qualitative and descriptive indicators covering social, cultural, economic, ecological, institutional, legal and policy elements (including local tenure).

Some indication of the increasingly complex range of factors that have to be taken into account by forest policy decision makers can be gauged from the criteria that were proposed for the Amazon region countries under the Tarapoto process. They include the evaluation of policies and benefits at the national, management unit, and global levels. The proposed criteria cover:

Environmental criteria

- biodiversity (genetic, species, ecological, and landscape)
- productivity (of the ecosystem)
- soil conservation (including erosion and natural hazards)
- water conservation (including water quality and quantity)
- forest ecosystem health and vitality (ecosystem functioning and processes)
- contribution to carbon sequestration and other global ecological services.

Socio-economic criteria

- institutions and infrastructure to facilitate SFM
- long-term supply of social benefits
- long-term output of multiple economic benefits
- recognition of full spectrum of forest functions and uses
- recognition of, and respect for, indigenous rights, and knowledge of historical and archaeological sites.

The process of evaluating the practicality and usefulness of various criteria and indicators is ongoing. These attempts to improve measurement of the various elements of forest sustainability constitute a significant advance over earlier approaches that were often limited to periodic assessment of logging operations by frequently weak forest administrations.

and have to be context-specific to include the social dimension. The Commission notes that some international processes (ITTO Guidelines, Helsinki Process, Montreal Process; Tarapoto Proposal; FAO Regional Processes) are assisting countries to develop national frameworks to assess progress on sustainable forest management; and that some countries (Bolivia, Mexico, Brazil, Indonesia, the Nordic countries, UK, Germany, The Netherlands, Belguim, Switzerland) have set up national certification programmes for imported and domestically produced wood. Since only 20% of forest products enter international trade, there is equally urgent need for establishing standards for certification for domestically traded products. The Commission advocates that all countries producing forest products should develop criteria and indicators specific to their situation, as well as participate in international certification schemes for their products that enter international trade.

With respect to internationally-traded products, it is essential that the various bodies of principles, criteria, indicators, and certification systems are harmonised to assure competitiveness for those countries and products adhering to sustainability standards. To this end, the Commission advocates that the various initiatives for development and application of criteria and indicators, certification and labelling, plan to ensure such harmonisation at the formulation stage itself. Also the Commission is concerned regarding the risk of lowering the standards of certification systems and bypassing stringent requirements in order to make the system more manipulative and acceptable. Harmonisation and monitoring standards of certification systems could be achieved through a FOREST MANAGEMENT COUNCIL, already mentioned in Chapter 3 as part of FORESTRUST INTERNATIONAL.

Certification of SFM

Many forest product consumers in Europe, USA and Japan – who between them account for more than 60% of world consumption of manufactured forest products – are increasingly insisting that the products they purchase derive from forests that have been certified as being managed sustainably.

Certification is perhaps the most powerful 'soft' policy instrument to be designed and implemented outside government. The key actors have been NGOs and the private sector. Although of recent origin, certification is already making a positive impact on private sector forestry.

criteria and indicators need to be harmonised

Forest product certification is a procedure by which written assurance is given that a product comes from a forest which is managed in conformity with specified environmental and social standards. Certification links market demands for sustainably produced forest products with producers who can meet those demands.

At present, the Forest Stewardship Council (FSC) and its accredited certifiers offer such a procedure. FSC was established for the purpose of forest certification (Upton and Bass, 1995). It operates an extensive certifying service: a forest management standard, an interna-

Since forest types vary, there can be no universal body of criteria and indicators for sustainability

tional accreditation programme for certifiers, a trademark which can be used in labelling products from certified forests and also a communication/advocacy programme. The International Organization for Standardization (ISO), through its ISO 14000 series, also offers a framework for the certification of forest management systems among other environmental management systems. The ISO certification covers similar issues to the FSC process, but it does not specify precise performance standards and it does not permit a label to be attached to forest products. The environmental management system is certified, rather than the forest product. Although not strictly a forest certification programme, the ISO approach also offers potential for assessing the environmental sensitivity of forest management. There have been calls for both processes to be integrated.

certification is already making an impact on private sector forestry

Many companies whose operations are now certified have adopted sound forestry practices for some time. Certification is having the effect of recognising and rewarding the performance of these companies by enabling them to maintain or improve their market share and marketability of their wood products. As certification becomes more widespread – encouraged by 'buyers groups' and consumers groups which are committed to trading only in products from certified forests – then many forest enterprises will either be shut out of environmentally discriminating markets, and thus might be forced to improve their forest management to enter such markets; or companies that do not meet certification standards will divert their products to less discriminating markets.

4.5 Controversial forestry practices

Some controversial issues dominate news headlines on the subject of forest management. Can clearcutting really be a sound management technique when so much has been written about its ostensible trail of destruction? Is there a place for tree plantations with few species? Should large areas of forest be set aside for environmental reasons?

This section attempts to position questions like these in the context of the principles for sustainable forest management advocated earlier.

Clearcutting

The pros and cons of clearcutting are anything but clear-cut. Clearcutting is an outcome of plantation forestry. Its advocates hold that it is important for economic viability and is justifiable where there are few species. There are many well-documented examples of the negative effects of large-scale clearcuts (Anderson *et al.*, 1976; Gimbarzevsky, 1988). Equally there are scientific studies that confirm that in some situations, clearcutting is an ecologically appropriate management practice.

The effect of clearcutting depends on the site, the size and pattern of the clearcuts, the amount of cut material left on the ground, and the subsequent treatment of the area. Except for very small cuts surrounded by intact forest, the effect of excessive clearcutting particularly on steeper slopes can be devastating both in temperate and tropical forests. If clearcutting is conducted over a large area, genetic diversity may be diminished, especially when no seed-bearing mature trees are left, or when the habitats of the mature trees are damaged to the point that mature seed-bearing trees no longer persist. Species diversity may decline rapidly in the clearcut area.

Within the forestry industry, clearcutting is the harvesting method of choice where the desired new forest is of light-demanding species whose light requirements are not satisfied by alternative harvesting systems. In humid climates and on wet, fertile sites, competition for light from shrubs may prevent the growth of light-requiring seedlings. The greater ease of applying some methods of weed control in clearcut than in non-clearcut areas (for example, because of the danger of damage to the residual trees) may also favour clearcutting on bushy sites.

Ultimately, whether or not clearcutting is appropriate depends on the character of the landscape within which it is being applied. Many specifics have to be taken into account. What are the effects on soil erosion? on water retention and flow? on forest regeneration? on wildlife habitat? What are the objectives and end products for which the site is being managed?

Private interests other than that of loggers and timber corporations, as well as the larger public interest, can be directly affected by the effects of clearcutting. However, given the considerations involved, the Commission can neither condemn the practice, nor unreservedly condone it. It is not helpful to universalise prescriptions about the practice because situations vary. This reality, however, only reinforces the need for wider participation in the decision-making process and for localising management of forests. It is in such a context that questions about whether to clearcut, where to clearcut, how much to clearcut, at what cost, and at whose cost can be appropriately addressed. Such an approach would in time yield a body of experience and understanding upon which guidelines can be developed by and for each country.

Plantation forestry

Tree plantations as a management issue is similar to clearcutting in terms of the controversy it generates. Reports of natural forests being razed to make way for commercial tree plantations has done little to help turn public opinion in their favour.

Simple plantation forestry – the relatively intensive management of simplified forest systems for a range of wood products – can return commercial wood yield many times greater than natural forest systems. Large-scale plantation forests are mostly a 20th century phenomenon though there are antecedents in both temperate (e.g. oak in Europe) and tropical (e.g. teak in India and other parts of Asia) environments. The majority of the world's plantation forests have been established in the past half-century, and the rate of planting has risen steadily. The most familiar plantation forests have been established as even-aged, single-species crops of trees with the primary purpose of wood and fibre production. They represent the most intensive form of commercial forest management, and many expect them to become an increasingly important source of industrial wood and fibre in the coming century.

It is estimated that the global area of plantation forests is approaching 135 million hectares. They are thus assuming increasing importance: as a land use, as sources of forest products, and as the

whether clearcutting is appropriate depends on the character of the landscape

The rich green mantle of forests is being replaced by a chequered landscape

means of delivering other forest benefits and services such as recreation, carbon sequestration, and environmental protection and rehabilitation. While low in biodiversity value, plantation forests are also often higher in carbon sequestration value compared with mature natural forests.

plantations: low in biodiversity high in carbon sequestration

Environmental concerns have been expressed about the potentially harmful social and economic impacts of plantation forests. There are well-documented instances of situations where inappropriately sited plantations have contributed to reduced water yield from catchment areas (Calder, 1996). There are also case studies of situations where large-scale industrial plantations have been established without regard to local community needs and land rights. Such impacts could be avoided if decisions about siting forest plantations are taken as part of overall landscape planning.

Notwithstanding the many legitimate concerns, scientific research carried out over several rotations of plantation crops such as *Pinus patula* in Swaziland, *Pinus elliotii* in Australia, *Eucalyptus* spp. in Brazil, and teak plantations in India, indicates that yields over time can be steadily increased. The technologies for achieving sustained yield plantation management are well documented. In particular the importance of leaving in place the 'lop and top' from harvesting operations to maintain soil organic matter and structure (Evans, 1992). There are also thousands of small farmers and private woodland owners, in both temperate and tropical regions, who derive substantial income and other benefits from plantation woodlots.

Plantations meet needs for some goods and services

By the year 2050 – when more than half of the world's industrial wood consumption will be cellulose fibre for production of wood-based pulp and paper (Solberg et al, 1996), and assuming quite conservative yields of 15 cubic metres per hectare per year – the implication is that all of that pulpwood could be produced from an area of less than 100 million hectares of plantation forests (equivalent to less than 3% of the world's remaining forest area).

Well-managed plantation forests are likely to continue as a major component of the productive forest resources in many countries, as long as they produce competitive returns on investment. Consequently they are more likely to seek out sites which are inherently more productive than marginal lands, and where costs of transport to wood processing plants are low.

The Commission acknowledges that plantations supply necessary commodities, and that they are useful as a means of relieving pressure on remaining natural forests. But the Commission has no hesitation in condemning the creation of plantations through conversion of any remaining primary forest lands. From a global environmental perspective, plantations should be planned and managed precisely to reduce pressures on remaining natural forests. This is the forest policy already being followed by China, as of 1998 – substituting the forest production from natural forests with that from tree plantations – in order to stop erosion of its natural forest capital.

We need to plan with such an objective in mind. A trend toward increased private sector investment in plantations in countries with favourable ecological conditions for plantation growth – such as New Zealand, Brazil, Chile, Argentina, Uruguay, Indonesia, South Africa, and Congo – is well advanced. A related trend is also under way toward the relocation of industrial activity to areas with favourable conditions for plantation growth and cheap wood production such as the southern states of the USA and parts of Vancouver Island in Canada. These trends need to be supported and enhanced for optimum public gain.

As in the case of clearcutting, the Commission cannot offer a blanket endorsement of tree plantations. Some important functions, especially ecological ones, cannot be provided by plantations, while others can. There is therefore a need for a more discriminating appreciation of what values can and cannot be secured by plantations. Again, the specifics are what matters, and they need to be decided in the context of the principles advocated earlier. Plantations do have a significant role to play in the future, but more attention will be required to make sure that they are established and managed with more sensitivity to the objectives of sustainable development than has been the norm to date. This implies greater direct involvement of local people in the planning and management, and in the sharing of benefits and products, more diverse species composition, and a wider range of products that could meet local needs.

The Commission advocates that plantations be promoted as an acceptable form of land use for production forests, but that plantations be sited so as to make

Box 4.9 Plantations: where are they? what do they grow?

About 75% of the world's existing plantation forests are in temperate regions and about 25% in the tropics and subtropics. Some 5% are found in Africa, a little more than 10% in each of the American continents, some 20% in the former USSR, and around 25% in Asia–Pacific and Europe. Around 10% of existing plantations can be classified as 'fast-growing', yielding more than 15 m^3 per hectare per year. Most of these fast-growing plantations are in the southern hemisphere, with around 40% each in South America and Asia–Pacific.

The majority of fast-growing plantations are of species such as *Acacia* or *Eucalyptus* grown on short rotations for relatively low-value uses of fuel, cellulose fibre or roundwood. Perhaps a third are longer-rotation crops, of either softwood or hardwood species, grown principally for sawn- or veneer-wood. A few other species – e.g. *Araucaria*, *Gmelina*, *Larix*, *Paraserianthes*, *Populus*, *Pseudotsuga* or *Tectona* – are of regional importance. Renewed interest in plantations of indigenous hardwoods has yet to lead to their large-scale establishment. The testing of a wider range of these species and the development of appropriate propagation technologies is a prerequisite to their more widespread use.

Around 90% of existing plantations have been established for industrial wood production, and most of the remainder to produce wood for use as fuel or roundwood to be used as building poles or fencing stakes. Some forest plantations have been grown for non-wood products such as essential oils, tannins, or fodder, but those grown as part of agricultural systems – e.g. rubber or coconut – have not generally been considered forest crops. The harvest rotations of forest plantations vary enormously, from annual or sub-annual for some non-wood products, to around 200 years for traditionally-managed high-value temperate hardwoods. With few exceptions so far, shorter rotation plantations have been grown for fuel, cellulose fibre or roundwood, and longer rotation plantations – typically upwards of 25 years – principally for sawn or veneer wood products.

use of degraded lands and not be created through conversion of remaining primary forest. Further, decisions about their location and establishment, and about their management, should be made in a framework of participatory land-use planning. In this way, plantations would be more likely to obtain local community support.

Plantation forestry should be actively promoted in the developing countries of the tropics as a major vehicle for economic development, given their comparative advantage in fast tree growth. This would also relieve the pressures on their remaining primary forests as sources of timber and fibre, and conserve them for sustaining their environmental services and realising the economic values that those services represent. (See Chapter 6 for a fuller discussion of this.)

Fire: menace as well as management tool?

Fire as a management tool

Attitudes towards forest fires have undergone a massive change in the last 10 years. In the past, forest managers and scientists viewed wildfire as a deadly foe. Fire management focused on removing the threat of fires from forests. However, now there is widespread acceptance that fire has historically been a part of the landscape, and should remain so. It is even suggested that using fire as a management tool can be more effective at carbon sequestration than fire suppression, and that fire management strategies could be more effective than afforestation (Guggenheim, 1997). Scientists and fire ecologists say that forest fire:

- clears old, dead or diseased trees
- kills pathogens (rot, insect, fungi)
- breaks rocks through heating and cooling, builds soil
- releases the nutrients phosphorus and calcium from leaf litter into soil
- stimulates growth of nitrogen-fixing plants
- allows individual trees and forest patches to survive, providing seed source, and wildlife habitat
- encourages conifer growth, as heat stimulates cone opening and thus ensures natural seed supply
- contributes to genetic diversity.

Drier forests, especially those in the temperate and boreal zones, benefit from periodic fires. Such types of forests have been regularly visited by fires, even before human intervention. Past successes in eliminating smaller fires have caused massive fuel build-up, leading to the catastrophic fires that are now occurring in temperate and boreal forests throughout the world. Moist forests, such as the coastal temperate rainforest of the Pacific Northwest in the USA and Canada, or the tropical rainforests of the Amazon, have a much longer natural fire cycle between 500 and 1000 years. Regular fires are not a feature of the ecosystem. Thus fires in these moist forests, such as those that occurred in 1998 in the Brazilian Amazon, are damaging rather than beneficial to the health of the ecosystem. Box 4.10 illustrates changing attitudes towards fire in the North American context.

The impact of fire also depends on the type of fire. Ground fires burn slowly through organic matter in the soil, whereas surface fires burn the top of the soil and the parts of underground plants that exist above the ground. Crown fires burn both the ground level vegetation and canopy of the forest and can be the most damaging, incinerating everything in their path and generating temperatures of 1000 °C.

Another management implication that new knowledge towards fire brings is the manner in which timber harvesting is carried out. Scientists are advocating the retention of patches of old-growth trees or

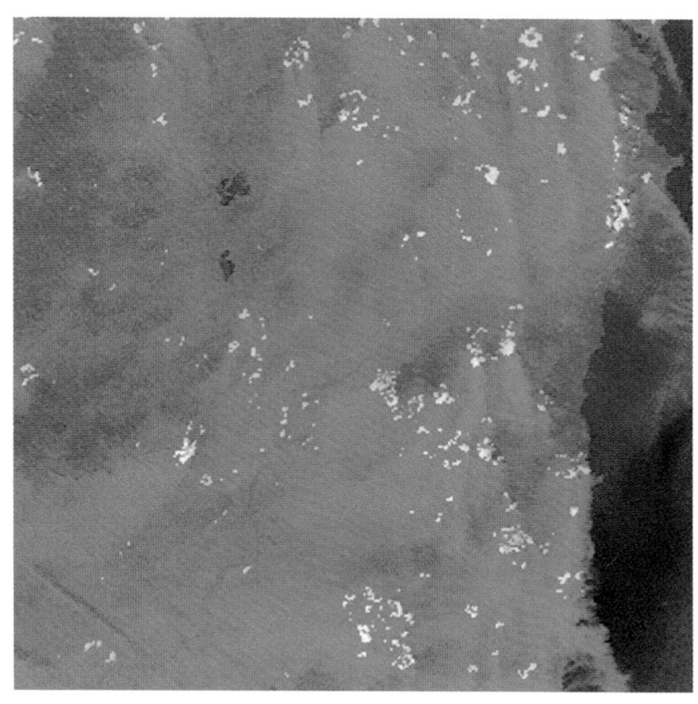

Satellite photo of widespread forest fires in fareast Russia – 14 August 1998. Heat signatures are red and smoke plumes are the blue haze

Box 4.10 Using fire to fight fire

Before European colonisation of North America, the native people regularly set fire to forests. Periodical burning served to create a younger forest that was more suitable for game and wildlife. Early European settlers also occasionally set fire to forests in order to clear land for building homes and for agriculture. Starting from the early 20th century, when forests began to be managed for timber, foresters made concerted efforts to suppress fires. The prevailing view was that fires damage timber, human life and property. After the Second World War, sophisticated technology – water bombers, helicopters and bulldozers – were harnessed to fight fires. In the USA, an intensive war-like campaign with Smokey the Bear as the mascot was very successful in ingraining into the public's psyche that all forest fires need to be fought vigorously. However, the old ways of thinking – referred to in the USA as the 'Smokey the Bear syndrome' – changed. Fire ecologists realised that fires are a part of the natural ecosystem, and if they are suppressed, then their benefits are also removed.

Also, it is now thought that most of the larger wildlife are able to flee a forest fire. For example, during the massive fires of 1988 in the Yellowstone National Park of the USA, only 335 of the 30,000 elk died in the fires, and burrowing animals whose nests were at least 7 cm underground survived.

The impact of fire on a forest depends on its fire cycle, that is the average frequency with which a fire returns to a forest. In the boreal and dry temperate forests of North America, the natural fire cycle (caused by lightning) varied between 25 and 200 years. Modern fire suppression efforts increased the cycle to 400–1000 years, which resulted in a build-up of fuel in the forest, resulting in greater intensity and damage on the occasion of a fire. The huge forest fires that have been sweeping across USA and Canada over the past few years have been attributed in part to the massive build-up of fuel due to fire suppression over time.

Source: Wildlands League; USA Today, 1998; Globe and Mail, 1998

Box 4.11 Fire out of control – in Brazil

In 1997, forest fires in Brazil ravaged 1.2 million hectares of forests. However, in the first months of 1998 fires exceeded the area affected in 1997.

The tropical Brazilian Amazon forest is home to half the earth's plant and animal species. The 1997 and 1998 fires occurred on the fringes of the rainforest in northern Brazil, which has vast tracts of grassland, or savanna. The fires destroyed about two-thirds of plant and animal life in an area the size of Belgium.

Each year, fires in the Brazilian Amazon burn an area larger than Rio de Janeiro state. Ranchers and subsistence farmers ignite their lands in an attempt to convert forests into fields, and reclaim pastures from invading weeds. Subsistence farmers migrated from all parts of Brazil to the fringes of the rainforest, lured by government promises of free land and a better life. But despite the lushness of the nearby forest, the soil is too poor to support intensive agriculture. They arrive armed with hope and chainsaws, clearing and burning land to farm the poor soil. The fires set by ranchers and subsistence farmers often get out of hand, inadvertently burning forests, pastures and plantations.

Normally, the fires are easily contained in the savannas. They usually do not reach the rainforest's humid edge, where moisture cloaks the air and daily showers would extinguish any flame. But 1997 and 1998 were different, due to combination of a seven-month drought and unusually high winds attributed to El Niño.

Compounding the fire problem is evidence of a drying trend in the Amazonian forests. The results of a 7-year study suggest that the Amazon rainforest is experiencing an acute drying trend, leading to increased susceptibility to fire. Recent tests involving digging for water at many sites had found dry ground, while similar tests 7 years earlier had revealed water close below the surface. "A lot of the Amazon has lost its capacity to protect itself from fire" warns Daniel Nepstad, a scientist at the Woods Hole Research Center in Massachusetts, USA which conducted the study. Environmental groups forecast irreversible damage to the Amazon, which already has lost about 13% of its 6 million km^2 basin to logging, burning, or other human activities over the last 15 years.

The world's rain forests produce 20–30% of the world's oxygen. In fires of the magnitude that occurred in 1997 and 1998, that process shifts, with the trees giving off more toxins than they absorb. The threat of large uncontrolled forest fires in Brazil, Indonesia and elsewhere has become critical due to climate change, deliberate burning and other forest clearing activities. On an average 15,000 km^2 of forests are burned each year in the Brazilian Amazon, contributing approximately 4–5% of the annual global flux of carbon into the atmosphere resulting from human activities. If half the Amazon were to burn, then approximately 35 billion tonnes of carbon would be released into the atmosphere, the equivalent of 6 years' worth of global fossil fuel emissions. This in turn could exacerbate changes in climate resulting in the increased possibility of more severe forest fires in the future.

Researchers at the Woods Hole Research Center have made several suggestions that could reduce the occurrence of fires in the Amazonian rainforest. Amongst them are community-based monitoring of fires, agricultural intensification so that subsistence farmers do not have to burn large areas for minimal returns, and restriction on road construction in the region, thus limiting the accessibility of the forests.

Sources: Nepstad et al., *(in press); International Herald Tribune, 1997*

mature older trees in clearcut stands. If fire occurs then these patches would survive and provide future habitat and seed source.

Should intentional fires be set in forests? Some scientists and foresters now advocate prescribed burns (intentionally set fires) more often, to maintain the natural composition of forests, to prevent fuel build-up, and to engineer a quick input of nutrients. However, many environmental groups are opposed to this. They point to the disastrous recent fires in Brazil and Indonesia as evidence of the devastation that fires can cause in moist, tropical rainforests, which can affect plant and animal species that might take up to 100 years to recover. In view of this controversy, there is need for more scientific research on the role of fire in ecosystems, and to identify specific scenarios in which intentional fires could benefit the ecosystem. Once again, conclusions about this controversial issue can only reasonably emerge in context and through application of the principles of SFM discussed earlier.

Protected areas

There has been much talk about an area – a 'magic number' – of forests that should be set aside and protected from the onslaught of unrestricted human use. At UNCED, for example, 12% of the total forest area was suggested. But there is no single, simple, scientific answer to the question of how much of the world's forests should remain in protected areas.

an obvious priority: to conserve what remains of the world's primary forests

The key issue in the new 'full world' is the protection of the biotic, chemical and physical integrity of the landscape. On steep slopes with easily eroded soils, there is little choice but complete protection from deforestation. On lesser slopes with soils less vulnerable, there may a basis for replacing forest over 10–15% of the area with perennial crops, or with agroforestry or other innovations in land management that preserve the stability of land, water flows, water quality, and nutrient budgets. In other drainage basins there may be a sound basis for allowing a higher degree of disturbance and replacement of forest with

Box 4.12 Fire out of control – in Indonesia

Conservative estimates put the total forest area affected by the 1997 forest fires in Indonesia at 2.4 million hectares. The fires were caused mainly by land clearing attributed to commercial oil palm and timber plantations, government-sponsored transmigration projects, temporary migrants, and local small farmers. An estimated 70 million people were affected by the fire haze in Southeast Asia. According to a study conducted by the Indonesia Program of WWF and the Singapore-based Economy and Environment Program for Southeast Asia, the haze cost the people of Southeast Asia about US$4.5 billion, mostly in short-term health costs (EEPSEA website).

Fires continued in early 1998, accelerating the already high rate of deforestation in Indonesia. They were explained by the persistence of El Niño which caused drought conditions in parts of the country. Over 120,000 hectares of forest burned in its East Kalimantan province, including 2,000 hectares in the Kuti National Park, renowned in the region for its rich biodiversity. Air quality in Singapore and Malaysia, which were blanketed by a deadly haze from forest fires in 1997, deteriorated leading to a noticeable increase in reports of asthma and other respiratory problems in those countries. The fires affected not only humans, but also wildlife. In Borneo and Sumatra, orangutans were forced to flee the forests due to the heat and smoke. Hunger too drove them out of the forests as the fires destroyed the fruits on which the orangutans feed.

Sources: Nepstad et al., *(in press); British Broadcasting Corporation, 1998*

row-crop agriculture. But in the normally forested zones globally, retaining landscapes that are dominated by forest is the first reliance in establishing the structural and functional integrity that is necessary for long-term stability of all human interests in environment. The requirement is not that forests be undisturbed, but that their functional integrity be preserved.

The key issue is the protection of the biotic, chemical and physical integrity of the landscape

The definition of 'functional integrity' is a new requirement, yet to be refined. But it is clearly definable and open to measurement in every instance. Its' definition, however, requires a new, acute interest in where the broadest public interest lies and a continuous definition and redefinition of that interest, locally and globally. A flat prescription of 10 or 12% of the area in forest is misleading in that it calls attention to the cost of conservation of forests without calling attention to the reason for conservation and the values to be preserved.

An obvious priority is to conserve intact, undisturbed, forests which are invaluable in terms of biodiversity and which are largely irreplaceable by human ingenuity or engineering – that is, what remains of the world's primary forests. This challenge rests principally with those countries which still retain some primary forests; however, it falls to all countries to cooperate in devising the political and social mechanisms that make it clear why such steps are necessary and desirable in the interests of all, as well as the financial mechanisms that would make it possible and worthwhile to do so.

The Commission welcomes the leadership of the World Bank/WWF Alliance for Forest Conservation and Sustainable Use to set targets for the year 2005 of an additional 50 million hectares of new forest protected areas, accompanied by more effective protection of 50 million hectares of existing reserves. The objective is desirable but totally inadequate as to area and purpose.

The fact that such innovations are possible is shown by the 22 countries that have already made a pledge to protect a minimum of 10% of their forests by the year 2000: Argentina, Armenia, Australia, Malawi, Mozambique, New Zealand, Nicaragua, Romania, the Russian Republic of Sakha, Slovak Republic, Tunisia, Uzbekistan, and Viet Nam. Globally ten million hectares of forests are now managed under the rules of certification. These are just the initial steps in moving toward stabilising the human habitat.

If forests are managed to protect the functional integrity of landscapes, other objectives in management of forests will become much simpler. These objectives include areas of forests to be dedicated to specific purposes, such as protection of medicinal plants and other non-wood forest products which are vital to the health and well-being of local communities. The Chang Mai Declaration of 1988, concerning the conservation of medicinal plants, affirms that medicinal plant conservation and the revitalisation of traditional knowledge on health care uses of plants must become matters of international priority. The principle of localised management would confer on local communities control in management of these resources for their own use and possible commercial benefit. Protected areas policy should seek to stem the continuing loss of medicinal plants and their natural habitats, the loss of cultural diversity and the loss of local control over natural resources and their management. Such policy should be complemented by international investments for *in situ* and *ex situ* conservation of medicinal plants and revitalisation of traditional medical cultures. Equally, priority should be given to protecting sources of non-wood forest products which provide income and livelihood to millions of people living near and within forests.

Everywhere, from the rainforests of the Amazon to the boreal forests of North America, the lungs are gasping

4.6 Private sector investment and management

The private sector has a critical role to play in sustainable forest management. In most of the major wood producing countries of the developed world, the private sector is the largest owner or manager of forests. In the USA, which is the largest wood producer in the world, 72% of forest lands is in private ownership. Though private ownership of forest lands in Canada, which has the third largest forest area in the world, is only 6%, most government-owned commercial forest lands are managed by private industry under long-term licences. The experience of Sweden reflects the way in which the private sector can be instrumental in rejuvenating forests (see Box 4.13).

The role of the private sector in furthering SFM in developing countries is also critical. In Brazil, which has the second largest forest area in the world, domestic private sector investment in wood products (including pulp) accounts for 85% of the total investment in the forest product sector. In Chile, the share of private sector investment is as high as 95%. In Indonesia, private sector investment in the forest sector is also very high. Domestic private investments in some African countries amounts to 35% of the total investments in the forest-based sector.

Private capital flows to developing countries, in the form of investment and lending, now amount to about 60% of development financing and has increased each year since 1991. The trends of decreasing public and increasing private investment are expected to continue. In the last few years foreign private sector investments in the forestry sector have rapidly increased in China, Papua New Guinea, Cambodia, Laos, Thailand, the Amazon Basin and Central Africa. The operations of transnational corporations (TNCs) in the forestry sector have also grown rapidly in the last decade. Today TNCs from about 30 countries are involved in the forestry sector in Africa,

Box 4.13 The experience of Sweden: from bust to boom

Sweden was a very poor country in the middle of the last century. Agricultural production was old-fashioned, inefficient, and inadequate for a rapidly growing population. Industrial development was in its infancy. Living conditions, especially in the rural areas, were harsh. Hunger as well as periodic famine formed part of the pattern of life. Land degradation was severe in many parts of the country. Deforestation was widespread and escalating. In southern Sweden, where population pressure was the most intense, forests were rapidly being converted into over-utilised and unsustainable farmlands and pastures. Remaining forests were subject to over-cutting for fuelwood, construction material and fencing. Natural regeneration was hampered by the practice of forest grazing. In the central parts of the country, deforestation had been systematic for centuries, mainly due to the constant demand for timber and charcoal from mining and processing activities (iron, copper and silver). Wood had become scarce in areas close to mines and related industries. Northern Sweden was sparsely populated and characterised by vast areas of old-growth forests in the first half of the 19th century. However, around the 1850s large-scale logging operations began, and extensive forested areas were purchased for very low prices from farmers. Forests most easily accessible to rivers or the coast were quickly logged to extinction.

This mismanagement and over-exploitation of the forests soon began to cause concern at the highest level. In the 1850s the problem of deforestation became a major topic of discussion in the Swedish Parliament. One speaker justified determined intervention by the State with the following words: "Everyone uses the forest but still nobody looks after it."

By the end of the 19th century, Sweden's forest resources were at an all-time low and most forest-related industries had begun to experience scarcity of raw material. In 1896, a new Parliamentary Commission was established to tackle the problem of deforestation, which resulted in a new Forest Act adopted by Parliament in 1903. County Forestry Boards were created for supervision of forestry and extension activities.

The general philosophy of this new legislation was that the forests should be managed in a way that did not jeopardise the sustainability of the resource. The new Forest Act made it mandatory for all forestland owners to guarantee satisfactory regeneration after logging, either by replanting or by natural regeneration. It contained provisions for non-compliance and provided economic incentives and assistance through the County Forestry Boards. The County Forestry Boards, though acting within the framework of national regulations, were truly locally based organisations, thus constituting a radical break from a traditional top-down model of state and public bodies.

Forestry became an increasingly important activity amongst Swedish farmers. Within a few decades, trees had become a valuable crop to be sown, managed and harvested like other crops. In southern Sweden, local organisations of concerned citizens took the initiative to plant forests on degraded areas. Logging was carried out in a planned manner and did not exceed regeneration. The forest industry started to grow. In spite of an efficient system of supervision, almost nobody had to be brought to court for violations of the law. It now paid to play by the rules.

These revolutionary forest management changes were aided by simultaneous reforms aimed at improving land tenure security and modernising agriculture. This resulted in increased efficiency in agricultural production, which meant that less land was needed to feed more people. Through the

(continues)

(Box 4.13 The experience of Sweden – cont.)

development of forestry, a large number of small farmers gained the opportunity to escape from the grip of rural poverty. During the first half of this century, the role of forestry in the impressive socio-economic development of the Swedish countryside could hardly be over-estimated.

What lessons can we take from this experience?

- Rising demand for wood and increasing fear of wood scarcity (emanating mainly from the forest industries) resulted in an economic incentive for Swedish farmers to grow trees. Thus the demand generated by forest industries, initially the cause of deforestation, later became the reason for people's involvement in regenerating forests.
- Improvements in agriculture led to higher yields, thereby reducing the need for clearing forest-land for cultivation.
- Due to increasing tenure security, small farmers also benefited from improvements in agriculture, which in turn contributed to the stabilisation of land-use patterns. Also, well-defined and secure tenure or usufruct rights to the forest resulted is an incentive for farmers to grow trees.
- The interest of the principal actors and stakeholders (farmers, industry, and government) to develop a system for sustainable forestry merged in Sweden. This merging of interests was reinforced by political will and legislation, which resulted in the new legislation being effective.

Source: Persson, 1998

Box 4.14 British Columbia timber producers to change practices

Three of the larger timber producers in Canada's British Columbia province, which together control more than half of the coastal forests of the province, recently announced shifts toward sustainable forestry practices:

Western Forest Products, Ltd. announced that it is pursuing third-party certification under Forest Stewardship Council guidelines through the British certifying body SGS Forestry Qualifor Programme.

MacMillan Bloedel, Canada's largest wood products company, announced it will phase out clear-cutting over the next 5 years. The company said it will pursue a stewardship strategy that focuses on retaining old-growth forests and conserving habitat in the roughly one million hectares of its BC operations.

International Forest Products (Interfor), which harvests timber in a number of the province's more pristine and ecologically significant coastal rainforests, announced it will follow MacMillan Bloedel's lead.

Source: Wilson, 1998

the long-term profitability of the private sector depends on adapting their management practices

Asia and Latin America. The most dramatic growth in TNC investment in the forest sector has been in Africa, accounting for more than 60% of the total forest investment.

The major role of the private sector in managing forests in developed countries, and the trends indicating growth in private sector investment in the forestry sector of developing countries, emphasise the critical role of the private sector in furthering SFM. Due to the increasing interest of buyers, especially in Europe and the USA, in products from sustainably managed forests, coupled with rising public concern regarding industry practices, there has been a small yet significant shift in the attitude of some forest companies towards more sustainable forest practices. Certification is also being increasingly adopted by industry to provide credibility regarding its management practices to the public, customers, governments, company shareholders and other interested parties. Leading retailers and manufacturers have formed buyers' groups (currently in ten countries) and are sending the message to thousands of suppliers that they care about the forests from which their products have been sourced.

The forest industry has also been participating in efforts to develop forest management standards, or codes of practice, in countries as diverse as: Norway, Finland, Canada, Chile, USA, Ghana, Malaysia, Indonesia, Brazil, New Zealand and Australia, Austria and Turkey. These efforts involve a variety of players including private wood-lot owners, forest companies, governments, conservation groups, local communities and a wide range of other forest users. Industry forest management experts from 33 forested countries recently completed work on an ISO Technical Report to help the forest industry apply the ISO 14001 Environmental Management System to forest management operations (ISO 14061, 1998; Rotherham, 1998).

The role of the private sector is critical to achieving sustainable utilisation of the world's forests, as private companies are the largest managers of forestland or are the largest investors in the forest sector. Their management practices are coming under more intense scrutiny from their customers and the public. The long-term profitability of the private sector will be dependent on how quickly they adapt their management practices to fit into the new paradigm of sustainable forest management.

4.7 Towards improved information, research and understanding

The Commission recognises that there is considerable expertise and experience among forest scientists in managing forests for timber, fibre, and other products. However, a different body of scientific knowledge and public policy is required if forest management is to serve the public purpose of sustaining environmental services in perpetuity and of ensuring that forests contribute to social objectives of poverty reduction and secure livelihoods. As the foregoing discussion has revealed, professional positions and practices do change as understanding grows.

Improved information, analysis and research are required to enable forest managers to meet the current challenge. During its work the Commission was struck by the inadequacy of forest data, as well as the incompatibility in definitions and measurements employed by those agencies involved in forest data gathering and analysis. Even 'official' forest data are suspect by those knowledgeable about the field, and the manner in which data are collected or submitted is also debatable. The proposal for a Global Forest Information Service (GFIS) discussed by forest scientists at an international meeting in Austria in September 1998 is a useful start to addressing this problem.

Currently, research into forest management is scattered across many disciplines, with little systematic attempt to combine data and integrate analysis. Moreover, there is still much uncertainty about the functioning of forest ecosystems, and understanding of forest/climate change relationships is in its infancy.

Clearly this situation must change in keeping with the new and urgent requirements for sustainable forest management. Fortunately the last decade has seen more effort and resources focused on data gathering and research (see, for example, Box 4.15). But a more systematic approach is required to make maximum gains from those efforts and resources and to adequately train and support forest planners and managers.

One of the main reasons for poor management of forest resources is the lack of professional and managerial capacity tuned to the times. This has to be recognised and the deficiency has to be remedied through appropriate training programmes with updated and relevant curricula. The institutional framework and infrastructure for expanded, relevant and updated training need urgent attention.

The Commission encourages those entities involved in forest research to establish an international network for research and training in sustainable forest management to correlate data and research results, to share information on different forest management practices, to engage in collaborative social research, to upgrade data on all types of forest, to interface with user communities, and to provide them with training and support. Such a network would facilitate policy makers, scientists, forest managers, community organisations, policy researchers, universities, forest companies in their respective and collective contributions to achieving sustainable forest management. Governments, industry and donor agencies should consider such a network a high funding priority.

Forest management now has different responsibilites than in the past

Endnote

1 'Landscape' is used in this report as more than a geographical term. It includes economic, political, social, cultural and institutional factors which are discussed throughout the report, and which must be taken into account in planning policies and decisions about forests.

Box 4.15 Innovation in research and training

The Iwokrama International Centre for Rain Forest Conservation and Development in Guyana is an autonomous international research and development centre that aims to promote the conservation and the sustainable and equitable use of tropical rainforests in a manner that will lead to lasting ecological, economic and social benefits to the people of Guyana and the world in general. The Centre seeks to meet its mandate by undertaking research, training and the development and dissemination of appropriate technologies.

The Centre is established by an Act of Parliament of Guyana on 400,000 hectares of tropical rain forest made available to the international community by the Government of Guyana. Programme work was initiated by a grant of US$3 million in 1993 from the Global Environment Facility. Its Operational Plan is supported by new commitments of some US$10 million from a growing partnership, including support from small developing countries such as Mauritius and the Maldives as well as the larger donors such as the UK, the European Union, the International Tropical Timber Organization and the Commonwealth Secretariat.

The Centre will address related issues of climate change, biodiversity loss and the conservation, management and sustainable development of forest ecosystems. Forest valuation studies, and the development of mechanisms that will allow the values of the forest to be appropriated in a manner that will support both the conservation of the forest ecosystem and sustainable forest-based development, will be some of its major concerns.

Key potential capturable values at Iwokrama include the sale of sustainably produced timber and non-timber forest products, ecotourism, carbon storage services, biodiversity prospecting, training services and developing mechanisms to tap individuals' willingness to pay for the conservation of both the reserve's Wilderness Preserve and its Sustainable Utilization Area. The Centre's Business Plan estimates that it should be generating some US$3 million per year within ten years which should be sufficient to both conserve and manage the Iwokrama Forest and meet the core research activities of the Centre as a whole. It is a unique experiment in sustainable conservation and management that will be of interest to all managers and policy makers interested in the future of the world's tropical forests.
Source: Iwokrama, 1998

5

SUSTAINING FORESTS AND DEVELOPMENT

The subject of forests is related to the entire range of environmental and developmental issues and opportunities, including the right to socio-economic development on a sustainable basis
(UNCED, 1992)

5.1 Concept, context and challenge

Achieving sustainable development involves a complex web of environmental imperatives, and social and economic needs. Although mutually reinforcing, the rapid growth of the human enterprise and the weaknesses of economic and political systems in addressing competitive aspirations, often place these dimensions of sustainable development at variance. While the direction is clear there is still a long way to go in applying the required principles and policies.

The wide range of essential environmental services which forests provide, as well as the wide range of material products which they supply for human living and comfort, make forests an extremely important strand in this web. The Forest Principles agreed at Rio in 1992 apply the concept of sustainable development to forests and create the framework for public policies and international cooperation that, if applied, would enable us to work towards integrating environmental, economic and social dimensions in ways that sustain both forests and development. Sustaining forests and development requires us to find ways of making use of the forest resource to meet human needs for forest products and to contribute to social goals in such a way that does not impair the ability of forests to continue their environmental functions. Failure to achieve that type of forest management would impoverish the planet and substantially diminish future prospects for human societies.

the continuous expansion of the human enterprise is out of balance with the shrinking forest resource

The global human habitat is already unstable, and threatened with further changes the effects of which are difficult to contemplate. The world's forests are central to both the cause and the correction of that instability. At the same time, climatic changes and widespread toxification of air and land by industrial pollution are affecting forests over large areas. The effects are a systematic impoverishment of forest stands with a reduction in their productive potential, internal structure and carbon content as well as their genetic diversity. Forest functions are already threatened, even as human numbers increase exponentially, human demands mount relentlessly, and human aspirations for wealth proceed unconscionably.

There is an increasing imbalance between a shrinking and deteriorating forest resource and a continuous expansion of the human enterprise, with its soaring demand for forest-related products. The challenges that arise are many, complex, and long-term. They are beyond the reach of forest managers and the forest sector *per se*. Understanding the challenges requires us to locate forests in the wider world: to see the forest, not just the trees.

In this Chapter, the Commission explores anticipated pressures on forests and assesses options for meeting those demands. It projects the likely consequences of those pressures if no changes are urgently made in policies and action. It proposes some key planning requirements that might better equip societies to make the policy decisions in the short term that might enable them, in the long term, to sustain forests and development.

5.2 Forests in a full world

The expansion in human numbers for the next half-century appears to be an unavoidable result of the present age-structure of the population. Human numbers are set to increase by 50% in the next half-century before there is any hope of stabilisation. It is projected that the global population will be 9.5 billion in 2050, with more than 8 billion in developing countries. This is enough to assure that the demand for material goods will rise, potentially overwhelming the productivity of forests.

The increased pressures on forests will result from the general pattern of consumption combined with the requirements for infrastructure for human settlements, and it is difficult to see how they can be met without some further loss of forests. At the same time, there is ample evidence that the environmental services of forests are already sufficiently diminished locally and regionally to present a global problem of immediate consequence.

The threats to forests and their normal functions in the biosphere are from three sources. Firstly, from competition from other land uses, especially from demands for additional land for agriculture. Secondly, from unsustainable logging to meet a growing demand especially for timber and pulp and fuelwood for energy. Thirdly, from a series of exogenous threats to forested land from climatic disruption and from industrial toxification.

Underlying these three sources of threats are the pattern and level of consumption. The latest Human Development Report of UNDP (1998) points out that the pollution and waste we generate exceed the capacity of the planet to absorb and convert them, that the natural resource base – water, soil, forests, fish, biodiversity – is deteriorating, and that these two trends are "nudging humanity to the outer limits of what Earth can stand". The shrinkage of forests is occurring predominantly in developing countries, but the products derived are used disproportionately in the industrialised countries. It is poor people in the less well-off countries who bear the costs of this unequal consumption.

Several levels of intervention will be necessary to bring these pressures under control and ultimately to achieve a better balance between the extent and quality of the forest resource and the needs to be satisfied. If, as seems clear now, there can be no substitution for the environmental services of forests, then the policies designed to accommodate that fact, and the formal planning to implement the policies, would do well to acknowledge early that securing those services must be paramount.

Cropland and food

The encroachments of agriculture on forest land arise from two processes: the expansion of demand for pastures, large-scale farming and a place for the landless poor to live and farm, and the continuing need to replace agricultural land impoverished through soil degradation or salinisation.

the diminished environmental services of forests is an immediate global problem

Historically, forested lands have been converted on a massive scale for agriculture, to great and necessary human advantage. But now we find ourselves in a full world in which there is a clearly intensified competition between human needs for a stable habitat and equally demanding needs for increased agricultural production. While the demands appear, at least on the surface, as competitive, they are also mutually dependent. There is a bleak future for agriculture in a world of continuous and progressive environmental, including climatic, disruption. There is an immediate need for limits on further transitions in forested

agricultural land used to be replaceable: now the realities of a full world must be faced

land to agriculture to protect agricultural production even as we seek to increase it. This symbiotic relationship needs to be recognised.

In the past agricultural land has been both renewable and, if not renewable, replaceable. Now, the realities of a full world have to be faced. Agricultural analysts observe that 80% of the expected increase in demand for agricultural production by the year 2010 will have to be met from an increase in agricultural yields and cropping intensity, and 20% from an expansion in the area of cropland. This expansion of cropland means an additional 90 million hectares or a 6% increase over present area (Alexandratos, 1995). Developing countries as a group will need to double their food production by 2020 if they are to feed their populations.

How much of this will be at the expense of forested lands? The answer requires a comprehensive and coordinated approach to land use, including judgement as to the further industrialisation of agriculture versus the spread of subsistence or smallholder approaches. Nevertheless, it is projected that by the year 2010 at least 40 million hectares of forest land will be threatened by that expansion; and that by 2050 about 127 million hectares of forests will be at risk, of which 71 million hectares – more than half – will be in Africa, with most of the rest in Asia and Latin America (Houghton, 1998).

Various innovations in land use restore some of the lost functions of forested land through agricultural landscapes while retaining agricultural productivity. The techniques of agroforestry have been developed successfully with those purposes in mind. The techniques include nitrogen fixation, green manuring, the production of fodder and shade for livestock, the establishment of living fences, and protection for drainage basins. While such techniques do not replace forests, they replace some of the environmental services of forests while enabling agriculture on otherwise marginal agricultural lands. The systems are advanced within the programmes of applied research institutions. More widespread development and application are clearly desirable and possible. Traditional plant breeding and genetic engineering could increase agricultural productivity outside forests to reduce pressures for conversion of forest lands to agriculture. This needs to be done compatibly with the concerns for farmers' rights and biosafety currently being addressed under the Convention on Biological Diversity.

Past approaches to agricultural growth from use of such technology have given cause for concern. For example, most of the successful breakthroughs in productivity have occurred in more favoured agro-ecological zones and have involved intensive use of irrigation water and modern inputs like fertilisers, pesticides, and improved seeds. The Green Revolution, which has played a major role in enabling many developing countries to feed themselves since the mid-1960s, has been limited largely to irrigated rice and wheat-growing regions.

Despite the unintended environmental consequences of the Green Revolution, hundreds of millions of hectares of forested land were spared as a result of the productivity increases it yielded. It enabled developing countries to avert famine, and incidentally to avoid encroachment on forest lands. Had it not taken place, an additional 280 million hectares of land would have been called into agricultural production. Much of this expansion of the agricultural frontier would have been into marginal lands, forests and already overpopulated upland watersheds. Such expansion would, importantly, have weakened the very substantial ability of forests to enhance food security for poor rural people.

Environmental concerns are real but not inevitable consequences of agricul-

With women taking the lead, village coops are managing tree nurseries in India, planting forests on what used to be barren land. They are seeing early benefits in reduced flooding, fuel for cooking and lumber for house construction

tural intensification. Now it is critically important for the world to take the best of that era's accomplishments and merge them with a new generation of ideas, technologies, institutional arrangements and better management practices for greater, less costly, efficient, and environmentally more sound agricultural production: that is, for the world to embark on a New Green Revolution.

the challenge is to make the new green revolution for poor farmers

Sustainable farming and forest stewardship go hand in hand. Land and water are shrinking resources for agriculture. Since population is unlikely to be stabilised before 2050, it will be essential to produce more food and other agricultural commodities under conditions of diminishing availability of per capita arable land and irrigation water resources. This will be possible only by achieving advances in productivity per unit of land and water.

The current high yields in most high-potential areas must not only be sustained, they must be increased if developing countries are to meet their food needs in the years ahead. Unlike the developed countries that now have agricultural surpluses, most developing countries cannot switch immediately to low-input farming systems because they cannot afford the associated reduction in yields. Productive lands lost through erosion and salinity from poor irrigation and drainage and over-use of fertilisers will have to be recovered. These lands are potentially productive with application of scientific principles and results of relevant research that would lead to selection of appropriate plant species and varieties. Such reclamation and reafforestation efforts could also attract external financial support, as has been done by Costa Rica.

A New Green Revolution

Technological advances in high-yielding crop varieties now widely used in developing countries have made the largest single impact on rural poverty in the last two decades. There is little doubt that the first Green Revolution averted a food crisis in Asia and has been the foundation for rapid economic growth in many Asian economies. Productivity of rice, wheat and maize have transformed farming systems in China, India, Southeast Asia, the Pacific, many parts of Latin America and the Caribbean. However, there is now an understanding that the first Green Revolution was more complicated than at first appeared, and like many technological advances there have been both winners and losers. There is also a growing body of work on the effects of the Green Revolution which has provided new insights into the social issues and the scientific and technology aspects. Armed with this information, and aware that there are an estimated 800 million food-insecure people in the world, the search is on for a second or New Green Revolution. How can this avoid the mistakes of the first and reach those still isolated from agricultural technology?

What is clear is that a New Green Revolution cannot just be a copy of the first. The challenge is to develop the technological packages which will make this a 'poor farmers' green revolution. This requires that productivity breakthroughs are made for crops such as sorghum, millet and cassava – the staple crops grown by poor farmers, often on marginal lands. It demands low-cost inputs, and higher returns from small-scale holdings with the minimum of risk. There is scope for developing crop varieties that are tolerant of saline or acid soils, are drought-tolerant, and resist pests and disease. The classical methods of plant breeding were the backbone of the first Green Revolution and the hope of great strides in biotechnology including genetic engineering have fuelled optimistic predictions of new gains in productivity. However, there is at present a lack of biotechnology focused on the needs of small-scale farmers in the tropics and the science is complicated by issues concerned with ethics, biosafety and intellectual property rights. It is estimated that it may take 20 years for innovations to reach farmers' fields. The more widespread use of fertilisers was a cornerstone of the first Green Revolution and there is a demand for technologies which efficiently recycle nutrients – making use of atmospheric nitrogen through legumes and from agroforestry practices. At the same time it is widely agreed that significant yield increases can be achieved by correcting the severe phosphate deficiencies of many African soils.

The New Green Revolution will focus less on crops and more on finding ways to diversify production using tree crops and livestock. It will also build on the successful technologies of integrated pest management and the new methods of land husbandry which stress low-cost soil conservation measures. Modest increases in irrigated agriculture especially in the form of low-cost, but high-intensity schemes are still possible especially in Africa and there are gains to be made in water management in most irrigated areas. Of special interest is the potential of peri-urban and urban agriculture which have in the past been ignored or actively discouraged in the developing world. The contribution of vegetables and small livestock production to the diets of urban dwellers and to cash in the hands of the urban poor is slowly being recognised.

However, one of the stark lessons of the first Green Revolution was that technological advances alone cannot solve the food security problem of developing countries. Greater equity does not arise automatically from greater food production. Therefore the New Green Revolution needs to have a different point of departure. Essential elements include:

- broad popular participation which will encourage farmers to select the technologies which are most appropriate to their local situation
- a strong political emphasis on agriculture which provides access to credit and markets and builds suitable institutions
- a recognition of the community's capacity for collective action to replace weakened government agricultural services.

Plant biodiversity is important for achieving food security

This is a very demanding agenda, especially when it is acknowledged that it is in Africa that lagging agricultural productivity has fallen behind population growth, and it is also in Africa that the parlous state of agricultural research makes advances difficult. If there is to be a New Green Revolution it will be based on intensification that can be sustained. There is empirical evidence that substantial growth is possible on currently unimproved or even degraded areas, and that regenerative and low-input (but not always no-input) agriculture can be highly productive if farmers participate fully in all stages of the technology development and extension.

Fortunately, architects of the Green Revolution are aware of its limitations, and are already at work on a New Green Revolution. The potential of this initiative for coping with the demand for food, while reducing the threat to forest lands, is an essential element in a comprehensive forest and land-use policy and plan. But the emphasis must move beyond agriculture and forestry *per se* to the landscape and the integrity of its function. Sound land management is an intrinsic part of the reality of a full world.

the emphasis must move beyond agriculture to the landscape and the integrity of its functions

Plant biodiversity

The relationships between biotic impoverishment and the perpetuation and spread of poverty have been key concerns for the Commission and for agencies engaged in economic development. The International Center for Agricultural Research in the Dry Areas, for example, feels that there is pressing need to preserve plant biodiversity if the world's growing population is to be fed in the next century and beyond and if drastic fluctuations in agricultural production, that lead to poverty and famine, are to be avoided. This need is urgent in the world's drylands where biodiversity is the key to better yields – and thus to food security and poverty alleviation – in these harsh environments.

In the past human societies utilised hundreds of plant species to safeguard their food and health security systems (National Research Council, 1989). Today, global food security depends on too few crops such as wheat, rice, corn, soybean, barley and potato, thereby increasing the vulnerability of food availability to biotic and abiotic stresses. Enlarging the food security base by including the excluded (a wide range of millets, grain legumes, tubers) and by strengthening the *in situ* on-farm conservation traditions of rural and tribal families with reference to agro-biodiversity will help to:

- revitalise the earlier farming systems where crops adapted to local agro-ecological conditions were grown and consumed, thereby helping also to conserve valuable agrobiodiversity
- enlarge the composition of the food basket by including a wide range of crops
- overcome the deficiency of micronutrients in the human diet, since many food crops like millets are rich in iron, calcium and other micronutrients.

All of these outcomes will contribute to reduction of poverty, increase in food security, improvement of nutrition, health and welfare, and sustaining rural livelihoods, while helping to ease the demand for conversion of more forest lands through improvement in agricultural productivity and sustainability. But meeting the need for increased food requires attention not only to agricultural production but also to equity in access to food. The issue of equity is important. It is an issue of distribution and price and of an individual's opportunity for independence. These are fundamental matters of social and political structure that define civilisation. They bear heavily on the potential for success in managing landscapes in such a way as to protect the public interest in long-term security from a wholesome environment in the face of intensified demands for food. They are intrinsic to any planning of land use that brings hope of success.

Land husbandry

Improved land husbandry involves the active management of rainwater, vegetation, slopes and soils, at a variety of scales, and embraces land under planted crops, pastures and plantations, and natural forest (Shaxson, 1997). Many of the techniques are already known and include: composting, green manure crops, vegetation erosion barriers, and agroforestry. The difficulty has been that these have often been developed in a research station environment with little if any farmer involvement. Pioneering work in Central America has dramatically shown how farmers can take and adapt those introduced technologies which are profitable. Agroforestry systems are central to these land husbandry ideas and contribute to food security, and play a major role in increasing land productivity and preventing land degradation. Trees can make a difference by:

- directly providing foods such as fruits, nuts, and berries, to supplement agricultural outputs
- providing fuelwood and charcoal for cooking and heating
- making marginal lands more productive
- supplementing sources of animal fodder.

Public policy, investment, and aid flows targeted at improvements in agricultural production in the developing world have for many years been channeled into the better endowed lands, which generally means the more humid agro-ecological areas, where the agricultural potential was perceived to be high. In the last decade, however, there has been a shift toward more marginal areas which generally means more arid zones and land on slopes. This has been in response to poverty-focused donor programmes, concerns about food security, migration to urban areas and, perhaps most persuasive of all, the notion that environmental degradation was increasingly out of control in these less favoured areas.

Early efforts to limit degradation by putting in place measures to prevent soil erosion were never very successful. This has been replaced by an ecological view of land damage which places emphasis on working with farmers to improve the care – the husbandry – of their lands and less on efforts to combat erosion alone. This approach reflects farmers' desire to raise yields and incomes as they stabilise or reverse land degradation. This is recognised as conservation for business, which does not require significant external investment and makes farm profitability the incentive. Farmers occupy centre stage as the husbanders of the land. Both men and women farmers become part of the process in that they participate in deciding what is needed to sustain family livelihoods, they select and reject, integrate and adapt the advice tendered by specialists. These ideas are transforming the lives of subsistence farmers in Kenya, Brazil and in Central America. Governments, scientists and donors now need to catch the wind of change and grasp the opportunity to improve sustainable rural livelihoods.

At present, value is ascribed only when the forest has been cut down

Industrial timber and fibre

Recent projections of future consumption of industrial wood to the year 2050 suggest an increase from the current level of about 1.7 billion cubic metres per year to anywhere between 2 and 3 billion cubic metres per year. Variations in projections like the ones shown in Figure 5.1 reflect a series of different assumptions about future GDP growth and price changes. By 2050 more than half of the world's industrial wood production will be for the man-

Figure 5.1 Projected demand for industrialised wood

Source: Solberg et al.*, 1996*

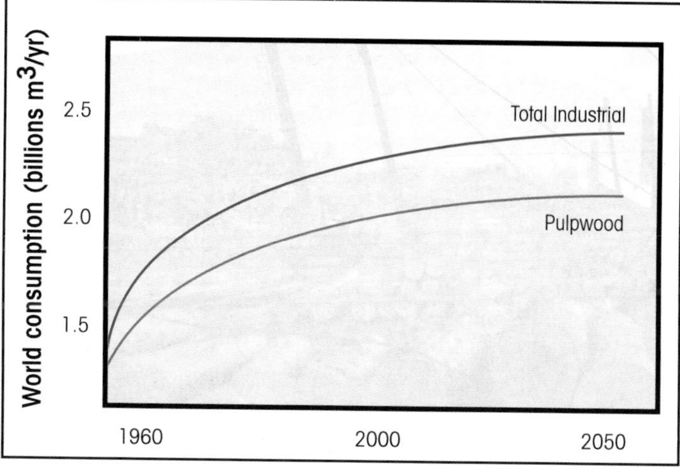

ufacture of pulp and paper. There is a challenge to ensure the productivity of forests for timber, fibre and fuel in the face of surging demand. The possibilities for meeting these needs lie in improved technology in the production and use of wood and in intensified productivity of forests.

Technology

As in the case of agriculture, there are exciting possibilities for technological improvements to reduce wasteful use of forest resources and to increase forest/tree productivity. The most obvious option is to reduce the amount of timber required to satisfy a unit of demand. The reduction is possible through modern technologies for efficient harvesting and conversion to timber, for recycling, and for substitution. Improving low-impact harvesting technologies will better enable forests to satisfy demands for industrial forest products while also meeting environmental standards. Recycling can do much to lessen the demand for new industrial wood. Already, 30% of the pulp and paper manufactured globally consists of recovered rather than new fibre. Another 5% comes from non-wood fibres. Market forces will play a large role in mapping out the future of recycling efforts. Consumers can influence these by signalling their preference for recycled products and materials.

Fossil fuel use is set to increase in the next 30 years

Potential of plantations

In Chapter 4 the Commission foresees the potential for intensified production systems to meet the growing demands for industrial wood from a relatively small land base. Tree plantations have a major role. They can most efficiently be established in warm climates where growth rates far exceed those in the temperate and boreal forests. Plantation forestry offers opportunity to contribute to multiple objectives: conserving remaining primary forests, increasing forest cover, increasing carbon sequestration, and creating income and employment.

By 2050, more than half of all industrial wood demand is expected, on the basis of current trends, to be for pulpwood fibre destined to become paper or utility grade construction timber. In the very long term, a combination of genetic improvement and intensified forest management could make it possible to meet all the world's foreseeable industrial wood requirements from a small percentage of today's global forest area. Such intensification would in turn make it possible to conserve other forests to meet the needs of local communities, to provide environmental services, and to compensate for the lack of biodiversity in plantation monocultures. Hence, ecological land-use planning based on sound evaluation of land suitability in tropical countries should define production areas for intensively managed, fast-growing, short-rotation pulpwood plantations. Land-use planning carried out with the participation of local people should also define other sites for community and conservation needs.

Energy

Forests are a major source of energy services through use of fuelwood. It is estimated that by 2050 demand for fuelwood will increase from 3.0 to 3.5 billion cubic metres per year, though projecting future fuelwood consumption is handicapped by the need for better data. While the lion's share of fuelwood is used in industrial activities, it is anticipated that rural well-being in many parts of the world will long continue to depend heavily on access to fuelwood supplies.

There are a number of technological advances that can be encouraged through more funding for research and development. Such resources should focus on options for satisfying the needs of poor rural people, such as:

- new and more efficient kinds of wood-burning stoves that are now available can be adapted to suit the needs of rural households; their wide distribution can be accomplished at little cost and will gradually show results
- the more widespread application of technologies for increasing energy efficiency
- new technologies for solar and wind energy which can be encouraged to move beyond niche markets to become competitive with conventional energy sources.

Equally, there will be need for even greater effort to stimulate the production of wood on-farm or at least close to the point of demand, such as:

- encouragement of agroforestry systems that produce fuelwood as a by-product
- encouragement of private entrepreneur involvement in producing fast-growing woody species to supply fuelwood to urban centres and relieve pressure on natural forests. This could be achieved through an economic stimulus such as a land subsidy or the imposition of fees on transport of timber. Such an injection of private funding is important as past experiences with fuelwood plantations for community use have not in many cases been successful.

The result of the above measures, for forest-dependent rural people, will be easier access to supplies for local usage and more time for collectors to allocate in other ways to generate family income. In addition to relieving pressure on forests, fuelwood plantations and more trees on-farm could make a major contribution to some one billion poor people who are without a reliable source of energy services.

Renewables

A possible scenario is that renewable energy sources could become significant by 2020 (Shell International, 1995). Fossil fuel use could increase steadily over the next 30 years, in support of the economic development of a majority of the world's population. By 2020–30 they reach their maximum potential and no longer contribute to growth. At that time a number of developing countries (e.g. China and India) having reached a sufficient level of industrial development, increasingly turn toward renewable energy sources. The Shell study suggests that renewable energy technologies will increase their market share as total energy demand grows. This allows growth in energy supplies to be sustained at a time when fossil fuels reach a plateau.

It is not necessary for our purposes here to discuss which renewable technology has the best prospects. Technologies will compete but the market will decide. However, by 2060 sources of energy services are likely to be more diversified than today. Perhaps ten different sources will each have a market share between 5% and 15%.

farms need to be stimulated to produce more wood

Among the several renewable energy sources expected to play significant roles in the future energy mix is that derived from fast-growing woody biomass plantations (see Figure 5.2).

The Shell report points out that the cost of sustainably growing biomass could be reduced by advances in clonal propagation and genetic enhancement of plants, notably woody crops; conversion, first into electricity, and later into liquid

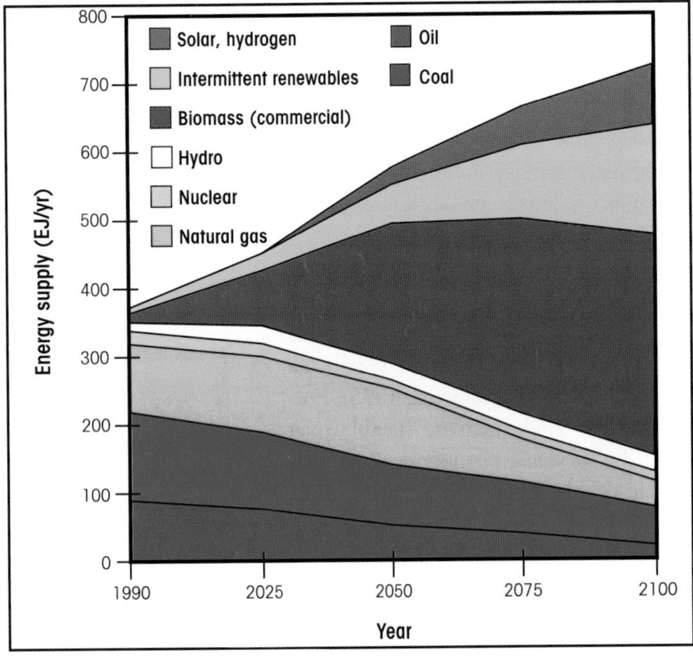

Figure 5.2 Energy projections for a biomass-intensive world

Source: IPCC, 1996

fuels, could become commercial through small-scale replicable facilities; and that over the last decade some commercial companies have developed experience in growing and enhancing trees for pulpwood and have been involved in the development of integrated biomass gasification for power generation.

Development and commercialisation of renewable sources of energy would not only relieve pressure on forests for fuelwood supplies, but would also positively contribute to the health and resilience of forests through reduction in fossil fuel use and greenhouse gas emissions.

Water

Water scarcity is likely to become a major constraint to development in the coming decades. Already, one billion people, mostly in developing countries, do not have access to abundant and clean water. Each year 2 to 3 million children die from water-related diseases. Population growth and industrial growth will increase demand for water resources even further.

Continuing forest decline exacerbates water shortages in many parts of the world, reducing the amount of water available for agriculture, fishing, industrial and domestic purposes. The losses will be an increasingly severe constraint on development in some countries. Deforestation, including intensive forest cutting without changes in land use, disrupts water supplies. The increased runoff from upland areas leads to increased sedimentation of dams and reservoirs. Sometimes forest clearance causes groundwater tables to rise and salinisation to occur. In Western Australia, about 400,000 hectares of agricultural land have been lost to salinisation because of the removal of eucalyptus and other forests over the past hundred years.

Water quality issues have taken on renewed urgency. Inadequate water supply and sanitation services cause ill health and human suffering. Pollution of water resources is reducing usable supplies and aggravating the scarcity problem. Thus quality and quantity issues have merged in a way that reinforces the need for a more integrated approach to water policy. Solutions will need to focus first on managing water as an economic good that is a product of the landscape where forests exert a major control on water flows and water quality. Some governments and international aid agencies are supporting innovative attempts to promote joint management of watersheds by local residents and government agencies. In northern Thailand, for example, community mapping of watersheds has contributed to developing a physical model of the watershed that serves as a basis for a joint zoning exercise for a network of participating communities. In the Phewa Tal Basin in Nepal, for example, villagers planted fodder grasses and fodder legumes in the major gulleys near farms on degraded upper slopes, which stabilised soil surface and reduced erosion, and significantly increased water catchment.

Exogenous threats to forests

Climate disruption

One of the most prominent environmental concerns of the moment is the prognosis about climate change as a result of emissions of greenhouse gases. Forests play a dual role in this phenomenon. They contribute to the release of carbon as carbon dioxide and methane, both heat-trapping gases, through the destruction of forests; and they remove carbon dioxide from the atmosphere through photosynthesis and store it in the plants and soil of forests for decades to centuries. Deforestation due to changes in land use from forest to agriculture and other non-forest uses contributes 20–25% of total carbon emissions into the atmosphere, ranking second only to the combustion of fossil fuels as a source of atmospheric carbon.

This complex relationship is compounded by the fact that climate change may in turn have a considerable impact on forests. The Large-Scale Biosphere–Atmosphere Experiment in Amazonia supported by the governments of Brazil, USA, and Europe, is investigating how changes in land use and climate affect the biological, chemical, and physical functioning of Amazonia, including the sustainability of development in the region and the influence of large-scale conversion of tropical rainforest on regional and global climates. The warming, if it proceeds as rapidly as anticipated and with the intensity anticipated (and experienced so far) in the higher latitudes of the northern hemisphere, will stimulate the decay of organic matter stored in the peats and soils of those latitudes and speed the warming (Houghton, 1998). The process becomes autocatalytic in that the warming speeds the further morbidity and mortality of trees at all latitudes and the further release of carbon into the atmosphere. There is a sufficient pool of carbon available in forests and their soils to affect the atmosphere significantly. It is important that steps be taken immediately to stabilise global climates by stopping the further accumulation of heat-trapping gases in the atmosphere. Forests and forest management have a significant role in this transition under the Framework Convention on Climate Change and the Kyoto Protocol.

What is at stake now is the stability of the biosphere as a major element in human welfare

While the consequences of a minor warming of short duration, perhaps as much as 0.5–1.0 °C over a few decades, may be predictable, the consequences of an open-ended warming at rates of 0.2–0.4 °C per decade, now under way, reach quickly into a realm where surprises are the rule. The surprises include the possibility of strong feedbacks that make the warming rapidly worse, sudden

Germany's Black Forest is threatened by air pollution

chronic disturbance causes progressive biotic impoverishment

sea level rise due to glacial melting and the slippage of ice from land to sea, changes in oceanic circulation, and major global changes in climate of the order of the changes observed during the El Niño of 1997-8 (Woodwell and Mackenzie, 1997). The impact of El Niño has underlined the uncertainty which accompanies climate change. While the exact nature of future weather patterns is contested, it is agreed that there is an increased likelihood of intense and unpredictable weather occurrences. The forest fires of Indonesia and the drought of 1992 in Southern Africa are examples. In this context the ability of the landscape to resist these short-term shocks and recover is impaired by dramatic and fundamental changes in land use, especially the removal of forest cover.

All of these consequences, obviously, run counter to the overall goals of sustainable use of the biosphere and any further economic development in the context of sustainability. Avoiding both the further loss in forest areas and the further impoverishment of the remaining forests is an essential component of any effective programme for stabilising the composition of the atmosphere and no less a central objective in protecting the public interest in a habitable biosphere. This ameliorating function of forests in sequestering carbon is at the core of intergovernmental discussions about why forests must be conserved, by whom, to what extent, and for what purposes. This is dealt with further in Chapter 6 on International Dimensions of Forests and Sustainable Development.

Biotic impoverishment

Chronic disturbance causes progressive biotic impoverishment. If the disturbance continues and is sufficiently widespread, species are lost. Extreme examples of impoverishment are now abundant in the world: the moon-like landscape downwind of smelters in Sudbury, Ontario, and in Monchegorsk on the Kola Peninsula and at Norilsk in Siberia, and a hundred other places around the globe, provide examples of chronic poisoning of the land and air. Deforestation has driven the landscape of Haiti and Madagascar and sections of China and India and extensive areas

Box 5.1 Imminent extinction

Biologists advise that we are already amid an extinction crisis unmatched in at least 65 million years and that, if current trends continue, one-quarter of the world's species may disappear in less than half a century. Assuming that the earth houses 10 million species today, a modest estimate, this rate of extinction means that over 130 species a day will disappear during that time. In the tropics, 15,000 species are disappearing annually, or more than 40 species per day.

Ecologist Walter Reid (1994) estimates that by the year 2020, up to 17% of the tropical forest species of Asia, Africa and South America may vanish unless deforestation rates drop substantially. If the rate doubles, Asian tropical forests could lose close to half of their remaining species in the same period.

To quote Edward O. Wilson (1992):
"The current reduction of diversity seems destined to approach that of the great natural catastrophes at the end of the Paleozoic and Mesozoic eras – in other words, the most extreme in the last 65 million years. In at least one important respect, the modern episode exceeds anything in the geological past. In earlier mass extinctions, which some scientists believe were caused by large meteorite strikes, most of the plants survived even though animal diversity was severely reduced. Now, for the first time, plant diversity is declining sharply."

elsewhere into the extremes of biotic impoverishment. The process is less extreme elsewhere but present in varying degrees in every corner of the earth (Woodwell, 1998). It is these losses of function that present the first concern in maintaining the human habitat.

Recent assessments suggest that present rates of species extinction are between 100 and 1000 times the natural rates. By the year 2020, up to 17% of species in tropical forests will vanish. Even more ominous, there are signs that extinction rates are accelerating. Species extinction, occurring at a time when humans have been deliberately narrowing the gene pool through intensive selection and breeding in order to increase timber and agricultural yields, reduces the resilience of forests to recover from natural or human disturbance. The fact is that before species are lost, the functional aspects of nature are severely impaired locally and there is ample warning that steps should be taken to avoid this most severe and irreversible loss, that of species. A study carried out in northwest Senegal revealed that biodiversity and tree densities there have declined in the last half of the 20th century, that population densities have risen above carrying capacity, and that the natural regeneration of local species would most effectively augment the land's ability to support people and lead towards sustainability (Gonzales, 1997).

Landscape attrition

The human life span allows only a brief snapshot of a landscape. It is easy to make misjudgements based on only a brief record of events. Droughts are followed by rain and a seemingly damaged, overgrazed and eroded land becomes green again. The blackened floor of a forest after fire by some miracle a year later presents a tangle of new growth. There is an appreciation that landscapes are dynamic, that there is a natural resilience which we may have underrated in the past. Now there is a more cautious approach to the forecasts of gloom which once excited the environmental lobby.

However, it would also be a terrible mistake to overrate this ability of nature to adjust too often or too quickly to major threats. Like a coiled spring extended too often too far, the ability to recover is finite and once exceeded may be beyond a point of return. Major and violent change or unremitting pressure on a landscape over decades could result in attrition which damages the ecological systems so severely that any natural resilience is undermined. The landscape then becomes dysfunctional. Large-scale conversion of and damage to forests reduce the productive capacity of the previously forested area as a result of soil erosion, nutrient depletion and loss of water retention capacity.

it would be a terrible mistake to overrate the ability of nature to adjust to major threats

When heavy equipment is used to clear forests in the tropics, already poor soils suffer further damage, especially when beset by severe, nutrient-robbing rains. In drier zones, deforestation is a con-

Heavy ecological footprints

tributory cause of desertification. If forest decline continues unabated, it is likely that the earth's deserts will expand in countries with dry climate and fragile soils. Desertification will be difficult to reverse. While desertification imposes heavy costs on the landscape, it also drastically affects the livelihoods of some of the poorest people in the world. The conversion of forest lands for food, human settlements and other uses, and resulting land degradation, often jeopardise the quality of the environment and future production prospects. These undermine the ability of rural poor people to improve their standards of living as well as their prospects for achieving sustainable livelihoods.

5.3 Consequences of business as usual

The overall consequence for forests of the above threats to forests and their functions are alarming, if anticipatory policies and actions are not urgently applied (see Box 5.2).

Box 5.2 The alarming consequences of inaction

Environmental disruption	
Accelerated forest decline	More forest loss and degradation, at higher rates.
Species loss	By the year 2020 up to 17% of tropical forest species of Africa, Asia and South America could vanish, reducing resilience.
Land degradation	Many forest lands suffering from deforestation and forest degradation are likely to become eroded, depleted of nutrients, and degraded.
Disruption of water flows	Increased water scarcity, already predicted to be a major 21st century issue; threatening billions who rely on water from upland watersheds.
More forest fires	More carbon emissions, further climate change, more forest decline, more forest fires.
Increased social hardship	
More poverty	Reduced opportunities and options for poor households to satisfy basic human needs.
Fuel scarcity	Over 2 billion people could suffer increased hardship in meeting their fuelwood needs, resulting in lower nutrition and health levels.
Pressure on marginalised groups	Vulnerable forest-dependent groups in society will be more exposed, including many women, children and indigenous peoples.
Increased economic hardship	
Squandered capital	Erosion of a valuable source of natural capital.
Fewer employment opportunities	Forest capital erosion reduces the potential for future subsistence and wage employment.
Reduced commercial potential	Forest capital erosion reduces the potential for future commercial production of wood and non-wood forest products.
Reduced non-commercial potential	Forest capital erosion reduces the potential for meeting subsistence needs from non-commercial forest products.

5.4 Planning to sustain forests and development

Landscape planning

In a world beset as it is at the moment by progressive environmental instability that threatens our future, its peoples have come to realise that human and natural systems interact in complex ways. Nothing but fundamentally new approaches to planning and management will enable societies to restore stability and assure a future that operates within the biophysical limits of a finite and fragile Earth. To deal with the range of essential needs, to integrate economic, environmental and social aspects of development, and to anticipate and deal with the feedback from one sector to another, will require a form of planning which takes all aspects of the landscape together as a totality.

This requirement implies that policy analysis and planning for use of forest lands requires radical change. Development planning on a sectoral basis is not equal to the task of satisfying an holistic concept such as sustainable development in a shrinking and complex world. Planning for forests requires projections for satisfying a variety of needs for food security, for water for domestic and industrial use, for energy sources and services, for living space and infrastructure. It also now requires consideration of where the largest public interests lie. This realm requires, not the classical compromises appropriate when resources were abundant relative to demands, but the far more difficult judgements as to what will work in a biophysical sense in keeping the landscape functioning under intensified use.

The very difficult task of comprehensive planning for and management of the overall landscape is required for meeting the vast range of human needs while designing policies for sustaining forests. The need is for issues management, for systems ecology, for a sense of the whole, not just for forest management in isolation from the wider world. There is no way that this transition can be achieved through forestry departments alone working on forest policies and programmes. These views have been echoed by forest scientists and policy analysts convened recently by the World Bank, as reflected in Box 5.3.

Participatory land-use planning

The current literature on natural resource management agrees on the need for some form of participatory decision-making. We have at least learnt from the failures of past approaches. Now we need the political will and the foresight to set in motion a different approach that responds to the

Box 5.3 Requirements of landscape planning

"Three elements of planning are essential for environmentally sound and socially acceptable forest management:

(a) that areas of forest to provide for all these uses should be set in a wider, national or bioregional, land-use context which provides adequately for all of them in suitable locations;
(b) that forests should be available to meet the various needs of society; and
(c) that each area of forest is carefully managed for the purpose for which it is suited and intended.

The exact details will vary greatly from country to country according to the area and nature of its forests, its population density, its state of development and many other conditions. This pattern should retain or even enhance the 'potential' of forests and give them the flexibility to respond to changing conditions whether social, economic or ecological. The best use of a forest cannot be considered in isolation. For example, forest plantations play an important part in producing timber and may thereby reduce pressure on natural forests; if established on degraded lands they may also increase biological diversity. In general, planning for agricultural expansion, for new settlements and for roads should take into account the possible effects of these developments on adjacent forests."

Source: World Bank, 1998

limitations revealed from experience.

The planning of land use is one of the tools which will make landscape management possible. A participatory approach to land-use planning avoids the possibility of centralised bureaucratic determination and control. It is also consistent with the themes of community management and empowerment of local people, and will serve as a consultative mechanism for the protection of the public interest, which the Commission advocates should become the principal objective of forest management.

not just the map but the method not just the plan but the process

It is recognised, however, that there is no perfect plan. Adjustments and refinements will always be needed. Participatory land-use planning provides an opportunity for both the initial involvement and subsequent interaction with the community in a structured way. The shift is from a plan as a blueprint prepared by scientists and foresters, to active involvement of interest groups in a process which recognises the public interest. Only such a process will allow, for example, the knowledge and experience of indigenous communities or women to be tapped. What is important is not just the map but the method; not just the plan but the process.

The above approaches allow community involvement in decision-making and management to be grafted on to scientific resource assessment. Key issues in 'community involvement' are: defining the community; willingness and ability to have a dialogue; presenting scientific information in a form which can be easily understood; reconciling local, national and perhaps global interests; and political will to respect and enforce the conclusions.

If we are to face up to the uncomfortable fact that pressure of population will make further forest loss unavoidable, then the best and most informed judgement on any changes in land use must be made. The world is strewn with agricultural and forestry projects which failed due to misunderstanding of what a dramatic change in land use would mean. Pictures of salted irrigation systems, dried peat swamps on fire, degraded pastures, and drought-stricken forestry plots attest to environmental horror stories. There does exist, however, a body of knowledge which can prevent at least the most extreme of these disasters and place a brake on unwise decisions.

However, the connection between the science of land evaluation and the decision-making over land use has been lost. This is in part due to a failure of the scientists involved to interact with the land users and the other interest groups. The marriage of sound evaluation of the land potential with a process of participatory land evaluation and land-use planning will increase the chances of informed decisions (see Box 5.4).

Reinforcing measures

This approach of landscape management within which participatory planning for forest lands is undertaken, needs to be reinforced through other measures, principally through education and information.

Education

Education provides the underpinnings for the direction which a society decides to take. It prepares citizens for occupying the political space which governance arrangements provide. It inculcates the values and ethics which a society elects to have. Education is fundamental to reducing both individual and national poverty and has a close relationship to the pressing issue of human population growth. It is a means to achieving the development goals of health, higher labour productivity, more equitable economic progress and the broader objective of social integration through participation in political and cultural affairs. It is central to orienting a society towards sustainable development.

Education is also the means through

Box 5.4 Participatory land-use planning

Ghana

Ghana has made remarkable strides in reconciling timber production with biodiversity conservation which has triggered international support and funding. Here the forest reserves were created as a result of a very thorough collaborative process. It is remarkable that the boundaries of Ghana's reserved forest drawn up in the 1920s and 1930s have largely been maintained. The decision on what to reserve was based firstly on technical specifications combined with a thorough process of consultation. These are the essential elements of any land use planning process. This tradition of sound planning based on strong community involvement is still alive in Ghana. It has underpinned the Ghana Environmental Resource Management Project funded by the World Bank.

Cameroon

In the Mount Cameroon project funded by ODA (UK), the same process (although by a different name) was used. At the beginning of this project a 'user group analysis' was carried out. This had embedded within it the essential land use planning elements: gathering information on resource use; identifying the main interest groups; agreeing with the communities on a plan for use.
Source: WCFSD Hearing, Yaounde

British Columbia

Beginning with the Provincial Land Use Charter in 1992, and a Statement of Principles and Process for Land Resource Management Planning in 1993, the Government of British Columbia has set out to create an overall Land Use Strategy for the Province. This works in tandem with a Forest Practices Code adopted by private industry. Within this framework a number of planning processes have been initiated and these are beginning to yield positive results in terms of agreed plans. An example is the Vanderhoof Land and Resource Management Plan published in February 1997, for an area of 1.38 million hectares in which some 10,000 people live. The Plan was developed over a period of 30 months by a core group of 35 people representing a wide range of values including water, fisheries, heritage, culture, recreation, tourism, access, and conservation. These groups were balanced by the direct land users such as agriculture, timber and mining representatives. In addition to this core group there was a public forum and regular communication through meetings and newsletters.
Source: Government of British Columbia, 1997

Brazil

Nine states have been engaged in preparing Integrated Environmental Management subprojects, with varying degrees of participation and levels of detail. The process of designing such plans has not been easy for any of the states despite the substantial technical assistance provided. There are few precedents to guide the environmental management of remote rainforest areas, and having a diverse group of federal, state, and municipal actors agree on a practical and realistic plan, with clearly defined roles for each agency has been especially difficult. These plans attempt to integrate existing environmental legislation with the identification of priority conservation areas and pay special attention to the institutional framework which will be required to implement the planning.

Education underpins the direction which a society decides to take

which individual citizens will appreciate the multiple functions for which forests are important, and the public policies which governments formulate to ensure continuation of these functions. It is public awareness through education that would lead to appropriate consumption patterns and levels for individuals and societies.

There are immediate and exciting possibilities. The growth of distance learning, the spread of Internet technology, and the encouragement of 'lifetime learning' has broken down the classroom barriers and allowed many adults to rediscover their potential. When these developments are linked to the need to increase awareness of environmental issues, the opportunities to engage societies in sustaining forests and development are apparent. Some of the main assertions of the Commission are that forestry goes well beyond silviculture; that sustainable forest management involves more than forestry; that an understanding of forest decline means addressing a multitude of issues; and that public awareness of the importance of forests for ecological, economic and social stability is imperative.

the education sector needs to be factored into plans to arrest forest decline

The education sector is therefore a potentially vital avenue through which the objectives of sustaining forests specifically and sustainable development more generally can be advanced. It needs to be factored into any programme that is intended to arrest forest decline.

Information

Reliable, timely and up-to-date information is essential for such an educational process as well as for landscape management and land-use planning. The present state of the basic data on forests leaves much to be desired. While there are many organisations which are engaged in observing forests and compiling and analysing data, there are gaps in coverage, spatially and temporally; efforts are unconnected and uncoordinated; and in many countries basic information about the state of forests is lacking.

There is enormous scope for enhancing the use of information technology in the management of information. The potential of Geographic Information Systems (GIS) technology is only now being realised in the forestry sector. Obvious improvements include the better planning of roads, the planning of tree selection and felling, and monitoring of regrowth. The biggest advance in the past decade has been the use of RADAR remote sensing technology for forest assessment in the tropics. These sensors are beginning to fill gaps in the existing knowledge at site, national and global levels. One of the most exciting possibilities is the ability of remotely sensed data to be processed and displayed so that a non-technical audience can understand. This is an invaluable tool for increasing understanding and if used sensitively can greatly enhance the involvement of other stakeholders.

Training in low-tech data processing, archiving and retrieving will also be necessary to make possible adequate use of increased and improved satellite data. This is an indispensable element in the process of pro-active landscape management and-participatory land-use planning as opposed to 'fire fighting' and inventorying the damages done to forests by illegal and/or poorly prepared forestry measures.

Eco-technologies based on a blend of traditional wisdom and technologies, and frontier technologies like biotechnology, information, space and renewable energy technologies, will be needed to stimulate and sustain an evergreen revolution in agriculture. Ecotechnologies need for their development a systems approach based on an integrated attention to the principles of ecology, economics, social and gender equity, employment generation and energy conservation. Ecotechnologies in the farm and forestry sectors are more knowledge than capital intensive. Hence, the tools of the information age should be fully harnessed for empowering rural families with the needed information and skills.

5.5 Forest Capital

How can we know with any confidence whether current efforts, and the comprehensive and intensive efforts which we hope to see in the immediate future to stem forest decline, are having a positive effect? How can we track what is happening to this stock of resources – the forest capital – over time?

Economists have been able to develop measures by which the world assesses the value of things. The concept and measure of Gross Domestic Product (GDP), for example, even with all its inadequacies as a measure and its methodological difficulties, allows us to put a rough value on national economic activity. This is used, not without challenge to be sure, to establish a benchmark for how any single economy is performing over time. It provides a basis for comparison among different economies at any moment. Even with its limitations, it has been a useful indicator to guide the economic policy decisions of countries and govern the financial and investment decisions of banking institutions and entrepreneurs.

A similar measure for reflecting the worth of the forests of a country, and by extension of the world – Forest Capital – is worth attempting. Work of a similar nature to estimate the annual value of the services that ecosystems provide is already in progress, and it is already "abundantly clear that ecosystem services provide an important portion of the total contribution to human welfare on this planet. We must begin to give the natural capital stock that produces these services adequate weight in the decision-making process, otherwise current and continued future human welfare may drastically suffer" (Constanza *et al.*, 1998).

In advancing this challenge, the Commission is conscious of what the UNDP has done for the concern about poverty through development of the Human Development Index. It has mobilised the range of intellectual inputs required and in less than a decade has created an acceptable and widely useful comprehensive measure encompassing important but previously inchoate information. The Human Development Index has thus provided the world – and individual countries – with a reference by which performance in improving the human condition can be tracked. UNDP continues to refine this measure in small increments each year in its Human Development Report. In a similar fashion, the 'Index of Social and Economic Welfare', which has been developed to compensate for the limitations of the conventional GDP, takes account of changes in social welfare and environmental quality, and reflects social and environmental costs as real losses.

a measure to reflect the worth of a country's forests is worth attempting

Similar creativity is unfolding in the context of the Framework Convention on Climate Change, where 'trading' in 'carbon emissions rights' has now become feasible, underpinning international legal commitments, and making possible a new mechanism in the global marketplace.

If indeed we value forests as an asset, and if ensuring 'the ability of future generations to meet their own needs' is not just rhetoric, it would be useful to have such a measure to appraise the effectiveness over time of all that we do in relation to sustaining forests.

Fortunately, we now have some tools in computer and satellite technology to assist in developing such a measure. A forest capital measure would be the first step in a process with potential for creating a mechanism for relative contribution/relative benefit by all countries to the interests of the public in essential environmental services performed only by forests. These ideas are expanded in Chapter 6.

5.6 Forests, the citizen, and security

The Commission was repeatedly presented in its public hearings around the world with moving descriptions of the relentless displacement of forest dwellers by logging interests. The appeal in Jakarta was from the remote Indonesian province of Irian Jaya; in Winnipeg it was from British Columbia, Ontario and New Brunswick, and from Mexico. In every case it was a last desperate cry: our land, our habitat, our age-old rights to life in the forest are being unilaterally destroyed and our government will not protect us. Our citizens are being killed and our land taken for timber and farms. It is our land and no one else's. The fact that the cry is age-old, classical, the same plaintive voice as that of a hundred and more Native American tribes whose very existence was erased, does not make it any more acceptable. The forests are home to someone who has rights and aspirations, too, and whose right to life we assert as no less, nor more, than our own.

At the same time the Commission encountered the even larger throngs of the dwellers of the forest margins, the swidden farmers, and the gatherers of herbs and game, rubber tappers, and others, all users of the forest, dependent on it for all or part of their existence. The success of these marginal dwellers in protecting their segments of forested regions such as the extensive Extractive Reserves of the western Brazilian Amazonian State of Acre is a notable success of a decade's duration. Here salvation has come to the forest and its dwellers through planning and through governmental decree in the establishment of the forest reserves. The forest dwellers, supported by an association, by university staff, by student projects, and by satellite imagery and educational programmes dealing with forest resources, and by relentless vigilance, have effectively protected their interests in the forest. They are rich in that they have a place to live and a better-than-subsistence living. They are poor in that they are only marginally part of the cash economy and struggling to enter it through the sale of non-timber forest products. They do know, however, that the one-time sale of their timber will cut off their ties to long-term markets in other forest products. The path to further economic development is unclear. What they have is sustainable, if marginal, but the value of the forest as a continuing source of support is clear.

Poverty remains a major challenge globally. There is no magic cure. The scale of the poverty problem seems overwhelming. About 3 billion people worldwide have US$2 or less per person per day to spend on meeting daily needs. Some 30% of people in developing countries live with US$1 a day or less per person. While globally there may be an abundance of food, nearly 840 million people lack the food they need to lead healthy and productive lives. About 40,000 people die of hunger every day, or from causes related to hunger, while 180 million or more pre-school children are significantly underweight. The number of chronically undernourished people in Sub-Saharan Africa has more than doubled in the last three decades. In some regions poverty is growing fast. Between 1990 and 2000 alone, the number of destitute people in Sub-Saharan Africa is expected to increase by 40%.

The percentage of the world's population living in absolute poverty (defined by the World Bank as living on less than $1 a day) has fallen since the mid-1980s. However, this decline was concentrated in Asia; other regions have not reduced the incidence of poverty to the same degree; and the total number of people living in poverty has risen, to just over 1.3 billion in 1993.

Many countries in which there is such poverty have large forest endowments. Forests currently contribute to poverty alleviation in many ways. Without that use of forests, there would be many more who live in abject poverty. The decline of forests threatens the life, living and livelihood of millions of people in marginal communities.

The extent and depth of poverty in the developing world, and the important role that forests, woodlands and on-farm trees play in contributing to poverty alleviation, were major themes of the Commission's Asia, Latin America and Caribbean, and Africa Hearings. There is a developing consensus around the drive to significantly reduce levels of world poverty in the next two decades. There is also increasing recognition that poverty can only be reduced by striving to achieve sustainable rural livelihoods. Natural forests, community forests, woodlots, plantations and trees on farms all underpin such an approach by providing fuelwood, fodder and other non-timber products, increasing food security, preventing land degradation, and offering employment.

Where people have relatively unrestricted access to forest products, it is the poorest of the poor who stand to benefit the most. As most small-scale processing and trading activities require little in the way of capital or skills to enter, they are usually accessible to the poorest members of the community. Forests could be their escape route from absolute poverty into greater food and economic security.

globally there is an abundance of food but millions lack the food they need for healthy lives

How can forests contribute even more to meeting the needs of communities who are directly dependent on them? There are many policy interventions available to governments for doing so. They include:

- supporting the efforts of the 2 billion or so small agroforestry farmers
- encouraging markets for non-timber forest products
- creating assets to enhance their ability to undertake reforestation
- providing technical assistance to these activities; supporting entrepreneurship for forest-based industries
- removing policy bias in favour of large-scale timber production, and giving the rural poor greater and more equitable access to forest raw material supplies
- granting local communities legal rights to land and land-based resources
- helping them build the village-level institutions required for their sound management
- extending support for forest-based poverty alleviation programmes, including especially the establishment of new micro-credit facilities
- involving communities in planning land use
- increasing public understanding of the importance of forests through educational channels.

The key to successful economic development includes a working landscape that provides a stable base for a variety of entrepreneurial activities. In the forested zones some of the forests will be used for timber and fibre and fuel; some will be used for non-timber forest products; some will be used as forest reserves and as water supplies. Such a scenario requires the approach to planning discussed above. Without a biophysically intact landscape, economic development has no place to stand.

The Commission recognises that forests must and will be used, as will other natural resources, to feed, clothe, house and otherwise satisfy basic human needs. Its concern is about the extent to which forests are used, in relation to their capacity for renewal to continue to satisfy indefinitely those human needs along with sustaining planetary stability through their environmental functions. On the evidence, and in spite of the incompleteness of the data available, forests can no longer be used in the same way now as they have been in the past. Radical adjustments in managing forests in a full world are required.

The question is then asked: but where is the money to come from to finance development? This is a necessary and legitimate question, especially on behalf of societies where large numbers of people exist in conditions of abject poverty. The answer is that the money is in the forest! The paradox is that at present value is ascribed only when the forest has been cut down and transformed through 'economic' activity.

How can forests contribute even more and in a sustainable manner to the resources required for financing development? In Chapter 2, it was evident that the 'opportunity cost' of squandering forest resources through ineffective policies and through give-away concessions is very high. The reform of timber concession policies alone to even remotely approximate the real economic value of forests, along with a general price level that more adequately reflects real values, is sure to yield significant revenues. At the minimum, the net effect of reducing extent of use and revaluing the resource should leave countries no worse off in financial terms.

The contribution of forests to financing sustainable development also has an international dimension, given the global services of all forests. The discussion on forests in relation to sustainable development in intergovernmental circles usually runs aground on the apparent conflict between insistence on conservation and imperative of development. What is needed are ways to realise the value of forests without the necessity to cut them down or reduce them to ashes. In the language of Chapter 2, markets and market mechanisms are required to deal in the value of forests beyond their value as timber and pulp. The Commission's proposal above of a Forest Capital measure will be relevant here, and will be discussed further in Chapter 6 on International Dimensions.

6

INTERNATIONAL DIMENSIONS OF FORESTS

Even as diplomatic prevarication continues, international understanding of the worth of forests – as crucibles of biodiversity and potentially valuable new products, as stabilizers of global climate, as conservators of soil and water, as aesthetic treasures, and as socio-economic pivots – is swiftly increasing. It is necessary to harness this knowledge and this awareness, and to translate it into concrete action

(Desa, 1998)

6.1 Continuing the search for solutions

International priorities

Because forests ensure the proper functioning of global environmental systems, the crisis about forests demands global attention. Solutions will involve all of the world's nations. The global significance of forests, regardless of location or political jurisdiction, means that all countries with forests must recognise that they hold in trust natural resources vital to people far beyond their own borders. Consequently, each society with sovereignty over a forested area becomes responsible in part for the global public interest which is threatened by forest decline. It is this concept which the Commission places at the core of its consideration of the international dimensions of the subject of forests and sustainable development. Other international issues of the forest crisis arise from the fact that forest products enter into international trade, and investment in forest exploitation is predominantly by large multinational corporations.

All of these issues were at the core of the debate on forests in the Earth Summit process. Considerable progress has been made since then through a series of bilateral and multilateral processes, and through the entry into force of three related international treaties. Altogether these agreements contribute significantly to the body of analysis and undertakings required to affect the way the world makes use of the earth's forest capital. However, lack of agreement on ways to deal with some of the global dimensions of the forest crisis has led to the continuation of the search for answers: by governments through the United Nations and other processes, within regional groupings, by international non-governmental organisations, by many public and private institutions, and through this Commission. Meanwhile, forests continue to be degraded and lost.

In previous chapters the Commission offers analysis and proposals on a range of issues relating to the forest crisis. The Commission is of the view that many of those proposals can be and need to be addressed at the national level.

At the same time, the Commission recognises that some issues require international dialogue and intergovernmental agreement and cooperation if they are to be resolved. These are the issues which the Commission discusses in this Chapter. Since they have also been, and will continue to be, the subject of intergovernmental discourse, the Commission addresses its discussion of these issues principally to the intergovernmental process.

The determination of governments to continue the UNCED search for solutions through the UN Intergovernmental Panel on Forests (IPF), and now through its successor the Intergovernmental Forum on Forests (IFF), was undoubtedly a step in the right direction. The very process of the IPF kept the issues alive, produced a comprehensive guide for all countries about what needs to be done within their jurisdiction for sustaining their forests, and increased the extent of collaboration and coordination among major UN bodies directly involved in supporting its work. All of these are desirable outcomes. There is now a huge body of literature that has grown out of the international dialogue on the global forest crisis, in which all the issues are extensively documented and debated. It is not the intention to review them here. The Commission instead limits this discussion to some truly global matters associated with forests that require international cooperation. Thus in this Chapter the Commission explores three international facets of the forest issue: multinational investments in forests, international trade in forest products, and global services provided by forests. The discussion is grounded in the recognition of the imperatives of preserving the global biophysical system as well as of eliminating poverty. Intergovernmental dialogue in which these are the motivating concerns and the priority agenda items may lead to more progress.

A plea for urgency

The Commission emphasises the need for more urgency in coming to conclusions and actions to respond to the crisis in forests. This is because, firstly, of the loss in forest cover and quality and the evident impairment of the environmental functions of forests and secondly, because of the livelihoods of numerous poor communities and groups that are directly and immediately threatened by that loss. This public interest, and these private interests of the most disadvantaged groups dependent upon forest use, have been the core of the Commission's concern.

The continuing intergovernmental discussion might therefore focus on a few priority issues which necessitate global attention, agreement and cooperation. Where everything is a priority, nothing becomes a priority. The political commitment made in Rio to forge a new level of international solidarity is yet to be realised; yet the elimination of poverty the world over depends upon that international solidarity. The Forest Principles assert and recognise the sovereign right of nations over their forest resources; yet securing the global public interest in a well-functioning biophysical system requires harmonised objectives and collaborative endeavour. Progress in these issues would make more fruitful the intergovernmental debate on whether or not a treaty on forests is required.

A plea for urgency... if 'ensuring the ability of future generations to meet their own needs' is not to be just rhetoric

6.2 Multinational investment in forests

As mentioned in Chapter 4, in recent years private sector investment in exploiting forests has far outstripped the capacity of public sectors to invest in forest management (Chandrasekharan, 1996). For the developing world, much of this comes from foreign multinationals in the wake of the globalisation of enterprises.

These firms are welcomed by developing countries, as such capital inflow is considered vital for their development process. At the same time, national authority to impose restrictions on foreign investment is weakened in the wake of liberalisation of trade, and further threatened by proposals contained in the Multilateral Agreement on Investment (MAI) being developed under the auspices of the OECD. If the MAI becomes part of international law, it could be used to challenge limitations on the use of natural resources. An example would be a regulation requiring that raw timber be processed in-country before it could be exported. Such a measure would be to protect domestic jobs and could be considered in violation of the proposed MAI. It would constrain the ability of sovereign nations to integrate economic, social and environmental considerations and to balance private interests with the public interest. It is not surprising that civil society organisations rose up with one voice to object to MAI and its fate is now uncertain.

erosion of national authority is happening at the same time as governments ought to impose restrictions on forest exploitation

These attempts at eroding national authority are occurring just at the moment when governments may need to impose far-reaching restrictions on exploitation of forests in the interest of sustaining the forest capital (see Box 6.1). This is cause for concern and would be an appropriate topic for intergovernmental discussion and resolution. Common approaches to dealing with this would strengthen the hand of those governments who are relatively weak in bargaining power with multinational firms. Governments should make this part of their agenda in the intergovernmental process.

The same public authority that is being eroded by powerful multinational corporations in the forest industry will be required to give effect to any multilateral or global agreement on forests that governments may agree. Governments ignore that at their peril. At the very least countries should require multinational corporations to behave according to a code of conduct designed to counter the unethical and corrupt practices illustrated in the cases from the field (see Chapter 3). They should all apply and enforce these codes. This requires cooperation between those countries from which the corporations extend their reach and those which they overrun.

The Commission heard repeatedly in its public hearings how some unscrupulous migratory logging companies have become powerful contributors to global forest decline. In the tropics and the former USSR, cash-strapped governments and politically weak local communities are especially vulnerable to the depredations

Box 6.1 Multinational investment and national authority

Significant decisions about economic management are already out of the hands of elected governments. National authority will be further eroded if the IMF does for capital what WTO does for trade. For example, Europe's decades-old special relationship with Caribbean economies has been ruled out of order because of international trade regulation. Meanwhile, the OECD is writing the Multilateral Agreement on Investment that will diminish the ability of host governments to manage the behaviour of big business in their back yards. For developing countries especially these developments create serious concerns as, given declining levels of ODA, they will increasingly rely on private sector investment – much of it from abroad – for managing their forests in the 21st century.

The World Bank estimates that the flow of private money to the developing world has surged from US$44 billion in 1990 to US$244 billion in 1996. World Watch Institute (1997) advises that "The bulk of this investment – which is much harder to track than public flows – is underwriting environmentally destructive forms of development including mines, coal-fired power plants, and logging projects destroying large areas of the planet's forests and threatening to accelerate the destabilisation of climate, in addition to disrupting indigenous peoples in many areas."

"I have a fear that by the end of the century the globe will be run by a handful of transnational corporations in search of the lowest wages, the loosest environmental regulations, the most docile and desperate workers. If this comes with no moral sympathy, or honourable code of behaviour, God help us all, large or small" – Anita Roddick, Chief Executive, Body Shop International.
Source: New Economics Foundation, 1997

of such powerful transnational corporations. The power relationship among these forces tend to be one-sided and inequitable, leading to the rape of the forests without sufficient reparations to the affected economy or community.

The environmental and social record of such corporations reportedly leave much to be desired. In general they apply destructive logging systems, are not held accountable for the erosion of a country's forest capital, do not adhere to management standards even where these are stipulated, and fail to transfer knowledge on advanced technologies to local workers. Many profit handsomely from give-away concessions and other subsidies thus preventing governments from capturing a greater share of the economic value of the forest resource. Further, they capitalise on the weakness of many public administration systems to regulate and monitor their activities.

Of course there are exceptions to this pattern. There are examples of firms that are voluntarily organising to interpret the concern for sustainability into their practices. Others are responding to the pressures and exposures by international non-governmental organisations. In this context, the initiative of the President of the World Bank to call together leaders of timber corporations to engage them in contributing to solutions is applauded. This effort needs to be continued with the more progressive firms in an effort to make the industry as a whole part of the solution.

In this regard the watchfulness of civil society through their organisations, and especially the vigilance of some international non-governmental organisations, give reason for hope that such depredations could be held in check (see Box 6.2). As governments are finding it more and more difficult to regulate corporations, NGOs and CSOs (civil society organisations) are stepping into the breach and demanding performance from

Box 6.2 Civil society: matching political posture with private practice

"Dear Vice-President Gore,

We, forty seven US and Russian environmental groups, are writing to express our alarm about the negative environmental consequences stemming from growing US federal financing of private companies logging Russia's primary forests, particularly in Siberia and the Russian Far East.

US taxpayers are now financing – through the Overseas Private Investment Corporation (OPIC), the Trade and Development Agency, the Export-Import Bank, and several government-sponsored enterprise funds – several private joint ventures in Siberia and the Russian Far East. The activities of these private timber ventures could destroy unique forest habitats. They could also undermine and contradict important biodiversity conservation programmes currently under way in the Russian Far East, programs which are backed by your office, and which are being implemented by other US federal agencies (USAID, US Forest Service, etc.) and non-profit groups such as some of our own.

These federally-backed plans will transform Siberia and the Russian Far East into a massive whole-log export colony. Taken together, they gravely contradict the conservation goal contained in your Joint Statement on Sustainable Management and Conservation of Natural Resources. They do not address the need to build ecologically sustainable, local economic industries in Russia, based on economic diversity and local value-added.

US agencies continue to refuse to disclose environmental and other information concerning their timber joint ventures to the public. As an example, in February 1995 the Pacific Environment and Resources Centre filed a Freedom of Information Act (FOIA) request to OPIC to obtain environmentally-relevant information about forestry-sector projects under consideration by OPIC in Siberia and the Russian Far East. Although OPIC is required by law to conduct environmental impact assessments of the given projects, the agency has to date refused to disclose its environmental reviews of the proposed ventures to either the US or the Russian public.

Normally, by US laws, environmental impact reviews are made available to the public so as to provide for open discussion of potentially environmentally destructive projects. OPIC is in violation of FOIA by refusing to provide full information. Without this information, US and Russian organisations are unable to judge the environmental sustainability of timber ventures proposed for OPIC funding. Such secrecy also prohibits public participation, sets a poor example for the Russian Federation about government openness and transparency, and sows seeds of suspicion among the public in the Russian Far East about the US Government's true intentions in the region."

Source: Excerpt from a letter made available to WCFSD

corporations in keeping with sustainability considerations.

This is a desirable trend: it will require the vigilance and engagement of civil society to make up for the authority wrested from governments in a world dominated by a few powerful countries and corporations. The set of mechanisms comprising FORESTRUST INTERNATIONAL described in Chapter 3 of this Report would contribute to this overall purpose.

But useful as non-governmental efforts are in calling attention to the concerns and exposing the unacceptable practices, they cannot supplant the authority or role of governments. Governments need to create the framework – domestically and internationally – in which private domestic and foreign investors operate consistent with larger societal goals, nationally and globally.

6.3 International trade in forest products

Two conditions must be satisfied before international economic exchanges can become beneficial for all. The sustainability of ecosystems on which the global ecoomy depends must be guaranteed, and the economic partners must be satisfied that the basis of exchange is equitable. Relationships that are inequitable and based on dominance cannot provide a sound and durable basis for interdependence. Neither condition is currently met.

It is important to note two basic parameters of the international trade in forest products: (1) between 20 and 25% of all commercial forest production enters into international trade, with a monetary value of about US$100 billion a year and (2) until recently, about 90% (over US$90 billion a year) of world trade in forest products emanated from industrialised countries, underscoring the great differences in commercial benefits received from forest production and trade today. Consequently, it would be appropriate for continuing intergovernmental discussions to aim to increase the scope for developing countries to enhance their share of trade in forest products and services.

International trade is also connected to forests through its impact on the prospects for sustainable forest management, to which forest production certification is relevant.

Market sharing

The lion's share of the international forest products trade is enjoyed by Northern temperate industrialised countries. A small handful of countries, including Canada, the USA and the Scandinavian countries, dominate the world market on the basis of their well-developed logging and wood processing industries. They have managed this despite having much longer growing cycles for trees compared with warmer climates. Given that only about 10% of the value of internationally traded forest products accrues to developing countries, conditions for an expansion in the share of trade for them are required. This would operate as an economic incentive to them to manage forests sustainably.

By 2050 it is predicted that more than half of the world's industrial fibre needs will be for cellulose fibre. The coming century will see a major shift in market demands and the location of timber and fibre production. As has been demonstrated on a large scale in New Zealand and Chile, cellulose fibre can be produced either from intensive fast-growing, short-rotation plantations which can be established in grasslands, degraded agricultural or forest lands at cheaper costs than sourcing it from natural forests, and from agricultural fibres such as bagasse and straw.

This trend is already ongoing. It will accelerate rapidly in the coming century because of the comparative economic advantage of growing cheaper fibre in the southern states of the USA, in countries of southern Europe such as Portugal, and in several countries of the southern hemisphere such as Brazil, Chile, Indonesia, and New Zealand. All of these have more favourable growing conditions than the colder countries of the temperate North. This trend has implications for reducing pressure on natural forests, especially on the boreal forests of the North that play a crucial role in sequestering global carbon.

Developing countries in warmer climatic zones are already gearing up to exploit this 'comparative advantage' in producing timber products quickly and cheaply. They therefore seek to increase their share in the world market. Some are succeeding: growth in exports has been particularly notable in Brazil, Indonesia, Chile, and Malaysia. But there are some obstacles preventing developing countries from competing for a larger share of international trade in forest products: poorly developed domestic forestry sectors; non-market barriers; technology; and financial capital.

Developing countries could benefit from international financing and technology cooperation to realise the comparative advantages of shorter growing cycles and lower wages, providing that the negative aspects of multinational investment discussed earlier can be overcome.

WTO and sustainability

There has been widespread concern about the effects of trade liberalisation on prospects for sustainable development. It should be a high priority of governments to examine and clarify the ways in which liberalised trade in forest products might negatively affect the forest capital and impair its ability to sustain the environmental, economic and social demands made on it. The existence of a Trade and Environment Committee in the WTO implies a recognition of this concern. However, there is widespread dissatisfaction among observers of the WTO process about the lack of progress by this Committee in advocating the interface between trade, environmental protection, and natural resource sustainability.

This Committee should not be regarded in WTO simply as an attempt to placate the environmental lobby. It is vital that we understand those linkages, anticipate the unintended consequences for forests of unfettered trade in its products, and take the necessary measures, within the WTO and outside it, to compensate for and eventually avoid those consequences. The WTO needs to integrate the issues of forests and sustainable development firmly into its workplan, and the environmental and social impacts of liberalised trade in forest products need to be carefully weighed in the WTO's rulings in trade disputes, so that the objectives and provisions of other international treaties are not negated through its operations.

short-term economic growth at the expense of long-term sustainability of the resource base is counter-productive

Governments value liberalised trade as an impetus to economic growth, but it would be counterproductive if short-term economic growth is achieved at the expense of long-term sustainability of the resource base. The world's governments when they are convened as the WTO must send signals that sustaining the range of economic, environmental and social services of forests is the bottom line, and that trade arrangements must subserve that bottom line, not the other way round. If trade arrangements impact negatively upon a nation's forests, countries must be able to protect their forest capital and rely on the WTO for support. The ongoing discussion in and around the WTO about an international agreement on 'process and production methods' is of central importance in this regard – any resulting 'trade and environment' or 'trade and sustainable development' agreement must give a country recourse to protect its forest capital (IISD, 1996).

These issues would benefit from full discussion in the continuing intergovernmental process.

Certification of forest products

criteria should be accompanied by penalties for practices not conforming to the standards

The forest certification issue has been under intense discussion and development during the 1990s. On-going work by the Forest Stewardship Council (FSC) and the International Organization for Standardization (ISO) is leading to development of broad frameworks of principles and management standards against which sustainable forest management can be judged. As has been mentioned in previous chapters similar efforts are under way at the national level in several countries, and consumers in Europe and North America, through 'buyers groups', are bolstering these efforts by building consumer awareness and retailer buy-in for products emerging from sustainably managed forests. A host of other efforts aimed at clarifying criteria and indicators of sustainable forest management also feed into various discussions on certification and labelling.

A major difficulty has been that the demand for certification is still highly uneven. Given the relatively small share of developing countries in global trade in forest products, there is little incentive in many countries to 'certify' forest production as deriving from sustainable methods, particularly in countries where priorities tend to focus more on meeting immediate human needs. Since the situation is complex and fragmented, a more systematic approach is needed, in which the following elements are given attention.

First, certification of forest products is also desirable for domestically traded products. This must be developed simultaneously and in harmony with certification processes for internationally traded products.

Second, harmonisation is also required in criteria and indicators for sustainable management, and certification and labelling for consumer guidance, by all trading countries – producers and consumers, exporters and importers. This is the only way to ensure a level playing field and fair competition. The proposal has already been made that the various independent initiators of certification mechanisms should constitute a Forest Management Council with the objective of making their respective mechanisms consistent, compatible and coherent (see Chapter 3 on FORESTRUST INTERNATIONAL).

Third, certification implies certain restrictions to respect and standards to be met. This can be expected to be easier for firms operating in countries with a well developed forest industry and well developed political structures than in countries where these have not yet matured. This is even more so where certification is based on criteria and indicators that incorporate social concerns. It is important therefore that supportive measures be offered to those countries less well equipped to comply.

Fourth, the benefits of certification mechanisms would be limited if they were not accompanied by penalties for practices that do not conform to the standards set, as well as by means to detect and prevent them from undermining the trade in certified products, domestically or internationally. These need to be thought through and agreed by governments, and consumers should be educated accordingly.

Fifth, local community involvement is desirable in verification procedures, as it is for forest management in the first place, especially to be able to assess the social aspects of management such as equity and sharing of benefits from use of the resource. Arrangements for their involvement and preparation for that role are required.

The above are some of the challenges involved in certification of forest products which require international attention.

6.4 Global services from forests

UNCED proposed that the financial responsibility for the global transition to sustainable development be differentiated among countries. This was an acknowledgement of past contributions of some countries to accumulated environmental disorder, as well as a recognition of different development priorities and imperatives according to place and circumstance. This proposal also recognised that a multitude of human beings in many countries still exist in deplorable material circumstances. Nations agreed that the poorest, most destitute and least empowered people cannot be asked to shoulder the same burden as the rich and powerful who consume most resources and make the largest demands on the natural capital and environmental integrity of the planet.

In the intergovernmental dialogue on forests, this is perhaps the most intractable international dimension. How can the world deal with the fact that forests provide common and indivisible environmental services for the whole world, irrespective of their geographical location, ownership pattern, or political jurisdiction? How can this financial differentiation, as it relates to forest conservation, be done objectively, rationally, fairly, respectably, and equitably?

Developing nations take the position that they should be compensated for the global ecological services which their current forest cover provides to the rest of the world. They argue that if industrialised countries have had the opportunity to fuel their development by using their forests, why should developing countries now have to forgo use of their forests in the interests of humankind and the planet. Meanwhile, it is noted, the general undertaking of UNCED about financing the transition to sustainable development has not been realised, and levels of ODA continue to be reduced. The intergovernmental debate on forests has remained fixated on these points.

This impasse in the debate on forests ignores some fundamental realities. First, the costs of deforestation for individual countries and for the world as a whole are becoming much greater than the costs of retaining forests for sustaining development and for stabilising the human habitat. Second, short-term costs of conservation are in reality investments for long-term environmental stability which is a necessary foundation for the continuing human enterprise – a basic need for all societies. Third, the fact that a multitude of the world's peoples still exist in utterly deplorable material conditions is inextricably tied up with the prospects for that stability. Fourth, the dialogue in the first place is supposed to be about common responsibilities for securing that stablity. Fifth, the urgency of the forest crisis demands immediate and concerted attention. Sixth, equity requires a pooling of resources among all nations to make possible the desired conservation and sustainable use of forests.

Some progress in fulfilling this notion of common responsibility has at least been made in the Kyoto Protocol to the Convention on Climate Change, in which it has been agreed to find ways to compensate the developing nations for at least one of the global ecological services that their forests provide, namely sequestration of carbon. Mechanisms of 'Activities Implemented Jointly' and the 'Clean Development Mechanism' are now being actively negotiated (see Box 6.3).

In a world of depleting natural resources, measures and mechanisms that reflect and establish the real value of natural capital must be tried; just as we have to experiment with new political and social institutions which are responsive to the challenges – eliminating poverty, achieving equity, ensuring participation, practising democracy – which emerge from the concept of sustainable development. Equity between nations requires that a method be found for assessing their respective and relative contributions to the forest capital of the world. Equity for future generations requires a mechanism for evaluating changes over time to the forest capital of the world. An ability-to-measure and therefore value forest services which do not now have markets needs to be actively and urgently sought as a basis for intergovernmental dialogue.

A Forest Capital Index (FCI)

The Commission proposes the development of a Forest Capital Index (FCI) based on the concept and measure of Forest Capital discussed in Chapter 5. The FCI (see Box 6.4) would provide a uniform numerical indicator of the state of a country's forest resources. This would facilitate a global framework for the proper valuation of forest ecosystem services, and would treat international comparisons of forest decline more equitably than absolute and contemporaneous measures of deforestation. Human activities have eroded global forest capital over

Box 6.3 The Kyoto Protocol and forests

Under the Framework Convention on Climate Change (FCCC) Parties have introduced new mechanisms to deal with global warming. In the recently adopted (December 1997) Kyoto Protocol to the Climate Change Convention, the Parties agreed to meet the commitments undertaken through new mechanisms known as emissions trading, joint implementation and the clean development mechanism. In addition, the Parties have also recognised the vital role that forests play both as sources and sinks of carbon.

Greenhouse gas emissions, of which carbon emissions make up a large part, contribute significantly to global warming by trapping heat from incoming solar energy in the atmosphere. By adopting the Kyoto Protocol, and by incorporating the mechanisms for cooperative implementation, the Parties have placed a global value on limiting the volume of carbon emissions that are discharged into the atmosphere. The industrialised countries have overall agreed to lower their emissions by 5% below the level of their greenhouse gas emissions in 1990. By differentiating this 5% reduction amongst them, the Parties recognised the need for flexibility in determining the appropriate responsibilities of different countries depending on their economic, social, and environmental circumstances.

With respect to both carbon sequestration and how the accounting is done for the role forests play as sources and sinks of carbon, through mechanisms such as the clean development mechanism and joint implementation, the Kyoto Protocol is of great consequence both for forests and biodiversity use and their conservation.

The FCCC has led countries to value a stable atmosphere. This is grounded in the best scientific understanding available. Now, with the fate of the world's forests in their hands, nations also face the challenge of introducing measures and mechanisms needed to reflect the global ecological services of forests.

centuries. Indeed, the progressive decline of temperate forests over time may be impairing vital ecological functions of the planet just as much as current tropical deforestation.

The recognition that forests provide global services is not new. It has been incorporated into the Global Environment Facility (GEF) in which 'incremental costs' incurred by developing countries for securing global benefits through curbing carbon emissions and conserving biodiversity are financed. However, this mechanism is applicable only for activities undertaken in the context of a project submitted and approved for funding under the GEF. The Forest Capital Index and a system of credits based on it would allow countries to benefit from their existing stock of forest resources, as well as the eventual effects of activities undertaken for purely domestic benefits and not necessarily eligible for financing under the GEF.

Box 6.4 Towards a Forest Capital Index

The forests of earth constitute a capital asset that sustains the world's population. To manage this capital wisely for the public good, societies need indicators of the status of the world's forests and estimates of their ecological and socio-economic value.

The Forest Capital Index is a tool for international forest policy. It will permit evaluation of the progress of each of the world's nations in renewing and sustaining its stock of forest resources – its forest capital. It will serve as a benchmark for assessing whether that capital is increasing, static or declining over time. It will underpin the concept of and concern for intergenerational equity. It will facilitate a global framework for valuation of forest ecosystem services and create a possibility for market mechanisms to compensate for those services.

The FCI will provide a uniform numerical indicator of each nation's current forest capital. A suite of indicators of forest qualities might be used, such as: surface area, standing biomass, net primary productivity, species richness, species diversity. Examining the changes in these indicators over time will treat international comparisons of forest decline more equitably than absolute measures of deforestation. These are first-order indicators: they reflect the most basic characteristics of forests. More detailed second-order indicators (such as age class of trees, leaf area index, soil fertility measures, soil organic matter content, the health of forest stands) will provide more detail on the state of particular forest ecological functions.

Condensing the suite of ecological indicators, appropriately weighted, into one dimensionless number offers a simple tool to compare the progress of countries across numerous categories. Imputing a dollar value to the services provided by the forest then becomes possible, and can then be reflected in a workable form in the international dialogue about compensation for global forest services.

Considerable research data are needed to characterise forest capital: *inter alia* an accurate estimate of global forest area based on a triangulation of data from forest inventories, remote sensing, and small plot studies; characterisation of vegetation before large-scale human disturbance; choice of ecological indicators to monitor; considerations for weighting of indicators; determination of the scale at which data will be reported.

The Commission, in collaboration with the Woods Hole Research Center (USA), has initiated a process of wider consultation about the concept of a Forest Capital Index and will catalyse a programme to properly value today's forests for tomorrow's generations.

Source: WCFSD/WHRC, 1998

dividing the world into developed and developing is no longer a useful construct when the benchmark is sustainability

In order to be useful in setting a global framework for valuing forests and therefore for establishing a basis for compensation for forest services, the FCI could generate a system of forest capital credits analagous to what is emerging for global carbon emissions under the Framework Convention on Climate Change (FCCC), as reflected in Box 6.3 on the Kyoto Protocol.

Many financially poor but forest-capital-rich countries, like Brazil, Indonesia and the Democratic Republic of Congo, would probably benefit significantly from a system of credits based on their forest capital. Yet all countries stand to benefit from such a framework, since it will provide a basis for recognising increments to their forest capital over time from their own efforts in conservation and afforestation. Countries in the fortunate position of having ample forest capital, such as the group including Canada, Sweden and USA, would be recognised for the global services they contribute. Likewise, countries poor in forest capital would have an incentive to manage their forest resources better in the future. Least Developed Countries (LDC) could be exempted for a period. A clearing house system would be applied to net out the balances in this global give and take.

Industrialised countries have been less than forthcoming in meeting their financial responsibilities under UNCED – arguing that more development aid is not the answer and that other financing mechanisms must be found. Developing countries should not be mendicant in areas for which they have something to contribute. This search for agreement on financial mechanisms to meet the UNCED requirements is still undermining the intergovernmental process. All countries should therefore work towards mechanisms that would make possible such transactions. FCI could provide an instrument for doing so.

Discussion on these international issues, among governments and others, have tended to situate the issues and the solutions in the conventional North/South divide. Dividing the world into North and South, developed and developing countries, is no longer a useful construct in a world where the benchmark for progress is sustainability. This categorisation obfuscates the real situation: that many 'developed' countries are indeed unsustainable; that many 'developing' countries are in fact declining materially; that disparities are increasing between them and within them; that ecologically they are in the same lifeboat; that economically they are mutually dependent.

The Commission feels that the North/South developed/developing formula for solution of global issues – if ever it could be regarded as such – has outlived its usefulness. It has become sterile. The differentiation in the Kyoto Protocol in carbon emissions credits among OECD countries indicates the need to become more discriminating in the way the burden of the transition is differentiated among countries. A Forest Capital Index would allow a defensible basis for differentiation of financial burden and financial rewards among countries based on changes in their forest capital.

6.5 A convention on forests?

The Commission supports use of international law in the service of societal goals. The Commission is in principle supportive of any instrument or process which could give relief to forests. Obviously, conclusions and commitments which have the force of international law would underpin the efforts that are required, providing that they address the fundamental issues, that they identify appropriate responses, that they secure the means for their implementation including financing, and that they are pursued with diligence and commitment to the overall purpose.

The Commission therefore considers that under those conditions a global forest convention would be a useful instrument for enshrining commitments capable of arresting the forest crisis, restoring and sustaining this resource indefinitely, and ensuring equitable sharing of benefits from its use, domestically and internationally.

Thus, the question to be asked is: what would such a global agreement address and include? If a convention is to be effective in responding to the forest crisis, it must incorporate and reflect the Forest Principles and:

- be designed to sustain the forest functions necessary for security of goods and services at both local and global levels and/or to minimise the international causes of forest problems that affect such security
- include provisions to ensure equitable sharing of benefits accrued from forests between nations and between present and future generations
- be able to strengthen processes that empower people from all levels of society to participate in decision-making about forests, and that ensure transparency and accountability in governance and administration of the forestry patrimony
- provide adequate financial resources through various mechanisms, including timber levies to finance non-market forest related benefits
- facilitate the monitoring of programmes for forest conservation and sustainable management
- recognise and make provisions for dealing with illegal and corrupt activities in the forest industry
- promote market access for all timber and timber products
- build upon existing forest-related agreements
- make use of existing global and regional institutional arrangements.

Enshrining commitments in a legally binding convention is no guarantee that those commitments will be carried out. This is a matter of political will. Given the record of governments to date in implementing existing treaties, there is little basis for confidence in the prospects for a forest convention being implemented with due diligence. In light of the urgency to respond to the crisis in forests, this record is a major reason for concern.

a considerable body of international law for sustainable development awaits implementation

The Commission could not ignore the considerable body of international law for sustainable development – reflected most notably in the three UNCED conventions (Biodiversity, Climate Change, Desertification) – which awaits implementation, and which would go a long way towards dealing with the objective of sustaining forests (see Box 6.5). Moreover, an objective analysis of the potential of these and other existing treaties which could contribute to the overall purposes of a forest convention should be a prerequisite for the discussion about a forest convention.

The Commission considers it of great importance that governments have been debating whether a convention on forests would enhance their political will and the ability of nations to adopt approaches for conservation and sustainable management of the world's forests, and whether it would strengthen international cooperation toward that end. The Commission urges governments to take into account the discussion and proposals of this Report in their continuing discussion on the role of a global forest convention and on the forest issues in general. It should be considered how a legally binding convention would benefit from the recommendations put forward by the Commission. The Commission again emphasises the importance of speedy conclusion of the present round of intergovernmental deliberations, given the global forest crisis, and the lives and livelihoods of communities that are now caught up in this crisis.

commitment by governments is a prerequisite for action

But in the meantime, the Commission insists that commitment by governments, within a convention or without one, is a prerequisite for urgent and effective action to deal with the issues raised in this Report, especially as the preponderance of actions and policies required can be undertaken by governments acting within their jurisdiction, or acting collaboratively, without the necessity for international law. Regional associations of countries which already exist provide political and policy frameworks within which multilateral cooperation for sustainable forest management could also proceed. Issues relating to the conservation and sustainable management of forests, and equitable use of forest resources, are best dealt with by such regional groups when the ecosystem transcends the political frontiers of individual countries in a region. Collaborative and concerted action within existing geopolitical groups (Box 6.6) would accelerate progress towards sustainable forest management. Some initiatives are already under way.

Box 6.5 Forest-related global and regional agreements

- The Rio Declaration on Environment and Development, 1992
- Non-Legally Binding Authoritative Statement of Principles for a Global Consensus on the Management, Conservation and Sustainable Development of All Types of Forests (The Forest Principles), 1992
- Combating Deforestation (Agenda 21, Chapter 11), 1992
- Convention on Biological Diversity, 1992
- Framework Convention on Climate Change, 1992
- International Tropical Timber Agreement, 1994
- General Agreement on Tariffs and Trade, 1994
- Convention to Combat Desertification, 1994
- Convention on Wetlands of International Importance Especially as Waterfowl Habitat, 1971
- Convention for the Protection of the World Cultural and Natural Heritage, 1972
- Convention on International Trade of Endangered Species of Wild Fauna and Flora, 1973
- United Nations Convention on the Law of the Sea, 1982
- Convention Concerning Indigenous and Tribal Peoples in Independent Countries (ILO #169), 1989
- Convention on Nature Protection and Wildlife Preservation in the Western Hemisphere, 1940
- African Convention on Conservation of Nature and Natural Resources, 1968
- Treaty for Amazonian Cooperation, 1978
- Convention on the Conservation of European Wildlife and Natural Habitats, 1979
- ASEAN Agreement on the Conservation of Nature and Natural Resources, 1979
- Central American Regional Convention for the Management and Conservation of the Forest Natural Ecosystems, 1993
- North American Agreement on Environmental Cooperation, 1993

6.6 Political leadership

Political will is, in the Commission's view, the crux of the matter, whether the concern is for national, regional or global commitment, arrangements and action. The Commission therefore draws attention not only to the serious crisis in the world's forests, but also to the crisis in political will to respond to it. The vacuum in political concern and commitment for forest conservation, protection and sustainable management is a serious shortcoming. The leadership of many countries appears not to be genuinely concerned about environment although 'green' issues have become compulsory issues in political rhetoric and manifestos.

Given these points of view and in light of this Report, while the debate on a forest convention continues in the Intergovernmental Forum on Forests, the Commission considers that additional ways must be sought to put the search for solutions to the forest crisis on a fast track.

The Commission on Global Governance (1995) pointed out that the Group of Seven (now G-8) is the nearest the world comes to having an apex body concerned with the global economy, but that it is neither representative of the world's population (having 12% of the world's population) nor very effective, and that the development issues that concern most of humanity have low priority on its agenda. However, it is to be noted that the G-8 addressed the issue of forests at its Denver Summit in June 1997 and released an Action Programme on Forests at the G-8 Foreign Ministers Meeting in London in May 1998. It remains to be seen whether their statements and conclusions will be reflected in political and policy leadership from which the forests of the whole world could benefit.

despite the rhetoric the leadership of many countries is not genuinely concerned about environment

The Commission advocates that there is need for mechanisms for leadership at the global level which focus on specific and pressing global concerns, which involve those who are most relevant to the issues in hand, which can

Box 6.6 Existing multilateral frameworks for cooperation

- African Timber Organization
- Amazon Treaty Organization
- Andean Pact
- Asia Pacific Economic Cooperation (APEC)
- Association of Caribbean States (ACS)
- Association of Southeast Asian Nations (ASEAN)
- Caribbean Community (CARICOM)
- Central American Commission on Sustainable Development
- European Union (EU)
- International Tropical Timber Organization (ITTO)
- MERCOSUR
- North American Free Trade Agreement (NAFTA)
- Organisation for Economic Cooperation and Development (OECD)
- South Asian Association for Regional Cooperation (SAARC)
- Southern African Development Coordination Conference (SADCC)
- South Pacific Regional Environment Programme (SPREP)

Member states of these organisations are listed in Annex 5.

overcome the limitations of the typical global inter-governmental process, which can make space at the table for civil society representatives and a range of relevant interest groups which seek to make policy more science-based, and which are capable of making progress at a much faster rate.

A Forest Security Council

a shared sense of responsibility and willingness to search for solutions should be the main criteria for membership of the FSC

The Commission therefore challenges a small group of countries to constitute themselves as a Forest Security Council to take up the mantle of leadership on behalf of their own, and the world's, forests and citizens (see Box 6.7). Its purpose will be to put the search for solutions on a fast track. The Commission holds the view that some countries, by virtue of the command which they have over forest resources, production and trade in forest products, and consumption of forest products have an extraordinary duty of care for forests on behalf of the world's peoples and the planet.

The Commission realises that it is an invidious exercise to propose names of countries for such a grouping, since there is no perfect solution, no ideal formula, no standard criteria. Nevertheless, the Commission takes the risk of proposing four key considerations, on the basis of which a preliminary group of countries is indicated. The intention in doing so is not to exclude others; it is to engender a renewal of concern and commitment to action on the part of a core group of countries whose forest circumstances make them indispensable to any effort to conserve and sustainably manage the world's forests. The hope is that they would exercise political and policy leadership that is commensurate with the urgency of the crisis and the responsibility it implies. Those countries which choose to take up this challenge and which exercise initiative to constitute a Forest Security Council will undoubtedly exercise a prerogative to develop the criteria and the selection further. Countries with special expertise or experience that would be especially relevant to the agenda of a Forest Security Council could also be considered as participants.

It has already been submitted by the Commission that the conventional North/South categorisation of the world creates a conceptual and a political obstacle to finding solutions to issues in a world that is so ecologically and economically interconnected and mutually dependent. Dividing the 'forest' world in this way will be even more irrelevant, inadequate, and ineffectual as a way of coming to grips with the world's forest crisis.

The core of the Forest Security Council would be made up of countries whose forest circumstances make them indispensable in any effort to alter the trend of forest decline and to get to the roots of the crisis. They would probably be more able and more disposed to define the issues with clarity and design the solutions with focus, and be more effective in giving leadership to the search for real and effective solutions. Such a group would therefore have the possibility of avoiding dilatory approaches and diluted policies, given what is at stake for their economies and societies.

Although leadership at the highest political and executive levels is essential for the Forest Security Council to come into being, the concept and the process should by no means be confined to governments of these countries. Work towards solutions to the forest crisis should proceed across several sectors of society concurrently, involving and interlocking the inputs and efforts of academia and research institutions, non-governmental organisations and forest industry corporations, scientists and foresters, and local communities drawn from the participating countries.

History reveals many examples of countries coming together to plan for the

Box 6.7 Selecting a Forest Security Council

Identification of countries to comprise a Forest Security Council could be based on four primary considerations:

1. Involve countries according to their prominence in forest cover, wood production, imports and exports of wood, production and export of woodpulp
2. Ensure that different types of forests are reflected
3. Ensure that all regions are represented
4. Draw upon expertise and experience relevant to key concerns (e.g. biodiversity conservation, community management).

Figures 6.1 to 6.8 accompanying this Box reflect the most prominent countries according to:

boreal and temperate forest cover: Russian Federation, Canada, USA, Australia, Japan, Sweden
tropical forest cover: Brazil, China, Indonesia, Democratic Republic of Congo, Peru, India

wood production (developed countries): USA, Russian Federation, Canada, Sweden, France, Finland
wood production (developing countries): China, India, Brazil, Indonesia, Nigeria, Malaysia

imports and exports of wood (developing countries): Malaysia, Chile, China, Indonesia, Brazil, India
imports and exports of wood (developed countries): Japan, USA, Russian Federation, Australia, Germany, Finland

production and export of woodpulp (developing countries): Brazil, China, Indonesia, Chile, India, Mexico
production and export of woodpulp (developed countries): USA, Canada, Japan, Sweden, Finland, Russian Federation

Consideration of special characteristics and regional balance:
Ethiopia is proposed to represent dry tropical forests and expertise in dryland biodiversity conservation
Ghana is proposed because of its well-developed community forestry
The need for adequate representation of the Amazon forest, being the second largest in the world, suggests the addition of other Amazon Basin countries not otherwise indicated – Bolivia, Colombia, Ecuador and Venezuela.

On the basis of the above considerations, the preliminary group of countries indicated, by region, is as follows:

Asia and Oceania:	Australia, China, India, Indonesia, Malaysia, Japan
Africa:	Democratic Republic of Congo, Ethiopia, Ghana, Nigeria
Latin America and the Caribbean:	Bolivia, Brazil, Chile, Colombia, Ecuador, Peru, Venezuela
Europe and the CIS:	Russian Federation, Finland, France, Germany, Sweden
North America:	Canada, Mexico, USA

The Commission considers it reasonable that members of the Forest Security Council be selected from the countries indicated above. The main criteria should be a shared sense of responsibility and willingness to commit to accelerating the search for solutions. The Commission reiterates its view that participating countries should exercise an extraordinary duty of care for forests, which will be reflected in the policy, planning and programme leadership they provide, and the way in which they accelerate responses to the crisis in forests.

management of resources which are strategic to them. Why not for the forest capital of the world? The Commission recalls that it was the strategic alliance among a handful of Western European countries to overcome rivalry that had caused two world wars and to safeguard their coal and steel resources that created

Figure 6.1 Countries with the most temperate and boreal forests

Source: FAO, 1997

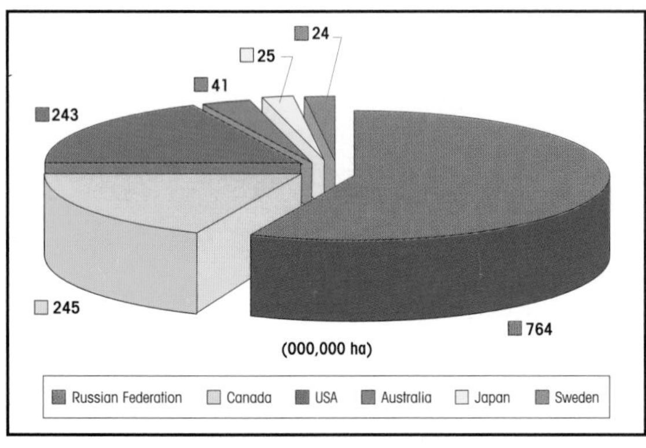

Figure 6.2 Countries with the most tropical forests

Source: FAO, 1997

68
65
109
110
133
(000,000 ha)
551
Brazil
China
Indonesia
Dem. Rep. of Congo*
Peru
India
*formerly Zaire

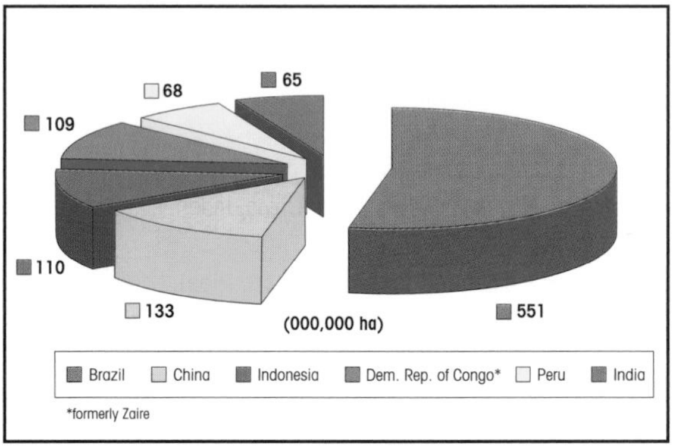

Figure 6.3 Largest importers and exporters of wood, developed countries

Source: FAOSTAT website

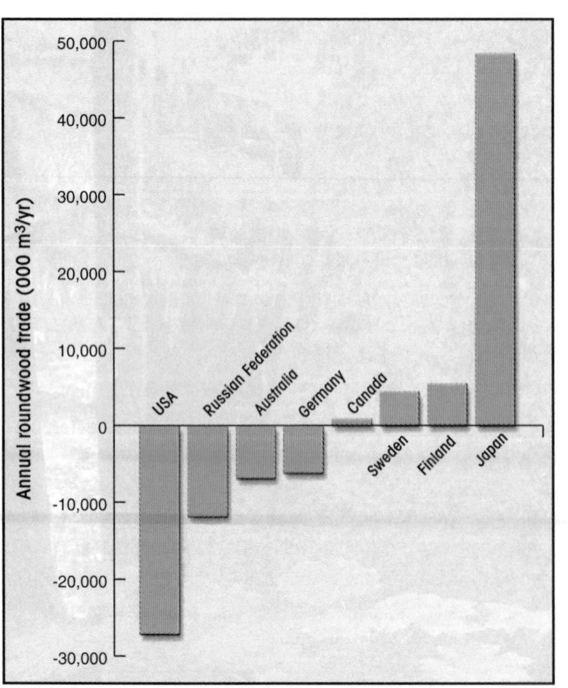

Figure 6.4 Largest importers and exporters of wood, tropical or developing countries

Source: FAOSTAT website

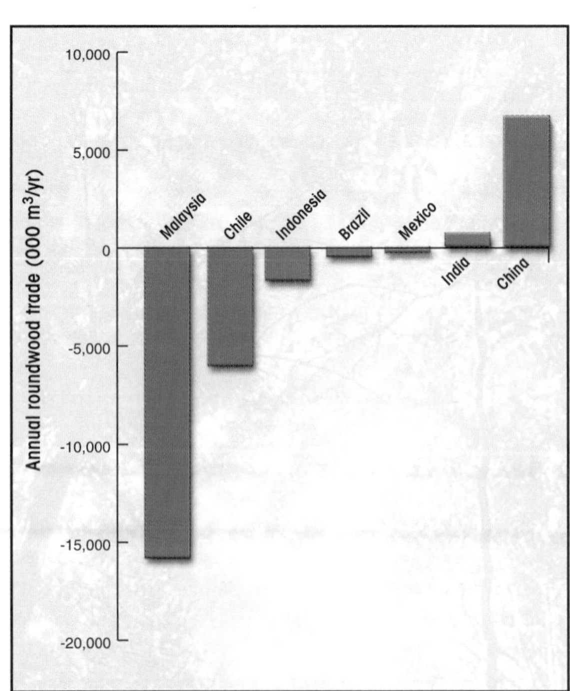

the nucleus for what has become the European Union. Similarly, a Forest Security Council could build the possibilities, options, and solutions for conservation and sustainable management of forests, which could provide a foundation for an eventual global effort in which all countries would be involved. The Commission holds the view that United Nations and other intergovernmental processes dedicated or closely relevant to forests (like the Intergovernmental Forum on Forests and the Convention on Biological Diversity) would benefit from accelerated policy development made possible by the operation of a Forest Security Council.

Figure 6.5 Largest wood producers, developed countries

Source: FAOSTAT website

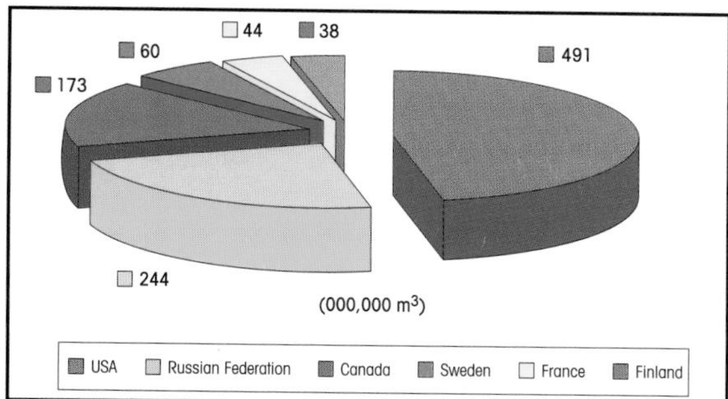

Figure 6.6 Largest wood producers, developing or tropical countries

Source: FAOSTAT website

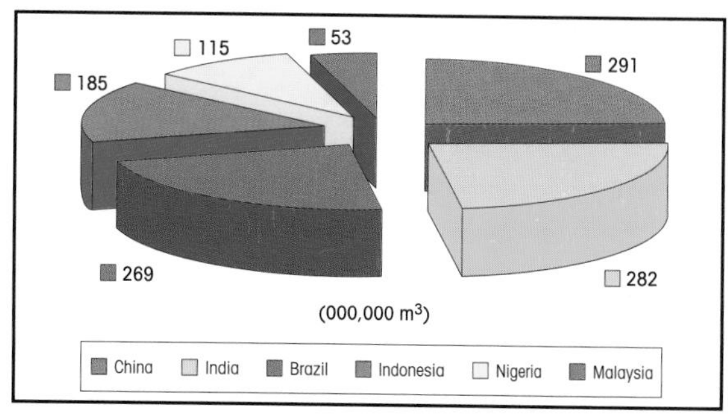

Figure 6.7 Largest woodpulp producers and exporters, developed countries

Source: FAOSTAT website

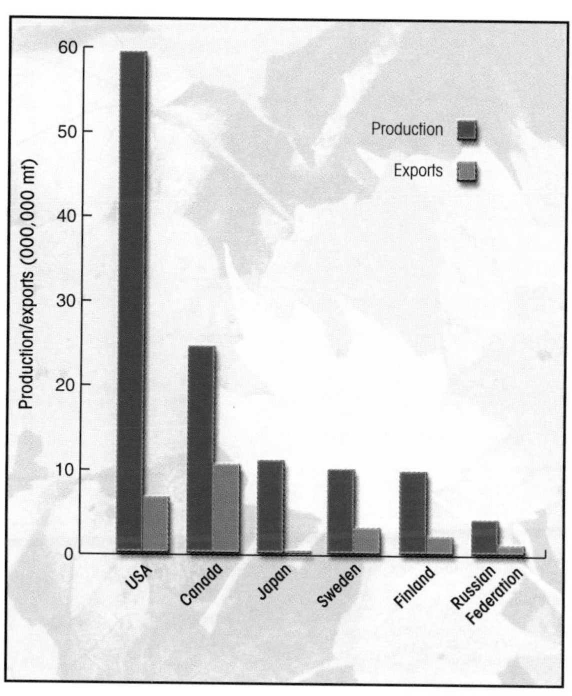

Figure 6.8 Largest woodpulp producers and exporters, tropical and developing countries

Source: FAOSTAT website

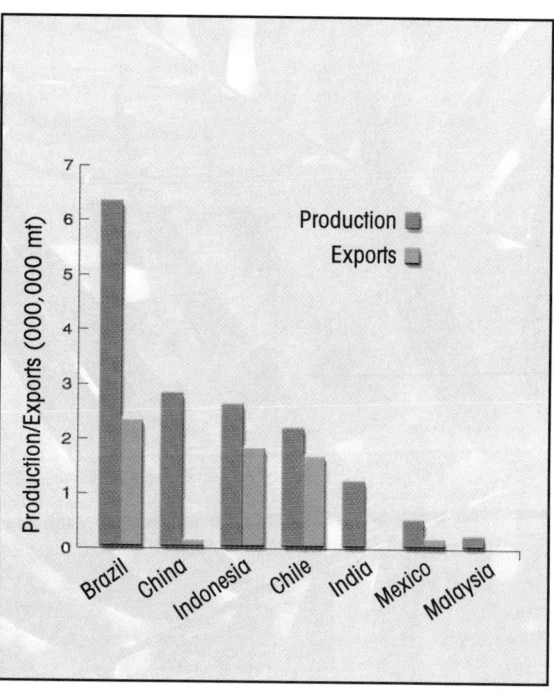

An obvious priority is to conserve what remains of the primary forests of the world

7

A FUTURE FOR OUR FORESTS

A touch of shameless idealism may yet prove to be the most pragmatic launch-pad for building a sustainable future.
(TOMORROW Magazine)

7.1 Overview

At one time development thought and practice used to reflect the concept of basic human needs exclusively in terms of necessities of food, clothing and shelter. Civilisation, however, stands at the close of the second millennium with a profound understanding of how the quality of the earth's environment, its resources and functions, influence and determine the ability of the world to meet these human needs now and indefinitely. The World Commission on Environment and Development (The Brundtland Commission, 1987), followed by The United Nations Conference on Environment and Development (UNCED, 1992) had led us to recognise and inscribe in public policy that human needs, satisfied through a process of development, can no longer be treated in juxtaposition with the need for a stable and optimally functioning environment. That understanding has increased so much further since UNCED that it is possible to conclude that most people and governments now accept that the stability and security of the environment is also a basic human need.

The benefits of global environmental services are shared by all societies, collectively and indivisibly. Their availability and enjoyment transcend distinctions of North and South; of developed, not so developed, and not at all developing; of industrialised and non-industrialised; of rich and poor. The services and benefits are relevant to all societies regardless of how wealthy they are, and to all individuals regardless of how well off they are. The recognition that a stable and secure biophysical environment is a basic human need – for all societies – is now well established in people's consciousness and reflected in statements of public policy.

We live in a full world. By the end of the 20th century the global human population will be approaching 6 billion and will be expanding by 85–90 million annually, nearly a billion people per decade in the first half of the 21st century. We know that the need for consumables will increase exponentially in the foreseeable future in response to an increase in population. Human numbers have the potential for doubling once again well before the middle of the next century. We shall be drawing upon the resources and services of a finite, impoverished landscape for meeting those needs, as well as the need for a stable and secure environment.

While human numbers may have a doubling time of 3–5 decades, the doubling time of demands on forests and forested land can take place in a few years or a decade or so. This acceleration of demand is the result of the compounding of rapid growth in population with the expansion and spread of technology (the ability to exploit resources), and the parellel expansion of human expectations. The effect is a growth in demands on resources that drives the environmental crisis and will continue to force it to the fore in governmental affairs.

We accept that food, housing, energy, living space, and paper, are basic human needs that must be met. But we recognise that forests are used as if they had only these limited purposes, and that in doing so forest lands are being squandered through subsidised activity and wholly marginal uses without concern for sustaining the human need for a stable environment. It is evident that societal values, economic policies, political realities, governance arrangements, and ethics – or lack thereof – underpin and permit that wastage.

At the same time human activities in burning fossil fuels and in the destruction of forests are changing the composition of the atmosphere and warming the earth at globally averaged rates of two to three tenths of a degree per decade. The rate is high enough to affect forests and to stimulate the decay of organic matter in soils. The process releases additional carbon dioxide and methane that will accelerate the warming. In many parts of the world future vigour of forests is in question even as demands on forests for timber, fibre, fuel, land for agriculture, and for services in stabilising the landscape, all soar. The room for compromise in assuring that forests endure is being diminished rapidly.[1]

We are aware that the causes of the crisis are varied and complex, embedded in the attractiveness of growth in all aspects of human affairs, and in the ways in which we organise our economic and political systems, reflecting the prevailing culture that emphasises the material over the spiritual, the human over other species, the rich over the poor, and private gain over public interest.

Nevertheless, there is some reason for hope. The Commission has been encouraged and impressed during its work by the range and variety of initiatives that are already under way at all levels to meet these challenges: by individual citizens, by communities, by forest scientists and managers; by civil society organisations, by national and international non-governmental organisations. We are impressed that governments are doing some things, if not enough; that some corporations are adjusting to a new threshold of performance, if not all. We recognise progress on a few fronts, and realise that this must be supported, extended, accelerated, and made more effective. We feel confident that this can be done. We perceive the beginnings of a whole new culture, especially among young people, more in keeping with the ethic of sustainability. We feel that despite the cause for concern there is still some reason for hope, providing we exercise the will and exert the effort to take the radical steps.

But we perceive a great gap between the extent of knowledge and understanding on the one hand and individual and political will, commitment, and leadership on the other. We are convinced that societies are not doing all that they know must be done, individually or collectively, to arrest the decline of forests and to better conserve and manage them. We consider that the world therefore needs to specify some objectives and actions, appropriate to the scale and significance of the forest crisis, and to summon the required commitment to pursue them with urgency.

We propose the following objectives and actions in the form of ten resolutions, which emerge from the work of the Commission and the wide range of representations to it, the basis for which has been discussed in the body of this report. Resolutions generally point us in a desirable direction, impelled by a historical moment or a searching experience. Resolutions embody conclusions of mind usually about ambitious undertakings, which inspire to new determination in the chosen direction. Resolutions tend to energise towards higher and nobler efforts which engender commitment to the actions required for their achievement. Resolutions, we know, are often made but not carried out; but that choice, we also know, is in one's hands.

7.2 Resolutions

1 that radical and urgent attention be given to arrest the decline in forests, since forests, their products and services, are threatened

We know that forests no longer cover the world. In the last two decades of the 20th century, the decades of the Brundtland Commission and the Rio Summit, the world has been losing an estimated 15 million hectares of forests annually to permanent deforestation, largely in the tropics. The rate of loss has increased as the frequency of fires has increased with the warming of the earth. We know that the decline is relentless, given business as usual. We suspect it could change the very character of the planet and of the human enterprise within a few years – unless we make some choices. Within the earth's landscape the capacity of forests to renew themselves is undermined by short-sighted excessive reduction in their mass and quality, and by human-induced climatic changes. We know that we have no choice but to make the radical adjustments in policies, practices, and preconditions that will sustain both forests and further economic development, and to do so with urgency.

The loss of forest lands is often measured in area terms, but more importantly it means losses in the variety of services that forests provide, all of them necessary for people's social and cultural needs, a functioning landscape and ultimately a functioning world. It is widely felt that among the natural resources or ecosystems of the planet, forests are extraordinary in their contribution to that basic human need for environmental stability and security, as well as in their contribution to the need for consumables in human society. The submissions to the Commission of scientists on the one hand and forest dwellers on the other confirm this.

It is clear that, over the past few centuries and especially over recent decades, the area covered by forests has dramatically reduced, and that the structural integrity of much of what remains has deteriorated. There is evidence that there has been a serious loss in the essential environmental services which forests provide. Such losses extract a heavy toll in human lives and well-being in the long term and on the habitability of the planet. We know that it is not too late for humankind to arrest the decline.

It is imperative that in the normally forested regions a generous area remains under the influence of forest to protect all public services, with a margin for error, a safety factor, built in. The fraction of forest will vary according to landscape and circumstance. The important factors will be the functional aspects – the rates of sedimentation in streams, the quality of water, and various other objectively measurable qualities of the landscape.

To give effect to this Resolution, the following major actions are recommended:

❒ a target to avoid further destruction or degradation of remaining primary forests, in order to secure their environmental services for all societies and species from what is left, now and for the future

❒ allocation and management through participatory land-use planning of forest lands for different purposes: conservation, corporate production, community forestry

- intensify wood production through expansion of plantation forestry on degraded and vacant lands and improve productivity in secondary forests
- reducte pressure on forest land for agriculture through improved productivity in farming by supporting efforts towards a New Green Revolution
- extensive support to community agroforestry to reduce the pressure on primary forests for supplying small-scale subsistence products.

2 that conserving and sustainably managing the world's forests go hand in hand with the priority of reducing poverty and sustaining livelihoods of millions of poor people and numerous communities who depend heavily on forests

Forests are habitat and basis for livelihoods and income for hundreds of millions of people. Forests currently contribute to their welfare in many ways. Without that use of forests, there would be many more living in abject poverty. The decline of forests thus threatens the life, living and livelihood of millions of people in marginal communities. Forests have the potential to contribute significantly more to their welfare and development. The Commission considers that there are many policy interventions available to governments to realise that potential. The poverty of about one billion of the world's poorest people in about 30 heavily deforested countries would be directly and urgently alleviated through community forestry to meet rapid afforestation and reforestion targets.

To give effect to this Resolution, the following major actions are recommended:

- intensified agroforestry efforts through application of technologies already developed and tested
- rapid afforestation and reforestion programmes, targeted to reducing poverty of about one billion of the world's poorest people, through community forestry
- removal of obstacles to community forestry by ensuring secure titles, tenure and access to forest lands and resources
- supports for community forestry through credit facilities, technology, technical assistance, marketing
- subsidies to support community forestry made available through a percentage of revenue from timber sales and timber concessions and licences
- creation and expansion of markets for non-timber forest products

- support of entrepreneurship for small and medium forest-based enterprises
- removal of policy bias towards large-scale timber production by introducing incentives in favour of community forestry, incorporating subsidies that favour communities rather than corporations
- support for village-level institutions required for sound management
- involvement of communities in the decision-making about allocation of forest lands
- creation of a Forum for Indigenous Peoples under the UN Commission on Sustainable Development

3 that the public interest in a stable and secure environment becomes paramount in decisions about use and management of forest lands

The causes of the crisis have their roots in economic and political arrangements and values. They permit policies, patterns of use and management, and distribution of benefits from forest use that ignore the needs of those who lack political and economic power. Prevailing governance arrangements exclude from consideration and decision-making many groups who are directly dependent on and affected by forest policies, uses and management practices. New and better forms of governance arrangements are required to reflect the range of needs and interests, to resolve inevitable conflicts, to contribute to equity and democracy, to allow the public interest to emerge and to be made the principal purpose for which forests are managed. **We need to get the governance right.**

We need to attend to our ethics. Underpinning governance failure is an ethical system that flies in the face of the precepts underlying sustainable development. Some of the most important reasons for forest decline have ethical roots: excessive concentration of wealth and power, both within countries and internationally; patterns of corruption, of consumption, of inequity, and of cultural discrimination which can be detrimental to the sustainability of forests. Ultimately economic and other pursuits cannot be separated from such ethical concerns. Corrupt and illegal practices which are rampant in forest industry activities are jeopardising the financial capacities of governments and societies to sustain both forests and development. **We need to bring our ethics in line with requirements of sustainable development: democracy, equity, gender equality; transparency, conservation and sustainability.**

The process of decision-making within a country about the use of its forest lands has to be opened up to widespread participation by interested and affected groups. New mechanisms are required to enable societies to have better scrutiny of what occurs in the forests, in order to secure the public interest. The public interest goes beyond the material interests of a single group and it exceeds the sum of all group interests. The public interest involves securing all the environmental functions of forests which are essential for humankind as a whole. We share those benefits, collectively and indivisibly: going beyond individuals to communities, beyond communities to entire societies, beyond individual societies to all societies, beyond humankind to the well-being of all other species, and beyond present to future generations.

Thus the ecological, economic and social significance of forests means that forests can no longer be managed primarily for supplying timber and pulp. Nor can their management be left only to private interests, as the public interest becomes more pressing as human demands increase while forest cover and quality decrease. Forest policy-making and management can no longer be left predominantly to governments and private corporations, though both of these have important roles and responsibilities in ensuring that forests are sustained. Governments have the responsibility to set up or facilitate mechanisms in which the public interest emerges, to represent the public interest, and to administer policies in ways that secure that public interest.

To give effect to this Resolution, the following major actions are recommended:

❒ creation and support of mechanisms that encourage and catalyse a larger role for non-governmental organisations and civil society that would permit scrutiny of the ways in which benefits from the use of forests are distributed

❒ creation of structured processes for civil society participation in policy-making and management

❒ creation and use of participatory processes by governments for policy-making for forests

❒ creation of arrangements for gender equity in decision-making, management, entitlements, access to credit, technical assistance and marketing supports

❒ creation of mechanisms for conflict resolution

❒ governance and other reforms that would limit opportunities for corruption and imposition of heavy penalties for corrupt practices

❒ creation of a FOREST OMBUDSMAN mechanism as a civil society body for resolving conflicts among different interest groups and passing judgement on the implementation of sustainable development policies in the forest area.

4 that we get to the roots of the crisis by bringing prices and policies in line to better reflect the range of values and uses of forests

Among the economic forces which lead to forest decline, the Commission emphasises the ways in which missing markets and the divergence between private values and public values distort investment and economic decisions away from conservation and towards extinction of forests. **Present market mechanisms are unable to reflect the ecological and social values of the world's forests. They consequently distort the pattern of consumption and production. We need to get the prices right.**

Land ownership and tenure help explain why some land uses appear to have economic values and others do not. **Clearly defined, secure and enforceable property rights are a fundamental requirement for encouraging sustainable use of forests.**

At the same time, government policies relating to timber concessions and subsidies, and to land ownership and tenure, exacerbate those market limitations. **Many policies and measures, applied to forest as well as other sector activities, are having unintended consequences that are detrimental to forests.** Forest sector policies should therefore arise from considerations that go well beyond forestry, anticipating the inevitable increase in demands for a wide range of goods and services.

To give effect to this Resolution, the following major actions are recommended:

- a comprehensive review of subsidies and other incentives, which originate within and outside the forestry sector
- reform or removal of subsidies that have perverse effects on forest lands and forest resources
- public sale of timber concessions, licences and leases through open auctions
- stumpage prices that properly reflect the diverse range of forest values
- a review of policies in agriculture, transportation, settlements, energy, and water, to alter those which have negative consequences for forests
- a review of land and resource tenure arrangements to make them more conducive to conservation
- support for work to value forest functions and to create market mechanisms for them.

5

that the threshold for responsible forest stewardship be raised to reflect the new responsibilities of forest management to integrate economic, environmental and social considerations and to make the public interest paramount

The Commission recognises that forests must and will be used, as will other natural resources, to feed, clothe, house and otherwise satisfy basic human needs. Its concern is about the extent to which forests are used, in relation to their capacity for renewal to continue to sustain planetary stability through their environmental functions, and to satisfy indefinitely those human needs. **Forests can no longer be used in the same way now as they have been in the past. Forest management now has different responsibilities than in the past.**

Radical adjustments in managing forests in a full world are required. Bringing prices and policies in line with sustainability considerations will largely determine whether forests are sustained or not. It is nevertheless imperative that the forestry sector itself urgently adapts its approaches and practices to the new and more complex objective of sustaining both forests and development, and not just sustaining timber yields. For this transition the Commission emphasises the principles of landscape planning and management, ecosystem-based management, participatory decision making, and localised management. **These principles would create a framework for controversial forest management practices and issues to be assessed in their environmental, economic, political, and social contexts.**

To give effect to this Resolution, the following major actions are recommended:

- ❒ involvement of communities in all stages of planning and implementation of forestry projects
- ❒ stipulating criteria for management and indicators of performance for all forest operators – public or private, corporate or community, domestic or foreign, large or small
- ❒ prescribing codes of conduct for timber companies which are consistent with the objectives of conservation, sustainability, equity and transparency
- ❒ imposing penalties for non-compliance with established standards
- ❒ adherence to social and ethical accounting practices by timber corporations
- ❒ investment in research to increase efficiency in the timber industry and to establish ancillary economic activities that make use of all 'waste' products from forestry operations
- ❒ adoption of third-party certification schemes for both domestically traded and exported products
- ❒ product labelling in accordance with certification standards and accompanied by consumer education programmes
- ❒ establishment of mechanisms for including local communities in monitoring performance through FORESTWATCH
- ❒ harmonising the various sets of criteria and indicators of sustainable forest management and coordinating forest certification systems through FOREST MANAGEMENT COUNCIL
- ❒ special efforts to reforest deforested land and land abandoned by agriculture through establishment of plantation and woodlots;
- ❒ recognition and reward to communities, corporations and countries for good practice in conservation and sustainable management of forests through a FOREST AWARD mechanism.

6 that new measures be created to keep track of the value of the capital stock of forests and to create a basis for compensation to countries for ecological services of forests

How can we know with any confidence whether current and future efforts to stem forest decline, are having a positive effect? How can we track what is happening to this stock of resources – the forest capital – over time? How can we get away from measuring systematic depletion of the forest resource as a net gain in economic growth? If indeed we value forests as an asset, and if ensuring "... the ability of future generations to meet their own needs" is not just rhetoric, it would be useful to have such a measure to appraise the effectiveness over time of all that we do in relation to sustaining forests. **We need a measure for the changing value of the forest capital of the world.**

Perhaps the most intractable issue in the international debate of governments on forests is how to deal with the fact that forests provide common and indivisible environmental services for the whole world, irrespective of their geographical location, ownership pattern, or political jurisdiction. The extent to which the forests of a single country do so and the particular environmental services they contribute, are the essence of international and intergovernmental negotiation. So is the net contribution of any country to forest decline on the one hand and forest services on the other. **We need new mechanisms to deal with global services from forests.** A forest capital index would facilitate a framework for estimating respective and relative contributions.

To give effect to this Resolution, the following major actions are recommended:

- development of the concept of Forest Capital
- development and use of a Forest Capital Index
- creation of financial mechanisms on the basis of such an Index to compensate countries for ecological services from forests.

7 that participatory planning for the use of landscapes, not just forests, be instituted to assure conservation objectives

It is urgent to move away from the linear and sectoral approach to planning and policy-making which has long been known to be inadequate and inappropriate in a complex landscape, and in an interconnected and interdependent, natural, economic and human world. A landscape planning and management approach, predicated on wide public participation, will stand a better chance of ensuring that the conservation targets will be realised, and that the right policies emerge and are applied. **Sustaining forests and development can come about only through planning for the entire landscape.**

The key to successful economic development includes a working landscape that provides a stable base for a variety of entrepreneurial activities. In the forested zones some of the forests will be used for timber and fibre and fuel; some will be used for non-timber forest products; some will be used as forest reserves and for water supplies. Such a scenario can come about only through planning for the entire landscape. But **without the planning and the biophysically intact landscape, economic development has no place to stand.**

We must reach beyond forestry – and beyond forests – if the whole is to work to a common purpose and if we are to sustain both forests and development. It is urgent to institute a landscape planning and management approach, supported by reliable data and scientific knowledge. The scientific and scholarly community must be encouraged with government support to undertake the analysis and research required. **We need to get the planning right.**

To give effect to this Resolution, the following major actions are recommended:

❒ opening up a new realm of analysis and research on landscapes and how to keep them stable and functional in support of the human endeavour

❒ implementing integrated planning and management approaches at the landscape level

❒ improvement in the reliability of time-series data for a variety of goods and services (food, fuel, fibre, water for domestic and industrial use, energy sources and services, living space and infrastructure)

❒ creation of mechanisms that would enable public administration systems to overcome the limitations of sectoral organisation and approaches

❒ creating and maintaining forest resource inventories

❒ engaging in participatory land-use planning.

8 that the information base about forests be enhanced and made more directly useful and applicable to policy makers, and in education programmes for the public

The Commission was struck by the inadequacy of forest data, as well as the incompatibility in definitions and measurements employed by those agencies involved in forest data gathering and analysis. Greater effort is required among public international agencies to bring about more coherence in the outcomes from the public resources they use.

Education provides the underpinnings for the direction which a society decides to take. It prepares citizens for occupying the political space which governance arrangements provide. It inculcates the values and ethics which a society elects to have. Education is fundamental to reducing both individual and national poverty and has a close relationship to the pressing issue of human population growth. It is a means to achieving the development goals of health, higher labour productivity, more equitable economic progress and the broader objective of social integration through participation in political and cultural affairs. It is central to orienting a society towards sustainable development. Education is also the means through which individual citizens will appreciate the multiple functions for which forests are important, and the public policies which governments formulate to ensure continuation of these functions. It is public awareness through education that would lead to appropriate consumption patterns and levels for individuals and societies. Education is central to efforts to sustain forests and development.

To give effect to this Resolution, the following major actions are recommended:

- ❐ efforts by UN and other international agencies involved in observation, measurement, monitoring and mapping of forests to achieve more compatibility in their definitions and terminology, and more comparability in their coverage and data
- ❐ better organisation and dissemination of information concerning forests to enable reliable monitoring of the state of forests
- ❐ emphasis on public awareness of the role of forests within formal and non-formal education
- ❐ campaigns for public education about forests, their role in meeting basic human needs, the pressures on forests, the part which consumption plays in those pressures
- ❐ incentives for reducing, reusing, recycling forest-related products
- ❐ incorporating indigenous and local knowledge in forest management
- ❐ disseminating forest-related information to local communities and forest users.

9 that research and training be adapted and accelerated to support the new responsibilities of forest management

The Commission recognises that there is considerable expertise and experience among forest scientists in managing forests for timber, fibre, and other products. However, enhanced scientific knowledge and public policy are required if forest management is to serve the public purpose of sustaining environmental services in perpetuity and of ensuring that forests contribute to social objectives of poverty reduction and secure livelihoods. **Improved research and training are necessary to support the process towards sustainability.**

To give effect to this Resolution, the following major actions are recommended:

- ❐ establishment by existing institutions and programmes of an international network within which research for sustainable forest management can be enhanced and training can be accelerated

- ❐ support by corporations of such a network as a means of enabling them to satisfy sustainable forest management requirements, standards and certification systems.

10 that additional avenues for political and policy leadership be explored to accelerate progress towards solutions

There is a crisis of credibility given the myriad international legal agreements, potentially useful in responding to some of the forest issues, that await serious implementation. **Political will and leadership lag behind knowledge and understanding.** Yet the need for attention to the forest crisis is so urgent that new and potentially more effective mechanisms, led by but not limited to governments, are necessary to accelerate the required reforms. Commitment by governments, within a legally binding convention or without one, is a prerequisite for urgent and effective action to deal with the forest issues, especially as the preponderance of actions and policies required can be undertaken by governments acting within their jurisdiction, or acting collaboratively, without the necessity for international law.

An extraordinary responsibility to secure the ecological services of forests for all humankind and other species rests with those countries which command or consume the lion's share of forest resources.

To give effect to this Resolution, the following major actions are recommended:

- ❐ constitution by those countries which dominate forest cover, production, trade and consumption of forest products of a Forest Security Council, to provide leadership in working out the economic, policy, and planning reforms required, and to seek solutions in a multilateral context which could be eventually extended to all countries

- ❐ undertaking a focused programme of actions by the Forest Security Council within which the contributions of governments, corporations, NGOs, communities, universities, research institutions, scientists and foresters are unified

- ❐ exploration of ways and means to curb the excesses of multinational timber corporations

- ❐ assessment of the extent to which liberalised trade negates efforts towards conservation and sustainable forest management

- ❐ providing feedback from these pilot efforts to ongoing intergovernmental and international processes in order to have more widespread application of approaches, policies and measures.

7.3 The fate of the forests is in our hands

The Resolutions submitted by the Commission call for more than technical adjustments in forestry practices. They call for a set of fundamental and far-reaching changes. As the Commission has said, the roots of the crisis are broad and deep, and the solutions go well beyond the obligations and responsibilities of the forestry sector. Correcting the root causes of forest decline will take much time, great patience, enlightened leadership, and considerable application. The effectiveness of these Resolutions and the effects of the actions may not be perceptible immediately. However, if the world is to prevent deepening of the forest crisis, initiatives already under way must be supported, and creative new ways to slow and ultimately reverse forest decline must be found. For those directly involved in planning, in policy analysis, in public service, or in political processes, a greater sense of urgency is required to build on current efforts and make them more effective. For those who are involved because they use timber and paper, the challenge for them is to reduce consumption. For those who walk in the woods and forests, the obligation is to encourage a wider appreciation of what could be lost. Everyone can be an actor, and all actors are encouraged to take on now the actions that they can implement or the forces they can influence. Individual actions will contribute to overall benefit, and short-term actions will determine long-term futures. We may not have a second chance. The choice is still in our hands.

Endnote

1 See Woodwell, G.M. editor. Forests in a Full World: Report of the Scientific Committee, World Commission on Forests and Sustainable Development (in draft) for a scientific discussion of the forces that underlie the global forest crisis and that are released by that crisis, which has informed the work of the WCFSD and upon which many of its findings and conclusions are based.

ANNEX

Annex 1 Glossary

afforestation
the establishment of a tree crop on an area from which it has always been or for very long been absent. Compare with reforestation.

Agenda 21
the internationally agreed plan of action on implementing sustainable development which emerged from the 1992 Earth Summit.

agroforestry
land-use system in which tree crops are planted on the same land used for raising agricultural crops or animals.

albedo effect
reflectivity for solar energy; high albedo means high reflectivity.

annual allowable cut or AAC
the amount of timber that is permitted to be cut annually from a particular area. It is used to ensure a sustainable supply of timber. It averages roughly the amount of new growth each year minus deductions for losses due to fire, insects and diseases.

biodiversity
biological diversity, which includes the diversity of species, genes and ecosystems and the evolutionary and functional processes which link them.

biomass
the dry weight of all organic material (i.e. animals, plants and microorganisms) living or dead and above or below soil surface.

boreal forest (or taiga)
the predominantly coniferous forests growing in the northern climatic zone characterised by short summers and long freezing winters.

broad-leaved forest
a forest composed predominantly of broad-leaved species, also known as hardwood, non-coniferous or angiosperm species. The species classification is botanical, based on the structure of seed and wood – not all broad-leaved species have broad leaves or hard wood. Examples of broad-leaved species include acacia, eucalyptus and oak.

canopy
tree crown cover.

carbon sequestration
the removal and storage of carbon from the atmosphere by green plants through the process of photosynthesis, in which carbon dioxide is combined with water to form carbohydrates that can be stored in plant tissues.

carbon sink
an area where the rate of carbon uptake by living organisms exceeds the rate of carbon release, so that carbon is sequestered in organic or inorganic forms.

certification
the process of evaluation or audits by independent third parties of forest practices carried out by forest owners and managers primarily engaged in wood production. The evaluation is usually carried out in relation to widely accepted standards of sustainable forest management. Some processes focus on certifying products, while others focus on forest management systems.

clearcutting or clear-felling
logging technique that involves the complete felling and removal of a stand of trees. Compare with selective logging.

climate change
an alteration to measured quantities (e.g. precipitation, temperature, radiation, wind and

cloudiness) within the climate system that departs significantly from previous average conditions and is seen to endure, bringing about corresponding changes to ecosystems and socioeconomic activity. Associated with greenhouse gas emissions, of which fossil fuel combustion and forest decline are contributors.

closed forest
forest with a minimum of 30% tree canopy cover.

community forest
a forest area primarily designated to serve community needs.

community forestry (or community forest management)
used as an all encompassing operational term. The common denominator in community forestry is the focus on the role of local communities (usually forest-dependent) in managing neighboring forests and sharing the benefits from those forests. An important role is to foster productive relationships between communities, government agencies, and NGOs.

concession
lease or contract to use a forest for the production of forest products. Concessions often take the form of commercial agreements granting loggers the right to harvest a given area of public forest land for industrial wood.

coniferous forest
forest composed predominantly of needle-leaved species (softwoods or gymnosperms) such as pine, spruce and larch. Mostly evergreen with a few exceptions such as larch.

criteria and indicators
criteria are rules, standards, norms, conditions, or behavior which are considered to be 'good' or 'ideal'. Indicators suggest what kind of measures are needed to judge the success or failure of a programme.

deciduous
exhibiting discontinuous, often seasonal tree leaf cover. Opposite of evergreen.

defoliation
loss of tree leaf cover.

deforestation
clearing an area of forest for another long-term use. Technically, a semi-permanent depletion of tree crown cover to less than 10%.

desertification
degradation of land that ultimately leads to desert-like land features.

designated forest
a forest area legally set aside for protection, production, or some other specified use.

economic
as in an economic cause of forest decline, a term that today often implies a profit motive but more properly concerns a wider consideration of the demand for and supply of scarce resources, both commercial and non-commercial.

ecosystem
a dynamic and inter-related community of biological organisms and the surrounding environment, linked through nutrient cycling and energy flows.

ecosystem-based forest management
an approach to forest management centred on maintaining or enhancing ecosystem integrity.

El Niño
which is also called the Southern Oscillation, or ENSO (El Niño Southern Oscillation) is the largest climatic fluctuation observed on earth. It occurs sporadically with a period between 2 and 10 years and is accompanied by unusually high sea surface temperatures, air pressures, and rainfall in the Eastern Pacific near the equator. ENSO influences both the atmospheric climate and the ocean conditions.

endemism
endemic species are those whose distribution is restricted to a particular area or region.

energy budget
the character of the energy flows which drive all natural processes from forest growth and

photosynthesis to wind and rain.

evergreen
exhibiting continuous tree leaf cover. Opposite of deciduous.

exotic species
foreign or non-native species introduced from another eco-zone. Opposite of indigenous species.

forest
communities characterised by a predominance of woody vegetation growing more or less closely together, whether 'closed' or 'open' in canopy, and whether fully intact ecologically or modified, fragmented or planted by humankind. Technically, forests are usually defined as ecosystems with a minimum of 10% tree canopy cover.

forest capital
a weighted measure of the extent and integrity of forest resources in a given region (say a country). Primary forests may be deemed to have greater integrity than other types of forests, and therefore be given more weight than modified, fragmented or planted forests.

forest capital credits
the notion that, since forest capital is of global value due to the global ecological services provided by forests, the forest capital concept could form the basis of a global market in tradeable credits for the global services provided by forests. The forest capital credits system could build on or complement experiences with the emerging international market in carbon emissions trading.

forest capital index
a comparative measure of the forest capital of different regions or countries.

forest capital trend
a comparative measure of the degree of forest decline experienced within a given region over a period of time, expressed in percentage terms.

forest decline
a blanket term encompassing deforestation(conversion of forests to other uses) and forest degradation (deterioration in health and quality).

forest degradation
a reduction in the biomass, productivity or biodiversity of a forest, and alterations in ecological functions such as habitat, climate regulation and soil and water protection. Sometimes also referred to as a lowering in the quality or integrity of a forest ecosystem. One example is a change in forest class, say from closed to open forest, which negatively affects the stand or site or lowers the production capacity.

forest fallow
the woody vegetation which follows after shifting cultivation.

forest goods and services
all benefits provided by forests, whether material (such as timber or non-timber forest products) or non-material (such as shade, biodiversity, climate regulation or aesthetic enjoyment).

forest health
a characteristic of forests that are naturally resilient to damage, based on factors such as biological diversity and ecosystem stability.

forest practices
any forest management activity applied directly to forest land, including silvicultural and harvesting treatments.

Forest Principles
the non-legally binding set of principles for managing forests which emerged from the 1992 Earth Summit. Despite calls to make these principles legally binding, governments only reached agreement on adopting them as voluntary measures. The Principles were therefore published separately from the text contained in Agenda 21.

forest products
all timber and non-timber goods derived from forests.

forest sector
that group comprising all direct stakeholders in the forest resource.

forest tenure
ownership or other claims to forest lands, trees or their usufruct (use rights).

forestry
the science and vocation of forest management. Traditionally regarded as a mostly technical endeavor, forestry is now broadening to include more political elements.

fragmented forest
a patchwork forest, in which forest cover still comprises most of the total area. (Usually includes many forests fragmented by logging or moderate clearing for agriculture.)

Framework Convention on Climate Change
the agreement signed at the 1992 Earth Summit at Rio under which climate change is monitored and addressed globally.

fully intact forest ecosystem
a natural forest which remains essentially ecologically unchanged by human activity.

global commons
natural resources which belong primarily to all living beings rather than to individual nations. These are generally considered to include the oceans and outer space. The inclusion of forests in this category is a contentious issue.

global ecological services
the role forests play in regulating global climate, energy and hydrological flows, and other key biophysical functions.

governance
the legal framework and institutions within which decisions are made in a society.

greenhouse gases (GHG)
gases which accumulate in the earth's atmosphere and trap heat. Some are naturally occurring gases, like carbon dioxide. Others are made by humans, such as halocarbons, which in addition to contributing to the greenhouse effect, also contribute to the thinning of the ozone layer.

growing stock
all live trees of commercial species, except rough or rotten trees.

habitat
place or type of site where an organism naturally lives.

hardwood
a broad-leaved or angiosperm tree species, or its wood. (see 'broadleaved forest').

harvesting pattern
the spatial distribution of felled areas and reserve (not felled) areas across the forest landscape.

IFF (Intergovernmental Forum on Forests)
the nineteenth special session of the UN General Assembly held in June 1997 decided to continue the IPFs (see 'IPF') intergovernmental policy dialogue on forests through the establishment of an ad hoc open-ended IFF under the UN Commission of Sustainable Development. The IFF decided at its first meeting in October 1997 in New York that it would meet four times by February or March 2000.

indigenous peoples
as defined by the United Nations and International Labor Organization (Convention 169 concerning indigenous and tribal peoples in independent countries. 1989) are "(a) tribal peoples in independent countries whose social, cultural and economic conditions distinguish them from other sections of the national community and whose status is regulated wholly or partially by their own customs or traditions or by special laws or regulations; (b) peoples in independent countries who are regarded as indigenous on account of their descent from the populations which inhabited the country, or a geographical region to which the country belongs, at the time of conquest or colonisation or the establishment of present state boundaries and who, irrespective of their legal status, retain some or all of

their own social, economic, cultural and political institutions."

industrial roundwood
all unprocessed wood fit for commercial use other than fuelwood.

integrated resource management
the identification and consideration of all values, including the social, economic and environmental, in natural resource management.

intensive forest management (or intensification)
the management of forests to maximise a particular outcome within a given area – usually timber or pulp fibre production.

IPF (Intergovernmental Panel on Forests)
an open-ended ad-hoc body established in 1995 by the UN Commission on Sustainable Development (CSD) to pursue consensus on the management, conservation and sustainable development of all types of forests. The fourth and final session of the IPF was held in February 1997.

Joint forest management (JFM)
a variant of community forestry (see 'community forestry') widely adopted in India for managing government-owned forests in which responsibility and benefits are shared between local user groups and government forestry departments.

Kyoto Protocol
is a treaty negotiated in Kyoto, Japan in 1997 between 159 countries setting out legally binding reduction targets for six greenhouse gases averaging 5% emissions below 1990 levels for industrialised countries between 2008 and 2012.

landscape
the geographical and ecological integrity and resilience of a particular land area, not merely its aesthetic qualities. Landscape is not just a geographical concept, but includes human, cultural, and traditional values that are associated with the land.

landscape management
involves managing an area or region by integrating a variety of values associated with the land that may be ecological, social, cultural or economic.

logging
felling and extraction of wood, especially as logs (excludes fuelwood harvested non-commercially).

modified forest
non-primary, ecologically-altered forest.

monoculture
cultivation of a single species or variety of tree or other plant.

monopoly or oligopoly
an economic arrangement in which one or a few interests capture a disproportionate amount of control over the supply of a resource.

natural forest
a forest composed of indigenous tree species; non-exotic.

non-timber forest products
medicinal plants, resins, mushrooms, rattans, wildlife and other non-wood goods obtained from forests.

old-growth forest
a mature forest, in which a significant proportion of trees are near their maximum age.

open forest
forest with between 10 and 30% tree canopy cover. Includes many savannah, tundra and dry forests.

participatory forest management
forest management in which the decision-making follows from a process of broad public involvement.

plantation
tree crop of one or a few species, usually planted and managed intensively for industrial

wood production, whether timber or fibre. Sometimes, plantations are also managed to produce fuelwood.

planted forest
any forest planted by humankind.

plywood
a composite material made of thin sheets of wood or veneer, glued or bonded together.

policy
a rule or norm usually prescribed by governments to help direct behaviour or decision-making.

precautionary principle
the maxim that prevention is better than cure – where there are threats of serious or irreversible damage, lack of full scientific certainty shall not be used as a reason to postpone action.

primary forest
a forest in a mature succession phase, whose structure and composition have resulted from unrestrained ecological processes rather than from human activity.

private interests
interests of individuals, landowners, communities, corporations, and other groups and stakeholders.

production forest
a forest area primarily designated to achieve economic objectives such as the sustained production of forest products. Forest structure is usually less diverse than a protected forest.

protected forest
a forest area primarily designated to serve ecological, social or cultural objectives. A protected forest is usually more diverse in species and structure than a production forest.

public interest
the broader interest transcending individual or group interest for the good of the whole.

pulp
the liquefied material used for making paper, prepared by chemical or mechanical means from woodchips.

rainforest
tropical or temperate forest growing in regions of high rainfall where the dry season is short or absent, characterised by a high number of plant and animal species and an abundance of climbers and epiphytes.

reforestation
the re-establishment of forests on land which was previously forested. Compare with afforestation.

rotation
planned number of years between establishment of a forest stand and its felling.

roundwood
wood in the rough or natural state, including both industrial roundwood and fuelwood.

sawlogs
logs extracted for sawing into lumber.

sawnwood
lumber.

secondary forest
forest ecosystems that regenerate after substantial natural or human caused disturbances (e.g. flood, fire, extensive logging or slash-and-burn farming), with relatively few mature trees.

selective logging
method of logging that only removes some trees from a forest stand, for instance, commercially important species or certain age classes. Compare with clearcutting.

shelterbelt
strip of trees providing shelter, generally from wind.

shifting cultivation
farming system in which land is periodically cleared, burned, farmed and then returned to fallow.

silviculture
the science and practice of cultivating forest crops.

softwood
a coniferous tree species (conifer), or its wood (see 'coniferous forest').

stumpage
the stumpage value is the difference between timber's market value and the operating and transportation costs necessary to get the wood to a designated market.

stumpage rate
a per unit volume charge paid to governments for wood harvested from public forests.

sustainable development
development that meets the needs of the present without compromising the ability of future generations to meet their own needs. It implies integrating traditional economic concerns with often-ignored social and environmental considerations.

sustainable forest management (sfm)
a process, rather than a fixed state. As such, universal prescriptions are oversimplistic. Elements may include participatory and equitable approaches to decision-making geared toward maintaining ecosystem and landscape functions while also meeting broad economic, social and cultural needs. The management context is all-important.

sustained yield
the yield that a forest can produce continuously at a given intensity of management for a specific set of objectives, as in 'sustained yield management'.

taiga (or boreal forest)
the predominantly coniferous forests growing in the northern climatic zone characterised by short summers and long freezing winters.

temperate forests
forests found in the mid-latitudes, between the tropical and boreal forests.

tenure
ownership or use rights.

timber licence
an agreement that provides for the establishment of timber harvesting rights and, in some cases, management and forest regeneration responsibilities in a prescribed forest area.

timber supply area (tsa)
an area specified by the land owning authority (usually governments) from which timber could be extracted. TSAs generally have a prescribed annual allowable cut.

timber utilisation
the dimensions and quality of wood that are actually cut and removed from an area. Low utilisation generally implies high wastage, and vice versa.

traditional commercial forest management
an approach to forest management focused on the production of industrial wood.

transfer pricing
the practice of placing artificially low export prices on timber sold to foreign subsidiaries or associates, usually for the purpose of avoiding taxes.

tropical dry forest
forest found in tropical regions with low rainfall.

tropical moist forest
forest found in tropical regions with moderate to high rainfall. Includes tropical rainforest and tropical moist deciduous forest. Mostly low-lying, generally closed.

tropical rainforest
evergreen forest situated in the more humid and low-lying parts of the tropical moist for-

est zone. Associated features include high biological diversity, valuable hardwood timbers and poor soils.

wasteland
land that is degraded or less productive than it could be.

watershed
the water catchment area of a river, stream or body of water, and its associated landscape features.

wood
the ligneous material of which tree stems and branches are made.

wood-based panels
includes veneer, plywood, particle board and fibreboard.

woodfuel
fuelwood or charcoal.

wood production
all wood harvested for human use, whether commercially or non-commercially

wood products
all wood-based material used by humankind, including fuelwood and industrial wood.

Annex 2 References

Adams, W.M. 1990.
*Green Development: Environment and Sustainability in the Third World***.** London: Routledge.

Alexandratos, N., ed. 1995.
World agriculture: Towards 2010, an FAO study. Rome: Food and Agriculture Organization.

Anderson, H.W., M.D. Hoover and K.G. Reinhart. 1976.
Forests and water: Effects of forest management on floods, sedimentation, and water supply. Berkeley, CA: U.S. Department of Agriculture Forest Service.

Arnold, J.E.M. 1992.
Community Forestry: Ten Years in Review. Rome: Food and Agriculture Organization.

Barnett Commission. 1989.
Report of the commission of inquiry into aspects of the timber industry in Papua New Guinea. Port Moresby: Government of Papua New Guinea.

Barrow, E.G.C. 1986.
The value of traditional knowledge in present day soil conservation practice: the example of the Pokot and the Turkana. Presented to the Third National Workshop on Soil and Water Conservation, Kenya.

Bass, S., J. Mayers, J. Ahmed, C. Filer, A. Khare, N.I. Kotey, C. Nhira, and V. Watson. 1997.
Policies Affecting Forests and People: Ten Elements that Work. Paper prepared for the Fifteenth Commonwealth Forestry Conference, 12–17 May.

Batt, E.R. 1997.
A forest of her own: SEWA demands. Presented at the Inaugural Feminize Our Forests National Workshop, May. Ahmedabad, India.

BC Environment Report,
British Columbia's Forest Crisis', a discussion paper by Jim Cooperman, Editor, BC Environmental Report

Bie, S., and M.S.Swaminathan. 1996.
Lessons from the green revolution – towards a new green revolution, World Food Summit Technical Background Document. Rome: Food and Agriculture Organization.

British Broadcasting Corporation. 1998.
BBC Homepage, Feb 20, 1998

Calder, I.R. 1996.
Water use by forests at the plot and catchment levels. *Commonwealth Forestry Review,* 75(1), 19–30.

Carrere, R., and L.Lohmann. 1996.
Pulping the South. London, UK: Zed Books.

Chandrasekharan, C. 1996.
Status of financing for sustainable forestry management programmes. *Workshop Report on Financial Mechanisms and Sources of Finance for Sustainable Forestry.* Pretoria, South Africa, June 1996. New York: UNDP.

Chomitz, K., and K.Kumari. 1996.
The domestic benefits of tropical forests: a critical review. London, UK: University of East Anglia and University College, Centre for Social and Economic Research on the Global Environment, Paper 96–19.

CGIAR. 1996.
Annual Report 1996. Consultative Group for International Agricultural Research. Washington, DC: CGIAR Secretariat.

Colchester, M. 1997.
Guyana, fragile frontier. London, UK: Latin American Bureau.

Commission on Global Governance. 1995.
Our global neighbourhood. Oxford, UK: Oxford University Press.
Cooperman, J. 1998.
British Columbia's Forst Crisis, a discussion paper. *BC Environment Report.*
Costanza, R., d'Arge, R., de Groot, R., Farber, S., Grasso M., Hannon, B., Limburg, K, Naeem, S., O'Neill r. V., Paruelo J., Raskin R. G., Sutton, P., and M.van den Belt. 1997.
The value of the world's ecosystem services and natural capital. *Nature* 387 (6630): 215–230.
Daly, H. 1993.
From empty-world economics to full-world economics: a historical turning point in economic development. In *World forests for the future.* K. Ramakrishna and G. M. Woodwell, eds., New Haven, CT: Yale University Press.
Day, B. 1997.
Economic distortions and their influence on forests. London, UK: Centre for Social and Economic Research on the Global Environment.
Desa, A. 1998.
The Prospects for an International Environmental Agreement on Forests. *International Environmental Affairs* Vol 10 No.1, Winter 1998.
Earth Council. 1996.
Subsidizing unsustainable development. San José, Costa Rica: Earth Council.
EC-UN/ECE. (European Commission - United Nations/Economic Commission for Europe) 1995. 1996. 1997.
Forest condition in Europe. Published under the auspices of the Convention on Long-Range Transboundary Air Pollution, Brussels/Geneva: EC-UN/ECE.
EEPSEA. (Economy and Environment Program for SE Asia) website
http://www.idrc.org.sg./eepsea/specialrept/specreptIndofire.htm
Evans, J. 1992.
Plantation forestry in the tropics. Oxford, UK: Clarendon Press.
FAO. (Food and Agriculture Organization of the United Nations) 1995.
Forest resources assessment 1990 – global synthesis. FAO Forestry Paper 124. Rome: FAO.
FAO. 1996.
Forest resources assessment 1990: Survey of tropical forest cover and study of change processes. FAO Forestry Paper 130. Rome: FAO.
FAO. 1997.
State of the world's forests 1997. Rome: FAO.
FAOSTAT website
http://apps.fao.org/cgi-bin/nph-db.pl?subset=forestry
Forest Ecosytem Management Assessment Team. 1993.
Forest ecosystem management: An ecological, economic, and social assessment. Report of the Forest Ecosystem Management Assessment Team. July 1993. USDA Forest Service and other federal agencies.
Friends of the Earth. 1997.
Green Scissors 1997 Report. Washington D.C.: Friends of the Earth.
Gillis, A.M. 1990.
The new forestry: An ecosystem approach to land management. *BioScience*, 40 (8): 558–562.
Gimbarzevsky, P. 1988.
Mass wasting on the Queen Charlotte Islands: A regional inventory. Land Management Report 29. Vancouver: British Columbia Ministry of Forests.
Glaeser, B 1984.
Ecodevelopment in Tanzania: An Empirical Contribution on Needs, Self-sufficiency and Environmentally Sound Agriculture on Peasant Farms. Berlin: Mouton.
Glaeser, B and V. Vyasulu. 1984.
The Obsolescence of Ecodevelopment? In *Ecodevelopment: Concepts, Projects, Strategies,* B. Glaeser, ed. Oxford: Pergammon Press, pp. 22–36.

Globe and Mail. 1998.
Smokey the Bear not altogether right', *Globe and Mail*, 8 May 1998.

Gonzales, P. 1997.
Dynamics of Biodiversity and Human Carrying Capacity in the Senegal Sahel. PhD dissertation. California, USA: University of California, Berkeley.

Government of British Columbia. 1997.
Vanderhoof Land and Resource Management Plan, January 1997.

Government of India, 1997.
Ministry of Finance Discussion Paper on Subsidies, prepared by National Institute of Public Finance, New Delhi, India.

Gregersen, H..M., Arnold, J.E.M., Lundgren, A.L. and A. Contreras-Hermosilla. 1995.
Valuing forests: context, issues and guidelines, p.15. FAO Forestry Paper 127, Rome: FAO.

Guggenheim, D.E. 1997.
Management of Forest Fires to Maximise Carbon Sequestration in Temperate and Boreal Forests, reviewed in World Resources Review, 9(1), March 1997. Washington, DC: World Resources Institute.

Hansen, K. G., ed. 1994.
Making budgets green. Winnipeg, Canada: International Institute for Sustainable Development.

Heywood, V.H. 1995
Global Biodiversity Assessment. Cambridge: Cambridge University Press.

Houghton, R. A. 1998.
Forest and the Warming of the Earth. In *Forests in a full world.* G.M. Woodwell, ed. Report of the Scientific Committee, World Commission on Forests and Sustainable Development. (in draft).

International Alliance of Indigenous Tribal Peoples of the Tropical Forests, Indigenous Peoples' Organizations of the Amazon Basin (COICA) and OPIAC. 1996.
Leticia Declaration. International Meeting of Indigenous and Other Forest Dependent Peoples on the Management, Conservation and Sustainable Development of All Types of Forests. Leticia, Colombia, December.

ICRAF. (International Centre for Research in Agro-Forestry) 1998.
More People, More Trees – The Future of Trees is on Farm in Africa. Paper by P.A.Sanchez, A. J. Simons, F.M. Place, M.G. Walsh, F.J.C. Chandler, C.A. Palm, P.K. Konuche, and R. Kindt, Nairobi, October 1998: ICRAF

IFPRI. (International Food Policy Research Institute) 1996.
Feeding the world, preventing poverty, and protecting the earth: a 2020 vision. Washington, DC: IFPRI.

International Herald Tribune. 1997.
International Herald Tribune, 17 Dec. 1997.

International Model Forest Network Secretariat, International Development Research Centre, Ottawa, Canada.
http://www.idrc.ca/imfn

IISD. (International Institute for Sustainable Development) 1996.
The World Trade Organization and sustainable development: An independent assessment. Winnipeg, Canada: IISD.

IPCC. (Intergovernmental Panel on Climate Change). 1996.
Climate Change 1995. Impacts, Adaptations and Mitigation of Climate Change: Scientific–Technical Analysis. Cambridge: Cambridge University Press.

ISO 14061. 1998.
Information to Assist Forestry Organizations in the Use of ISO 14001 and ISO 14004. Geneva, Switzerland: International Organization of Standardization.

Iwokrama. (Iwokrama International Centre for Rainforest Conservation and Development. 1998.
Personal Communication.

IUCN. (The World Conservation Union). 1980.
World Conservation Strategy. Gland, Switzerland: IUCN.
IUCN. 1996. *1996*
IUCN red list of threatened animals. Gland, Switzerland: IUCN.
IUCN. 1997. 1996
IUCN red list of threatened plants. Gland, Switzerland: IUCN.
Jeffery, R 1997.
Organizing Sustainability: NGOs and Joint Forest Management Agreements in India. Centre for South Asian Studies, University of Edinburgh, Edinburgh.
King, G. C., Hobley, M., and D. A. Gilmour. 1990.
Management of forests for local use in the hills of Nepal: Towards the development of participatory forest management. *Journal of World Forest Resource Management,* 5(1): 1–13.
Kitching, G. 1982.
Development and Underdevelopment in Historical Perspective: Populism, Nationalism, and Industrialism. London, Methuen.
Krishnaswamy, A 1995.
Sustainable Development and Community Forestry Management in Bihar, India. *Society and Natural Resources* 8: 339–350.
Ludwig, D., Hilborn, R., and C. Walters. 1993.
Uncertainty, resource exploitation and conservation: Lessons from history. *Science* 260(5104): 17.
MacNeill, J. 1996.
Keynote Address. *Workshop on Financial Mechanisms and Sources of Finance for Sustainable Forestry*, Pretoria, South Africa, June 1996. New York: UNDP.
Maini, J. 1996.
Keynote Speech. *Proceedings of the International Conference on Certification and Labeling of Products from Sustainably Managed Forests,* 26–31 May 1996, Brisbane, Australia.
Nepstad, D.C., Verissimo, A., Alencar, A., Nobre, C. Lima, E., Lefevre, P., Schlesinger, P., Potter, C., Moutinho, P., Cochrane., M., and V. Brooks. (in press)
Large scale impoverishment of Amazonian forests by logging and fire. *Nature.*
New Economics Foundation. 1997.
New Economics Foundation Magazine, Issue 44, Winter 1997. London: New Economics Foundation.
National Research Council. 1989.
Lost Crops of the Incas: little known plants of the Andes with promise for worldwide cultivation. Report of an ad-hoc Panel of the Advisory Committee on Technology Innovation, Board on Science and Technology for International Development, National Research Council, USA. Washington, DC: National Academy Press.
Overbay, J. C. 1992.
Ecosystem management. In *Proceedings of the National Workshop: Taking an Ecological Approach to Management.* Washington, DC: US Department of Agriculture Forest Service.
Pearce, D. W. 1998.
Can non-market values save the tropical forests? In *Tropical rain forest: a wider perspective.* B. Goldsmith, ed. London: Chapman & Hall.
Pearce, D. W. 1994.
Assessing the social rate of return from investment in temperate zone forestry. In *Cost-benefit analysis.* R. Layard, and S. Glaister, eds. Cambridge: Cambridge University Press.
Persson, R. 1998.
Paper prepared for Swedish International Development Agency. Unpublished.
Poffenberger, M and B. McGean (eds.). 1994.
Policy Dialogue on Natural Forest Regeneration and Community Management. Research Network Report No. (April). Honolulu: Asia Sustainable Forest Management Network.
Reid, W.V. 1994.
The Economic Realities of Biodiversity. In *Issues in Science and Technology* 10 (2): 48–55.

Reitbergen, S. 1997.
Project proposal for IUCN – The World Conservation Union. Unpublished.

Repetto, R. 1993.
Government policies, economics and the forest sector. In *World forests for the future.* K. Ramakrishna and G. M. Woodwell, eds. New Haven, CT: Yale University Press.

Rotherham, T. 1998.
The Forest Industry Applies Sustainable Forest Management Principles. Background paper prepared for WCFSD Secretariat. Montreal, QC. Canadian Pulp and Paper Association.

Sachs, I. 1979.
Ecodevelopment: A Definition. *Ambio* 8 (2/23): 113.

Sharma, N. P. (ed.) 1992.
Managing the world's forests: Looking for the balance between conservation and development. Dubuque, Iowa: Kendall/Hunt.

Shaxson, F. 1997.
Better Land Husbandry: Re-thinking Approaches to Land Improvement and the Conservation of Water and Soil. Natural Resources Perspectives, No. 19. London: ODI.

Shell International. 1995.
The evolution of the world's energy system 1860–2060. Extracts of a study. London, UK: Shell International.

Shepard, G., Shanks, E., and M. Hobley. 1993.
Management of tropical and sub-tropical dry forests. In *Earthscan Reader in Tropical Forestry.* S. Rietbergen, ed. London: Earthscan.

Shvidenko, A. and S. Nilsson. 1996.
Expanding forests but declining mature coniferous forests in Russia. International Institute of Applied Systems Analysis Working Paper WP-6-59. Laxenburg, Austria: International Institute of Applied Systems Analysis.

Singh, K.D., and A. Marzoli. 1995.
Deforestation trends in the tropics: a time series analysis. Paper presented at *Conference on Potential Impact of Climatic Change on Tropical Forests*, April 1995. San Juan, Puerto Rico: World Wide Fund for Nature..

Slocombe, D. S. 1993.
Implementing ecosystem-based management, *BioScience* 43(9): 612–622.

Solberg, B., Brooks, D.,Pajuoja, H., Peck, T.J., and P.A. Wardle. 1996.
Long-term trends and prospects in world supply and demand for wood and implications for sustainable forest management. Joensuu, Finland: European Forest Institute and Norwegian Forest Research Institute.

Third International Forestry Roundtable. 1997.
Discussion draft. Concepcion, Chile, January.

UNCED. (United Nations Conference on Environment and Development). 1992.
Non-legally binding authoritative statement of principles for a global consensus on the management, conservation, and sustainable development of all types of forests (The Forest Principles). New York: United Nations.

United Nations. 1996.
World population prospects. The 1996 Revision (draft). New York: United Nations.

UNDP. (United Nations Development Program) 1997a.
Forest management to support sustainable livelihoods. UNDP Project Document GLO/96/104/E/11/31. Unpublished. .

UNDP. 1997b.
Energy After Rio: Prospects and challenges. New York: UNDP.

UNDP. 1998.
Human Development Report, 1998. Oxford, UK: Oxford University Press

UN/ECE. (United Nations Economic Commission for Europe) 1998.
Convention on Access to Information, Public Participation in Decision-making and Access to Justice in Environmental Matters, June 1998.

Upton, C., and S. Bass. 1995.
The forest certification handbook. London, UK: Earthscan.

USA Today.
Foresters meet resistance to plan for intentional fires', 19 May 1998.

USDA. (United States Department of Agriculture) 1997.
Forest Service admits logging losses. Associated Press, redistributed by ENN Daily News, 24 Nov. 1997.

Vincent, J. R. 1990.
Rent capture and the feasibility of tropical forest management. *Land Economics* 66(2): 212–223.

WCED. (World Commission on Environment and Development – The Brundtland Commission) 1987.
Our Common Future. Report of the WCED. Oxford: Oxford University Press.

Wilson, E. O. 1992.
The diversity of life. Cambridge, MA: Belknap Press.

Wilson, A. 1998.
Environmental Building News, Jul–Aug 98.

Wolfensohn, J.D and K.S. Fuller, 1998.
'Saving Our Trees of Life', *The Washington Post*, 26 May 1998.

Woodwell, G. M., ed. 1990.
The Earth in transition: Patterns and processes of biotic improvement. Cambridge: Cambridge University Press.

Woodwell, G. M. ed. (in draft).
Forests in a full world. Report of the Scientific Committee, WCFSD.

Woodwell, G. M. and F. T. Mackenzie (eds.). 1997
Biotic Feedbacks in the Global Climatic System: Will the Warming Feed the Warming? 1995. London: Oxford University Press.

World Bank. 1998
No Forest without Management. Paper issued by a consultation arranged by the World Bank, 2–7 October 1998, at Graves Mountain Lodge, Syria, Virginia, USA

WCFSD/WHRC. (World Commission on Forests and Sustainable Development/ Woods Hole Research Center). 1998.
Global Forest Capital: proposed scientific and policy initiative (in draft), June 1998.

WCMC/IUCN/WWF. (World Conservation Monitoring Centre/IUCN – The World Conservation Union/World Wide Fund for Nature). 1998.
World List of Threatened Trees, 1998. Gland, Switzerland: IUCN.

WRI. (World Resources Institute) 1992.
World Resources, 1992–93: a report by the World Resources Institute. Oxford: Oxford University Press.

WRI. 1996.
World Resources, 1996–97: a guide to the global environment. Oxford: Oxford University Press.

WRI. 1997. Bryant, D., D. Nielsen, and L. Tangley
The last frontier forests. Washington, DC: World Resources Institute.

WRI. 1998.
World resources 1998–99: a guide to the global environment. Oxford: Oxford University Press.

Worldwatch Institute. 1997.
News release, 23 April 1997. Washington, DC:Worldwatch Institute.

Worldwatch Institute. 1998.
State of the world 1998. Washington, DC: Worldwatch Institute.

Annex 3 Credits

Photographs

(page)
1 H.J. Burkard/First Light
28 upper Joanna B. Pinneo/Aurora
28 lower R. Charbonneau/IDRC
29 CIDA Photo/Virginia Boyd
31 CIDA Photo/Pierre St. Jacques
33 CIDA Photo/Michel Faugère
39 Denis Marchand/IDRC
45 CIDA Photo/Roger LeMoyne
47 CIDA Photo/Hélène Tremblay
53 Nicholas Kristof/NYT Pictures
64 Stephanie Colvey/IDRC
66 Sherman Hines/Masterfile
75 IDRC/5364
79 CIDA Photo/Roger LeMoyne
86 IDRC/3849
91 Jan Toye Johannson/Masterfile
93 Ron Watts/First Light
94 Jan Toye Johannson/Masterfile
96 CIDA Photo/Michel Faugère
97 U.S. National Oceanic and Atmospheric Administration (NOAA)
100 CIDA Photo/Roger LeMoyne
101 CIDA Photo/Hélène Tremblay
105 Denis Sing/IDRC
107 C. Mayo/IDRC
111 CIDA Photo/Michael Wild
113 CIDA Photo/Dilip Mehta
115 CIDA Photo/David Mowbray
116 Joanna B. Pinneo/Aurora
119upper CIDA Photo/Roger LeMoyne
119lower Miles Ertman/Masterfile
121 Lloyd Sutton/Masterfile
126 Denis Marchand/IDRC
131 Mike Macri/Masterfile
133 Neil McKee/IDRC
150 J.A. Kaulis/Masterfile
151 Mike Macri/Masterfile
165 upper CIDA Photo/Pierre St. Jacques
165 middle CIDA Photo/Stephen Homer
165 lower CIDA Photo/Patricio Baeza

Background photographs for figures

7 CIDA Photo/Roger LeMoyne
43 CIDA photos
115 CIDA Photo/David Mowbray
148 (6.3) Ed Gifford/Masterfile
148 (6.4) CIDA Photo/Brian Atkinson
149 (6.7) Eastcott & Momatiuk/Masterfile
149 (6.9) CIDA Photo/Patricio Baeza

Book design and DTP

John Cropper

Cover design and figure illustrations

Ian Darragh Communications

Annex 4 Contributors

Members and advisers of the Organising Committee

The Organizing Committee met twice. The first meeting was held in Ottawa, Canada, in November 1994 at the invitation of IDRC and hosted by its President, Dr. Keith Bezanron. The second and final meeting at which a Work Plan and a Proposed Agenda were adopted was held in New Delhi in April 1995 at the invitation of the Indian Government and hosted by its Minister of Forests and Environment, Mr. Kamal Nath.

Kazuo Aichi, Member of Parliament, Former Minister of the Environmental, Japan
Hans d'Orville, Coordinator, InterAction Council (UN), USA
José Goldemberg, Professor, Former Minister of Education, Environment, Health, Science and Technology, Brazil
Razali Ismail, Ambassador to the UN, Chairman of the UN Commission on Sustainable Development, Malaysia
Ashok Khosla, Development Alternatives, India
Michael Tabong Kima, Ambassador, Former Minister of Mines and Power, Cameroon
Jim MacNeill, Secretary General, World Commission on Environment and Development
Jag S. Maini, Assistant Deputy Minister, Forest Environment, Forestry Canada, Canada
Christian Mersmann, Coordinator TWRP, Chair of Forestry Advisors Group, Germany
Olusegun Obasanjo, Former President of Nigeria, Nigeria
Kilaparti Ramakrishna, Director, The Woods Hole Research Center, USA
Shridath Ramphal, Former Commonwealth Secretary General, Guyana
Eneas Salati, Secretariat of Science and Technology, Brazil
Emil Salim, Professor, Former Minister of State for Population and Environment, Indonesia
Maurice Strong, Secretary General, United Nations Conference on Environment and Development (UNCED), Canada
Ola Ullsten, Ambassador, Former Prime Minister and Foreign Minister of Sweden
Alvaro Umaña, President of INACEA, Former Minister of Mines, Energy, and Natural Resources, Costa Rica
Nikolay N. Vorontsov, Member of Parliament, Former Minister of Environment, Russia
George M. Woodwell, President and Director, The Woods Hole Research Center, USA
Bernardo Zentilli, Senior Forestry Adviser, UNCED, Chile

Financial Contributors

Canada
CIDA
IDRC
IISD
Ministry of Foreign Affairs

European Union
The European Commission

Indonesia
Government of Indonesia

International Organisations
African Development Bank
Asian Development Bank
Inter-American Development Bank
UNDP

Japan
Ministry of Environment
Ministry of Foreign Affairs
Nippon Foundation
JFGE

Korea
Government of Korea

Netherlands
Ministry of Development Cooperation
Ministry of Forestry

Norway
Ministry of Environment

Sweden
Ministry of Foreign Affairs
SAREC (now part of SIDA)
Skogsindustrierna

UK
ODA

USA
Ford Foundation
MacArthur Foundation
State Department
US AID

Contributions through Woods Hole Research Centre

The John Merck Fund financed a scientific conference at the Woods Hole Research Center which started the process of establishing an independent commission on forest issues. Before the Commission could establish its own Secretariat, activities such as preparing for the meetings of the Organising Committee, fundraising, assisting in the recruitment of members to serve on the Commission, etc., were coordinated and partly financed by The Woods Hole Research Center, Massachusetts, USA. Financial support for these initial activities was received from the Homeland Foundation, The Gap Foundation, The San Francisco Foundation, German Federal Ministry for Economic Cooperation and Development, International Development Research Centre, Swedish Agency for Research Cooperation, United Nations Development Programme, The MacArthur Foundation, The Pew Charitable Trusts, Rockerfeller Brothers Fund, W. Alton Jones Foundation, and the United States Department of Agriculture Forest Service.
Dr K. Ramakrishna assisted by Research Assistant Linda Jacobsen, had the main responsibility for those activities. Dr. Ramakrishna remained a Special Advisor to the Commission's two co-chairmen throughout the work of the Commission.

Staff

June 1995 – January 1998

John S. Spears, Secretary General
Arnoldo Contreras, Forest Resource Economist
Ameena Dennis, Personal Assistant
Sara Brownlow, Secretary
Gunnar Larson, Personal Assistant

Since February 1998

Ajit Krishnaswamy, Researcher, Project Coordinator for follow up activities, IISD
Victoria Kellett, Special Projects Officer, IISD
Jacqueline Pilon, Administrative Assistant, IISD

Institutions

The Commission and its staff interacted with many more institutions than the ones listed below. Institutions that contributed written submissions to the Commission or supplied the Commission with facts and figures are in the hundreds. The following list contains those institutions with whom the Commission stood in regular contact during special phases of its work or throughout its duration.

First Nations Environmental Network
FAO, Forestry Department, Rome, Italy
Business Council for Sustainable Development, Geneva, Switzerland
CIFOR, Bogor, Indonesia
COAMA, Bogota, Columbia
Desertification Secretariat, Geneva, Switzerland
Environmental Defense Fund, New York, USA
Forest Stewardship Council
The Forest Adviser Group, Frankfurt, Germany
GLOBE International, Brussels, Belgium
ICRAF, Nairobi, Kenya
IDRC, Ottawa, Canada
IIED, London, United Kingdom
IISD, Winnipeg, Canada
INBio, San José, Costa Rica
International Fund For Animal Welfare
IPF/IFF Secretariat, United Nations, New York
ITTO, Yokohama, Japan
IUCN, Gland, Switzerland
Japanese Tropical Forest Action Network
KEHAI, Jakarta, Indonesia
M.S. Swaminathan Research Foundation, Chennai, India
Model Forest Programme, Ottawa, Canada
Mount Cameroon Project, Cameroon
ODA, London, United Kingdom
Onadef, Yaoundé, Cameroon
SIDA, Stockholm, Sweden
SAREC, Stockholm, Sweden
Skogsindustrierna, Stockholm, Sweden

Sustainible Development Institute, Washington, DC
Tacis, St. Petersburg, Russia
UNDP, New York, USA
UNEP, Nairobi, Kenya
UNEP, Geneva, Switzerland
Woods Hole Research Center, MA, USA
The World Bank, Washington, DC, USA
WRI, Washington, DC, USA
WWF, Gland, Switzerland

Resource Persons

Support and advice were given by many more people than the ones listed below. This group is chosen because they all attended one or several of the Commission's meetings (8 in all) or otherwise stood in regular contact with the Commission and its staff.

Valter Angell, Institute for Foreign Policy, Norway
Mike Apsey, Council of Forest Industries, Canada
Michael Arnold, UK
Steven Bass, IIED, UK
William H. Banzaf, Society of American Foresters, USA
Joseph Besong, Mount Cameroon Project, Cameroon
David Brown, ODA, UK
Neil Byron, CIFOR, Indonesia
Joji Carino, Int. Alliance of the Indigenous Tribal Peoples of the Tropical Forests,
Andrea Claudia, Sustainable Development Institute, USA
Marcus Colchester, Forest People Programme, UK
Indrajit Coomaraswamy, Commonwealth Secretariat, UK
John Cropper, Trinidad and Tobago
Hans d'Orville, UNDP, New York, USA
Brett Day, Center for Social and Economic Research on the Global Environment, UK
Cris Elliot, WWF, Gland, Switzerland
Victoria Kellet, IISD, Winnipeg, Canada
Guy de Lusignan, Transparency International, Washington DC, USA
Lennart Ljungman, FAO, Rome, Italy
Moh Garba, Secretary General African Timber Organization, Gabon
Don Gilmour, IUCN, Gland, Switzerland
Hans Gregersen, University of Minnesota, College of Natural Resources, USA
Mikael Grut, Consultant, UK
Narul Emmy Hafild, Wahana Lingkungen Hidpu, Indonesia
Claes Hall, Aracruz, Brazil
Karl Hansen, IISD, Canada
Matt Heering, Consultant, The Netherlands
Martin von Hildebrand, COAMA, Colombia
Vineta Hoon, M.S. Swaminathan Research Foundation, India
David Humphreys, Open University, UK
Nels Johnson, WRI, Washington DC, USA
Ron Kemp, UK
Brian Kerr, Commonwealth Secretariat, UK
Jim MacNeill, Chairman, IISD
Yolchi Kuroda, Director, Japan Tropical Forest Action Network, Japan
Sergio Madrid, Mexico
Bill Mankin, Global Forest Policy Project, Washington DC, USA
Hollis Murray, Head of the Forestry Department, FAO

George Nagel, British Columbia, Canada
B. Nde, Professor, Secretary General, CIEFE, Cameroon
Norman Myers, Consultant, London. UK
Sten Nilsson, Professor, IIASA, Sweden
Dubois Oliver, IIED, UK
Ellen Permato, Consultant, The Philippines
Mark Poffenberger, University of California, Berkley, California, USA
Kilaparti Ramakrishna, Woods Hole Research Center, Massachusetts, USA
Ralph Roberts, CIDA, Canada
Glevys Rondon, Mine Watch, UK
David Runnalls, Editor of Earth Summit Times, IISD, Canada
Elvira Sancho, INBio, Costa Rica
N. Saxena, National Commission for Minorities, India
Jeff Sayer, CIFOR, Bogor, Indonesia
Ralph Schmidt, UNDP, New York
Gill Shepard, ODI, UK
Nigel Sizer, WRI, USA
H. L. Stoll, Hinrich Feldmeyer GmbH & Co., Germany
Roger Stone, Sustainable Development Institute, Washington DC, USA
Peter Stratten, Stratten & Associates, South Africa
Fred Swartzendruber, USAid, Washington DC, USA
Anatoly Swidenko, IIASA, Russia
Bai-Mass Taal, UNEP, Kenya
Kees van Dijk, National Center for Nature Management, The Netherlands
Wouter Veening, Plantage Middenlaan, The Netherlands
Anders Wijkman, Assistant Administrator, UNDP
Stefan Witén, Skogsindustrierna, Sweden
Wolvekamp, 'Both Ends', Denmark

Participants in the Commission's public hearings

Of the five Public Hearings that the Commission organised the one in Jakarta for the Asia Region and the one in Winnipeg for North America were attended by several hundred people. They are not all listed here. The three following hearings were deliberately kept smaller to allow for more dialogue. Most of those attending those hearings would be listed here.

Jakarta, Indonesia, March 1996

Abbas Adhar, President, International Timber Corporation, Indonesia
Maria Adriana, Environment and Forestry Conservation, Jakarta, Indonesia
Herlina Agusti, Islamic Students' Association
Sayed Mudhabar Ahmad, Leuser International Foundation, Indonesia
Nur Amalia, Indonesian Women Association for Justice, Indonesia
M. Ali Basyah Amin, Faculty of Economic, University of Syiah Kuala, Indonesia
Firdos AN, KDM Foundation, Indonesia
Meita Andaru, Kampus Diakoneia Modern Foundation, Indonesia
Kastam Aptasuyanda, Department of Transmigration and Forest Settlement, Indonesia
Diana Awailah K., Islamic Students' Association
Charles Barber, World Resources Institute, The Philippines
Judge Tos Barnett, Deputy President, Administrative Appeals Tribunal, Australia
Morten Bjorner, Danish Timber Trade Federation, Denmark
Dieter Bucher, Asian Development Bank, The Philippines

Arie Budiman, Biology Research and Development Centre – LIPI, Indonesia
Yari Bun, Executive Director, Foundation of the Peoples of the South Pacific, New Guinea
Pius Bwariat, Don Bosco II High School
Jeff Campbell, Ford Foundation, India
Barney Chan, Sarawat Timber Association, Malaysia
Debashsih Chatterjee, JUNGLEES, India
Sonali Chowdhuri, IBRAD, India
Norlela Abde Dapa, Kampus Diakoneia Modern Foundation, Indonesia
Asril Darussamin, Plantation Biotechnology Research Centre, Indonesia
Natallia K. Deuxiemi, Agricultural Institute of Bogor
Helmi Ratna Dewi, Faculty of Forestry, Agricultural Institute of Bogor, Indonesia
Upik Djalins, Ekolabel Agency of Indonesia
Yohanes Dogopia, Students Communication Forum of Irian Jaya, Indonesia
James Douglas, World Bank, Washington D.C.
Phil Erari, Irian Jaya Human Rights National Awareness Forum, Indonesia
Krishna Ghimire, UNRISD, Switzerland
Tiurmaida A. Carolina Gulton, Students' Association of Forest Resources Conservation (HIMAKOVA), Faculty of Forestry, Agricultural Institute of Bogor, Indonesia
Kim Nam Gyun, Chief, Forestry Administration, Korea
Narul Emmy Hafild, Wahana Lingkungan Hidup Indonesia (WALHI)
Jorgen Hansen, Nordic Consulting Group, Norway
Bambang Tri Hartono, Department of Forestry, Indonesia
Bob Hassan, Indonesia
Max Henderson, Pacific Heritage Foundation, New Guinea
John Hendrik V., Legal and Organization Bureau, Department of Forestry, Indonesia
Korinna Horta, Environmental Defense Fund, USA
Siver Hutabarat, Directorate of Program Management – Directorate General of Forest Management, Department of Forestry, Indonesia
Nobuo Ichihara, Deputy Director, Environment Agency of Japan, Japan
R. Anwar Ishwan, Leuser International Foundation, Indonesia
Hira Jhamtani, Director, KONPHALINDO, Indonesia
Kosasi Kadir, Department of Forestry, Indonesia
Heradi Kartowisastro, National Standardization Board – LIPI, Indonesia
Hans E. Kawulusan, Strategic Studies Agency, Indonesia
John Edy Kennedy, Setia Budi Utama Foundation, Indonesia
Widya Kentjana, Ekolabel Agency of Indonesia
M. S. Kismadi, Sustainable Development Foundation, Indonesia
Padmi Kramadibrata, Department of Biology, University of Indonesia, Indonesia
Kusubandio, Department of Transmigration and Forest Settlement, Indonesia
Sarwono Kusumaatmadja, Minister of Environment, Indonesia
Piare Lal, Bhadrachalam Paper Boards Ltd., India
Darmawan Liswanto, Titian Foundation, Indonesia
Abu Hanifah Lubis, Titian Foundation, Indonesia
Frida Lumy, Kampus Diakoneia Modern Foundation, Indonesia
Amri Marzali, Faculty of Social and Political Sciences, University of Indonesia, Indonesia
S. T. Mok, Timber Trade Federation, Malaysia
Sandra Monlaga, Wahana Lingkungan Hidup Indonesia (WALHI)
Muflizar, National University, Indonesia
K. Mulyadi, Students' Association of Forest Resource Conservation (HIMAKOVA), Faculty of Forestry, Agricultural Institute of Bogor, Indonesia
S. H. Munarman, Palembang Legal Aid Agency, Indonesia
N. Mundu, Indian Confederation of Indigenous & Tribal Peoples, India
Silvanus Ngampun, Masyarakat Adat Benuaq/Bina Benua Puti Jaji Foundation, Indonesia
A. Munir Oesman, Department of Industry and Trade, Indonesia

Keiko Ohmori, Environment Agency, Japan
Bishnu Hari Pandit, Executive Director, Nepal Agroforestry Foundation, Nepal
Ihutan Pane, Student Solidarity Forum of Medan, Indonesia
Prof. Jaganath Pathy, South Gujarat University, India
Fitra Jaya Piliang, Adil Sejahtera Foundation, Indonesia
Philip Pupuka, Development Services Exchange, Solomon Islands
Aryanto Purwadi, Strategic Planning Division, BNI Bank, Indonesia
Hardjono Purwandono, Bina Usaha Lingkungan Foundation, Indonesia
Haryanto R. Putro, Agricultural Institute of Bogor, Indonesia
Sumerham Rambe, Centre for Political Studies and Public Advocacy, Indonesia
Widodo S. Ramono, PHPA Directorate General, Department of Forestry, Indonesia
Kanok Rerkasem, Chiang Mai University, Thailand
Mohammad Rifaat, Studi Tanah Air Foundation, Indonesia
Nin Rismini, Resources Development Centre, Indonesia
M. Eko Rudianto, Department of Transmigration and Forest Settlement, Directorate General of Housing and Environment – Program Management, Indonesia
Intan Ruwaidah, Konsumen Hijau Indonesia Foundation, Indonesia
Parkas Sagala, Banjar Baru Reforestation Technology Bureau, Indonesia
Iwan Fuad Salim, Ekolabel Agency of Indonesia, Indonesia
Do Dinh Sam, Director, Research Centre for Forest Ecology and the Environment, Vietnam
Melkianus Y. Samon, Kampus Diakoneia Modern Foundation, Indonesia
Richard Sandbrook, Director, IIED, UK
Yanto Santosa, Faculty of Forestry, Agricultural Institute of Bogor, Indonesia
Ibnu Sanyoto, Directorate of Multilateral Economic Cooperation, Department of Foreign Affairs, Indonesia
Didin Sastrapradja, Indonesian People's Advisory Assembly/Indonesian Legislative Assembly, Indonesia
Cherla Sastry, IDRC, India
Amalinda Savirani, Gadjah Mada University, Indonesia
Iskandar Sembiring, Regional Studies and Community Development Centre, Indonesia
Ranil Senanayake, Co-Executive Director, ELCI/NSRC (Sri Lanka), Kenya
Agus Setyarso, Faculty of Forestry, Gadjah Mada University, Indonesia
Soeyitno Soedirman, APHI, University of Mulawarman, Indonesia
Tafakurrozak Soedjo, Indonesian Islamic Intellectuals Association
Soelaksono, IUC Life Sciences Organization, Institute of Technology of Bandung, Indonesia
Mohamad Soerjani, National Research Board, Indonesia
Soesatyo, Department of Forestry, Indonenisa
Solagratia Slumy, Kampus Diakoneia Modern Foundation, Indonesia
H.L. Stoll, Hinrich Feldmeyer GmbH & Co., France
Subagyo, Department of Industry and Trade, Indonesia
Subardi, Pengembangan Akhlaq Mulia Foundation, Indonesia
Enny Sudarmonowati, Biology Research and Development Centre – LIPI, Indonesia
Sudiarto, Herbal and Medicinal Plant Research Bureau, Indonesia
Otto Sumarwoto, former Executive Director of BSCD, Indonesia
Winks Sutton, Chief Executive, Fletcher Challenge Forests, New Zealand
Achmad Sumitro, Faculty of Forestry, Gadjah Mada University, Indonesia
Djamaludin Suryohadikusumo, Minister of Forestry, Indonesia
Usep Sutisna, Biology Research and Development Centre – LIPI, Indonesia
M. Hassan Su'ud, Leuser International Foundation, Indonesia
Tan Keng Tong, Asian Agri, Indonesia
Prasert Trakansuphakon, IMPECT, Thailand
Sugeng Triutomo, Board of Technology Research and Development, Indonesia
John Valentine, Ministry of Forestry, New Zealand
Jalada Vokta, India

Odius Wanimbo, Kampus Diakoneia Modern Foundation, Indonesia
Sofyan P. Warsito, Faculty of Forestry, Gadjah Mada University, Indonesia
Lis Wibisono, Standardization Centre – LIPI, Indonesia
Bambang Widianto, Resources and Environment, University of Indonesia, Indonesia
Danoer Doro Widyawan, Patra Pala Foundation, Indonesia
Hisar Wijaya, Faculty of Economic, University of Indonesia
Damianus Wilil, Kampus Diakoneia Modern Foundation, Indonesia
Eddy Prabowo Witanto, Department of Archeology, University of Indonesia
Yulius Yulianto, KDM Foundation, Indonesia
Ervizal A.M. Zuhud, Faculty of Forestry, Agriculture Institute of Bogor, Indonesia

Winnipeg, Canada, October 1997

Gilbert D. Abraham, Saskeene First Nations, Canada
Emilio Amaro, National Rural Confederation, Mexico
Michael Anderson, Manitoba Keewatinowi Okimakanak, Inc., Canada
Teme-Augama Anishnabai, Canada
Frank Augustine, Friends of Christmas Mountains, Canada
Ralph Archibald, Ministry of Forests, BC, Canada
Michael Arndt, Washington State Fiber Research Team, USA
Silvano Aureoles, Red Mexicana de Organizaciones Campesinas Forestales, Mexico
Bill Banzhaf, Society of American Foresters, USA
Harry Bombay, National Aboriginal Forestry Association, Canada
G.P. Buchert, Genetics of White Pine and Implications for Management & Conservation, Canada
Rosendo Caro, Union Nacional de Organizaciones de Foresteria Comunal, Mexico
Fernando Arenas Casas, Union Nacional de Organizaciones de Foresteria Comunal, Mexico
Victor Sosa Cedillo, Natural Resources and Fisheries, Mexico
Chris Christensen, United Paperworks International Union – Local 1375, Canada
Amelia Clarke, Friends of the Christmas Mountains, Canada
Lindy Clubb, First Nations Env. Network & Indigenous Env. Network, Canada
Adena Cook, Blue Ribbon Coalition, USA
Raul Hernandez Cortez, San Pedro El Alto Zapotec Community, Mexico
Donald Couch, Riverside Forest Products Limited, Canada
Claudia D'Andrea, Sustainable Development Institute, USA
Carol Daly, Flathead Economic Policy Center, USA
Jeff Delaney, Canadian Institute of Forestry, Canada
James Ehnes, University of Manitoba, Canada
Kenneth Emberley, Crossroads Resource Group, Canada
Sam Etapp, Grand Council of the Crees, Canada
Brock Evans, National Audubon Society, USA
Gary Filmon, Premier of Manitoba, Canada
Mary Flanderka, Women for Sustainable Communities, USA
Gloria Flora, USDA, Forest Service, USA
Phil Fontaine, Grand Chief, Assembly of Manitoba Chiefs
Jerry Fontaine, Sagkeeng First Nations, Canada
Grand Chief Phil Fontaine, Assembly of Manitoba Chiefs, Canada
Donald Girton, National Woodland Owners Association, USA
Arlin Hackman, World Wildlife Fund Canada, Canada
Arthur Hanson, IISD
Kevin Hanson, Forest Alliance of BC, Canada
Mike Harcourt, Former Premier of British Columbia, Canada
Joyce Harder, Forest Alliance of British Columbia, Canada
John Heissenbuttel, American Forest and Paper Association, USA
Bill Henderson, Repap Manitoba, Canada

Gustavo Heredia, Chihuahua Model Forest, Mexico
Sandra B. Hill, District of Columbia Government, Department of Public Works, USA
Jennifer Hillard, Consumers Assoc. of Canada, Canada
Arthur Hoole, Manitoba Natural Resources, Canada
Marilyn Hoskins, USA
John F. Hossack, Communities for a Great Northwest, USA
Vicky Husband, Sierra Club of BC, Canada
Tom Isle, Pulp and Paper Workers Resource Councile, USA
Kathleen Jachowski, Communities Forest & Great Northwest, USA
Victoria Santos Jimenez, Organization of Forestry Ejidos of Mayan Zone, Mexico
Ria Julien, Manitoba Eco Network Youth Caucus, Canada
Darrell Keating, The Used Building Materials Association, Canada
Sheila Keller, Communities for a Great Northwest, USA
Michael Kilgore, Minnesota Forest Resources Council, USA
Aaron Koleszar, Youth for Social Justice, Canada
Manju Lodha, Preservation, Peace & Pleasure, Canada
Donald Ludwig, University of British Columbia, Canada
Linn Macdonald, Noranda Forest Inc., Canada
Beni Malone, Save Our River Environments, Canada
Kathryn P. Maloney, Department of Agriculture, USA
George T. Marek, Ontario's Boreal Forest Ecosystem, Canada
Elizabeth May, Sierra Club of Canada, Canada
Hugo Medrano, Calakmul Model Forest/Bosque Modelo de Calakmul, Mexico
Francisco Chapela Mendoza, Estudios Rurales y Asesoria A.C., Mexico
Ovide Mercredi, Assembly of First Nations, Canada
Harry Mesman, Manitoba Federation of Labour, Canada
Kim Lee Morrisseau, Sagkeeng First Nation, Canada
Michael Morton, Share BC, Coalition for Sustainable Development, Canada
Don Motanic, Intertribal Timber Council, USA
Jack Munro, Forest Alliance of British Columbia, Canada
Francis Nepinak, Pine Creek First Nation, Canada
Harvey Nepinak, Waterhen First Nation, Canada
Brian Oborne, Manitoba Conservation Districts Association, Canada
Andreas Obser, Germany
Ellen Pekilis, Canadian Standards Association, Canada
Rita Pimlott, Elder, BC Forests, Canada
Irene Pisanty, Ecosystem Protection, Commission for Environmental Cooperation, Canada
James (Jim) Potton, Manitoba Forestry Association, Canada
William Pruitt, Department of Zoology, University of Manitoba, Canada
David Rapport, University of Guelph, Canada
Shannon Robertson, Consultant, Canada
Gerald A. Rose, Minnesota Department of Natural Resources, USA
Peter Salonius, Canadian Forest Service, Canada
Gerardo Segura, National Autonomous University of Mexico, Mexico
Gerardo Segura, The State of Mexico's Forest Resources Management and Conservation, Mexico
Merran Smith, Sierra Club of BC, Canada
Muriel Smith, United Nations Association in Canada, Canada
Steve M. Smith, Weherhaeuser Canada, Canada
W.D. (Bill) Snell, Pine Falls Paper Company, Canada
Victor Sosa, Perspectivas Gubernamentales, Mexico
Greg Stevens, ILS Consulting, Canada
Karen Stock, University of Manitoba, Canada
Larry Strachan, Manitoba Environment, Canada
William Strong, Pulp & Paperworkers Resource Council, USA

Donald V. Sullivan, Manitoba Future Forest Alliance, Canada
Stephen Tolnai, University of BC, Canada
Robert Tippeconnie, USDA-FS, USA
Warren Ulley, IWA Canada, Canada
Bruce Vincent, Communities for a Great Northwest, USA
David Walker, MP, Winnipeg North Center, Canada
Dan Welsh, Canadian Forest Service, Canada
Don Wesson, Pulp & Paperworkers Resource Councilo, USA
Gaile Whelan-Enns, Endangered Spaces Campaign World Wildlife Fund Canada, Canada
Harvey Williams, Time to Respect Earth's Ecosystems – TREE, Canada
David Walker, Member of Parliament, Canada
Rosalind Wu, Colorado State University, USA

San José, Costa Rica, December 1996

Jesús Alemancia, Congreso General Kuna, Panamá
Valter Angell, Norwegian Institute of International Affairs, Oslo
Marco Vinicio Araya, Fondo Nacional de Financiamientos Forestales, Costa Rica
Jorge Ardila, IICA, Costa Rica
Guillermo Arias, Cooperación en el Sector Forestal y Maderero, Costa Rica
Liliana Arrieta, Defensoría de Habitantes en Asuntos de Medio Ambiente, Costa Rica
Rodrigo Artavia, CANAIMA, Costa Rica
Rocío Ballestero, ECO News, Costa Rica
Jorge Barba, Universidad San Francisco de Quito, Ecuador
Alicia Bárcena, UNEP-ROLAC, Mexico
Carlos Barrera, Smurfit Carton de Colombia, Columbia
Rafael Bejarano, Asociación Indígena Guaymí, Costa Rica
Edgardo Benítez, Federación Tawanka de Honduras, Honduras
Rafael Bolaños, Centro Científico Tropical, Costa Rica
Leopoldo Garcia Brandao, Founder of Aracruz Foresteral, Brazil
Vincente Brecklaire, European Commission, Belgium
Carlos Brenes, Programa Bosques, Arboles y Comunidades, Costa Rica
Oscar Brenes, CATIE/WWF, Costa Rica
Gerardo Budowski, Universidad para la Paz, Costa Rica
Ronnie de Camino, Universidad para la Paz, Argentina
José Joaquín Campos, Manejo de Bosques Naturales, CATIE, Costa Rica
Carlos Marx Carneiro, INEFAN, Ministerio de Agricultura y Ganadería, Ecuador
Sesto Chauque, ORIAWA, Argentina
Eugenia Ponce de Leon Chaux, Columbia
Alberto Chinchilla, CICAFO, Mexico
Hector Cisneros, Cámara Nacional Forestal, Perú
Thomas M. Clonts, Ston Forestal, Costa Rica
Juan Fernando Cordero, La Nación, Costa Rica
Juan Carlos Cruz, OTS/Esta Semana, Costa Rica
Maria de Lourdes de Freitas, Brazil
Roberto Delmastro, Forestal Valdivia S.A., Chile
Keister Evans, Tropical Forest Foundation, USA
Luis Ferraté, Banco Interamericano de Desarrollo, Costa Rica
Denis Fraser, Barama Company Ltd., Guyana
María de Freitas, Brazil
Rosendo Caro Gómez, Unión Nacional de Forestería, Mexico
Reynaldo González Segura, Asociación de Desarrollo Bribri de Talamanca, Costa Rica
Rodrigo Gámez, Instituto Nacional de Biodiversidad, Costa Rica
Héctor Huertas, Centro de Asistencia Legal Popular, Panamá

Quírico Jiménez, INBio, Costa Rica
David Kaimowitz, CIFOR, Jakarta
Alexander Kastì, COSEFORMA, Costa Rica
Ron Kemp, Overseas Development Administration, UK
Miguel Laforge, PFA, Costa Rica
Atencio López, Asociación Napguana, Panamá
Israel Losada García, Ministerio de la Agricultura, Cuba
Sergio Madrid, Mexico
Patricia Marchak, University of British Columbia, Canada
Glenda Medina, Caribbean Conservation Association, Barbados
M. A Mulder, Amazon Teak Foundation, The Netherlands
Valerio Nuñez, Congreso General Kuna, Panamá
Tirso Moldonado, Fundación Neotrópica, Costa Rica
Rubén Pasos, ASOCODE, Costa Rica
Rodolfo Peralta, PORTICO, Costa Rica
Alfio Piva, Instituto Nacional de Biodiversidad, Costa Rica
Gunars Platais, USAID, El Salvador
Eugenia Ponce, Colombia
Sergio Ramírez, Confederación Nacional Campesina, Mexico
Carlos Reiche, Proyecto IICA/GTZ, Mexico
Ralph Roberts, CIDA, Canada
Jorge Rodríguez, Programa Frontera Agrícola Panamá, Costa Rica
Jorge Mario Rodríguez, Fondo Nacional de Financiamientos Forestales, Costa Rica
Nidia Rodríguez, Fundación Iriria Tsochok para el Desarrollo Sostenible, Mexico
Glevys Rondon, Mine Watch, Kent, UK
Alberto Salas, UICN/ORMA, Costa Rica
Fabián Salas, Junta Nacional Forestal Campesina, Costa Rica
José Luis Salas, Consejo Centroamericano de Bosques y Areas Protegidas, Costa Rica
René Castro Salazar, Ministro de Ambiente y Energía, Costa Rica
Lorena San Román, Consejo de la Tierra, Costa Rica
Aquileo Sánchez, El Financiero, Mexico
Susanne Schmidt, UNDP, New York, USA
Beatriz Schulthess, Coordinadora Programa Pueblos Indígenas, Costa Rica
Eden Shand, Caribbean Forest Association, Trinidad and Tobago
Raúl Solórzano, SINAC, Costa Rica
Bernard de Souza, Guyana Natural Resources Agency, Guyana
Eladio Susaeta, Chile
Alejandro Swaby, Fundación Iriria Tsochok para el, Mexico
Franz C. Tattenbach, Fundación de Desarrollo de la Cordillera Volcánica Central, Costa Rica
Enrique Toledo, Peru
Tomi Tuomasjukko, UICN, Costa Rica
Alvaro Umaña, INCAE, Costa Rica
Frank Wadsworth, USA
Olman Varela, CICAFO, Mexico
Vera Varela, Fundación Neotrópica, Costa Rica
Edwin Vásquez, AIDESEP, Peru
Avelino Villa Salas, Planfosur/Simposon International, Mexico
Danilo Vindas Chaves, Asociación de Profesionales Forestales, Costa Rica
Matthew Wenban Smith, Forest Stewardship Council, Mexico
Toni Williams, A. Mazaharally and Sons Ltd, Guyana

Victor Mukete, Mukete Plantations Ltd, Cameroon
Florence Munget Munoh, CIFOR, Cameroon
Bertin Mvondo Essah, MINEF, Cameroon
Etienne Mvondo, Ministère de l'éducation nationale
Michel Tanyi Nana, Environmental Studies, Cameroon
Dr. Nde, CIEFE, Cameroon
Lydie Nde, Organisation d'action Feminine, Cameroon
Richard Ndemanou, MINEF, Cameroon
Michel Ndjatsana, WWF Cameroon, Cameroon
Théophile Ndjodo Nga, MINEF, Cameroon
Assitou Ndinga, IUCN/CEFDMAC, Congo
Ada Ndeso-Atanga, Global Environment Facility, Cameroon
Jael Christine Ngo Nkana, MINAGRI, Cameroon
Dieudonné Njib Ntep, ONADEF, Cameroon
Mbalo Ndiaye, Environnement et Développement du Tier-Monde, Senegal
Clothilde Ndomb, Banque Mondiale, Cameroon
Ousseynou, Ndoye, CIFOR, Cameroon
Jeanne Yarmick Ndzie, Peace Managers NGO, Cameroon
Neba Ebenezer, Family Federation for World Peace, Cameroon
Ngoh Martin Nganteh, ONADEF, Cameroon
Augustin Ngirabatware, Institute for Advanced Studies in Economics and Management, Gabon
Hilaire Ngnontsoye, Ste d'Exploitation Forestière, Cameroon Sud Ndjoum
Maurice Hilaire Ngnontsoye, Sud-Bois, Cameroon
Etienne Ngouffo, Ministère de l'environnement et des forêts, Cameroon
Louis Norbert Ngoung Adams, Bois du Sud, Sud Cameroon
Lucas Ngouo, CIEFE, Cameroon
Martin Saba Mjiniya, Centre Cameroonais d'Actions Sociales, Cameroon
Samuel Alain Nguiffo, CED, Cameroon
Martin Cyrille Laurent Nkie, ONADEF, Cameroon
Elisabeth Nkoa, Association d'Assistance, Cameroon
Jacques Nitha, L'Environnement et Forêts du Centre, Cameroon
Appolinaire Nkoulou Ndanga, MINEF, Cameroon
Jacqueline Nkoyok, CONGAC, Cameroon
Issah Nsangou Njoya, MINEF, Cameroon
Edward Osei Kofi Nsenkyire, Forestry Department, Ghana
Fantalie Nyemb, Cameroon Nature Environment, Cameroon
Zachee Nzoh-Ngandembou, CERUT, Cameroon
Luc Roger Oinona Assiga, ONADEF, Cameroon
Godwin Uyi Ojo, Environmental Rights Action, Nigeria
Jonathan Okafor, Tree Crops and Tropical Ecology, Nigeria
Catherine Okotiko, Shadrack Ondoua Ekotto, Gouvernement du Cameroon, Cameroon
Francois Ortiani Keou, Enviro-Protect, Cameroon
Mr. Onyeagucha, Oil Watch Africa, Nigeria
Elie Ondoa Zanga, ONADEF, Cameroon
Francois Oba Bikolo, Fondation Martin Paul Samba, Cameroon
Albin Obougou, ONADEF, Cameroon
Jean Francois Poulain, CIRAD, Cameroon
Ahmed Rhazaoui, UNDP, Cameroon
Guy Suzon Ramagason, Projet DJA, Cameroon
Njiniya Martin Saba, CECAS, Cameroon
Camille Somo, ONADEF, Cameroon
Jacques Siakeu, E.P.P.N., Cameroon
Kofi Smith, Ministry of Lands and Forestry, Ghana
J. Williams Sollo, ONADEF/MINEF, Cameroon

Fred Swartzendruber, USAID, USA
Djeidi Sylla, UNDP, Mali
Nazaire Taboue Siani, Université de Yaoundé, Cameroon
Gladys Mah Taminang, Minstry of External Relations, Cameroon
Jean Baptiste Tandjeu, Association des professionnels de l'Environnement et des Forêts, Cameroon
Hilaire Tchoffo Tameghi, Volontariat pour L'environnement, Cameroon
Dieudonné Thang, ONG 'Global Village Cameroon', Cameroon
Keou François Tiani, ENVIRO-PROTECT, Cameroon
Souane Thirakul, Le Roy Gabon SA, Gabon
Li Umeh, African Development Bank, Côte d'Ivoire
Martial Mathurin Wa, Compagnie Industrielle du Bois au Cameroon, Cameroon
Mwangi Wachria, The World Bank, USA
Zacharie Wandja, Association des jeunes Exploitants Forestiers, Cameroon
Raphael Willemain, Douala Union, Cameroon
Kojo Wireko-Brobby, Ghana Timber Millers Organization, Ghana
Bello Yadji, MINEF, Cameroon
Idrissa Zeba, NATURAMA, Burkina Faso
Jean Marie Claude Zingui, Protocole Ministère des Relations Extérieures, Cameroon

St Petersburg, Russia, October 1997

Oluf Alde, Director of Forestry, Royal Ministry of Agriculture, Norway
Genrikh Chibisov, Director, Institute for Forest and Forest Chemistry, Arckhangelsk
Dmitry Efremov, Director, Far Eastern Forestry Research Institute, Khabarovsk
Vadim Gorshkov, Komarov Botanic Institute, RAS, St Petersburg
Victor Gorshkov, Nuclear Physics Institute, RAS, Leningrad Region, Gatchina
Björn Hägglund, Chairman of 'Stora' Forestry Concern, Sweden
Victor Ipatiev, Bielorus Institute of Forests, NAS, Gomel, Bielorus
Alexandr Isaev, International Forestry Institute, Moscow
Administration of Krasnoyarsk Region, Krasnoyarsk
Oleg Kirillov, Chairman, Committee on Development of Forest Industry Complex, Grigory
Vladimir Kargopoltsev, Head, Chita Forest Management, Chita
Kira Kobak, State Hydrological Institute, St Petersburg
N. K. Koltzov, Inst. Of Development Biology, Russian Academy of Sciences, Russia
Leonid Kondrashov, Far Eastern Forestry Research Institute, Khabarovsk
Natalia Kondrashova, State Hydrological Institute, St Petersburg
Kirill Kondratiev, Scientific Research Center of Ecological Safety, St Petersburg
Nikolai Kozhukhov, Director, VNIILM (Institute for Silviculture), Moscow Region, Pushkino
M. Krotov, Tacis, Russia
Eugeny Kuzmichev, Deputy Head, Federal Forest Service of the RF, Moscow
Andrei Laletin, NGO 'Siberian Forests Friends', Krasnoyarsk
Dominique Larismont, Tacis, Russia
Peter Loiko, Deputy Chairman, Russian Federation Committee on Land Resources and Land Management, Moscow
Marjukka Mähönen, Finland
Markov, Head of Dept., Khabarovsk Region Management, Khabarovsk
Nikolai Nevolin, Head, Vologda Forest Management, Vologda
Alexandr Oblivin, Rector, Moscow State Forest University, Moscow Region, Mytischi
Matti Palo, Finnish Forest Research Institute, Finland
Victor Payanskly-Gvozdev, Forestry Committee of Leningrad Region, St Petersburg
Anatoly Pisarenko, Federal Forest Service of the RF, Moscow
Fedor Pleshikov, Deputy Director, Institute of Forest, RAS, Krasnoyarsk
Vladimir Pominov, Head, Khabarovsk Forest Management, Khabarovsk
Yury Pykh, INENKO, St Petersburg

Jan Remröd, Director General, Swedish Forest Industries Association, Sweden
Vjacheslav Rojkov, Deputy Director, Dokuchaev Soil Institute, RAAS, Moscow
Kaj Rosèn, University of Agriculture, Uppsala, Sweden
Raymond Rowe, ICRAF, Kenya
Frank Schwalbal-Hoht, Tacis, Brussels
Alexandr Shelgauz, Deputy Director, Far Eastern Economic Institute, Khabarovsk
Eugeny Shwartz, Chairman, Biodiversity Conservation Center, Moscow
Sven Sjunnesson, Forest Director, The National Federation of Forest Owners, Sweden
Pavel Sokolov, State Committee for Ecology of RF, Moscow
Vladimir Stepanov, Council of Forest Exporters, Moscow
Arkadll Tishkov, Project 'Biodiversity Conservation in Russia', Moscow
Anna Toropova, State Hydrological Institute, St Petersburg
Trombitsky, CIS Ecological Commission, Russia
Ljudmila Turchinovich, State Hydrological Institute, St Petersburg
Sergei Vavilov, Forestry Committee of Leningrad Region, St Petersburg
Stanislav Vompersky, Director, Institute of Forestry, RAS, Moscow
Vladimir Yagodin, Head, Forestry Committee of Leningrad Region, St Petersburg
Vasily Yarmishko, Deputy Director, Komarov Botanic Institute
Tamara Zlotnikova, Chairperson of the Ecological Committee of the State Duma, Russia
Victor Zubakov, Institute for Nature Conservation of the Arctic and North, St Petersburg

Annex 5 Member States of existing multilateral frameworks

African Timber Organization
Angola
Cameroon
Central African Republic
Congo
Côte d'Ivoire
Equatorial Guinea
Gabon
Ghana
Liberia
São Tome and Principe
Tanzania
Zaire

Amazon Treaty Organization
Bolivia
Brazil
Colombia
Ecuador
Guyana
Peru
Suriname
Venezuela

Andean Pact
Bolivia
Columbia
Ecuador
Peru
Venezuela

Asia Pacific Economic Cooperation (APEC)
Australia
Brunei Darussalam
Canada
Chile
People's Republic of China
Indonesia
Japan
Republic of Korea
Malaysia
Mexico
New Zealand
Papua New Guinea
The Philippines
Singapore
Chinese Taipei
Thailand
United States of America

Association of Caribbean States (ACS)
Antigua and Barbuda
The Bahamas
Barbados
Belize
Colombia
Costa Rica
Cuba
Dominica
Dominican Republic
El Salvador
France (in respect of Guadeloupe, Martinique, French Guiana)
Grenada
Guatemala
Guyana
Haiti
Honduras
Jamaica
Mexico
Netherlands Antilles
Nicaragua
Panama
St Kitts/Nevis
St Lucia
St Vincent and the Grenadines
Suriname
Trinidad and Tobago
Venezuela

Association of Southeast Asian Nations (ASEAN)
Brunei Darussaliam
Cambonia
Indonesia
Laos
Malaysia
Myanmar
The Philippines
Singapore
Thailand
Vietnam

Caribbean Community (CARICOM)
Antigua and Barbuda
The Bahamas
Barbados
Belize
Dominica
Grenada